Oxford Socio-Legal Studies

Contrasts in Tolerance

OXFORD SOCIO-LEGAL STUDIES

GENERAL EDITORS

Donald R. Harris   Keith Hawkins   Sally Lloyd-Bostock
Doreen McBarnet

Oxford Socio-Legal Studies is a series of books published for the Centre
for Socio-Legal Studies, Wolfson College, Oxford. The series is
concerned generally with the relationship between law and society,
and is designed to reflect the increasing interest of lawyers, social
scientists and historians in this field.

Already Published (by Oxford University Press)

Contrasts in Tolerance

*Post-war Penal Policy in The Netherlands
and England and Wales*

DAVID DOWNES

CLARENDON PRESS · OXFORD
1988

Oxford University Press. Walton Street, Oxford OX2 6DP
Oxford New York Toronto
Delhi Bombay Calcutta Madras Karachi
Petaling Jaya Singapore Hong Kong Tokyo
Nairobi Dar es Salaam Cape Town
Melbourne Auckland
and associated companies in
Berlin Ibadan

Oxford is a trade mark of Oxford University Press

Published in the United States
by Oxford University Press. New York

British Library Cataloguing in Publication Data
Downes, David, 1938–
Contrasts in tolerance : post war penal
policy in the Netherlands and England and
Wales. —(Oxford socio-legal studies).
1. England. Penal system. Compared with
penal system of Netherlands 2. Netherlands.
Penal system. Compared with penal system of
England
I. Title   II. Series
364.6'0942
ISBN 0-19-825608-6

Library of Congress Cataloging-in-Publication Data
Downes, David.
Contrasts in tolerance.
(Oxford socio-legal studies)
Bibliography: p.   Includes index.
1. Criminal justice, Administration of–Netherlands.
2. Criminal justice, Administration of–Great Britain.
3. Corrections–Netherlands.   4. Corrections–Great Britain.   I. Title.   II. Series.
HV9960.N4D68 1988   364.6'0942   88-5264
ISBN 0-19-825608-6

Set by Burns & Smith, Derby
Printed in Great Britain
at the University Printing House, Oxford
by David Stanford
Printer to the University

In memory of
Ronald Orr-Ewing
(1913–1988)
Friend and mentor

Contents

Acknowledgements

THE research on which this book is based was conducted intermittently over a period of several years, mostly in The Netherlands. It would have been impossible without the support and goodwill of all those who consented to be interviewed—in the main academics, administrators, and judges, who gave up time from busy schedules to talk to yet another visitor from abroad interested in their criminal justice system. Their patience, generosity, and hospitality have been memorable. The prisoners whom I interviewed in both countries could have withheld their consent, and in a few cases, felt anxiety about the purpose of the interview. In the event, their co-operation, insight, and often penetrating analysis of their situation and its context was for me the most valuable part of the research. I hope they will not regard the time they gave to it as entirely wasted.

I should like to thank in particular Nico Keijzer, formerly Professor of the Faculty of Law, The Free University, Amsterdam, now of the Supreme Court, the Hague, for his unflagging encouragement and advice. Jan van Dijk, head of Research and Documentation Centre of the Ministry of Justice at the Hague, provided stimulating criticism and more material than I could assimilate. Maurice Punch, Professor of Sociology at Nijenrode University, gave invaluable insights into policing work in Holland and Britain. And Pia Mitchell, who acted as research assistant on the project until April 1982, supplied translations and summaries of material available only in Dutch of a quality sorely missed after that date. In London, Paul Rock, Professor of Sociology at the School, tirelessly gave constructive criticism when it was most needed.

In addition I should like to express particular thanks to the following, who gave valuable time and insight to what must always be the uncertain course of this sort of research: Ms Sheila Welsh, formerly of the Graduate School, London School of Economics, for early assistance in compiling sentencing trends in England and Wales; Professors J. Remmelink, Herman Bianchi, and Erhard Blankenberg, and Dr Ulco van der Pol and Dr Sibo van Ruller, Department of Law, The Free University, Amsterdam; Judge Schroeder, Amsterdam; Dr Hans Tulkens, former head, Mr Erik Besier, Drs Jos Verhaegen and Leendert Erkelens, Prison Department, Ministry of Justice, The Hague; Dr Dato Steenhuis, former head, Drs Jack Essers, A. C. Berghuis and C. van der Werff, Research and Documentation Centre, Ministry of Justice, The Hague; Ms N. Spaniersberg, Department of TBR and Reclassering, Ministry of Justice, The Hague; Professor Alfred Heijder, Van Hamel Institute, University of Amsterdam, now of the Department of The

Attorney General, The Hague; Professor Jacqueline Soetenhorst de Savornin-Lohman, University of Amsterdam; Professor Tony Vinson, University of New South Wales, Australia; Professor Constantin Kelk, and Dr Paul Moedikdo, Pompe Institute, Utrecht; Dr A. M. Roosenburg, former Director of the Dr Henri van der Hoeven Clinic, Utrecht; Professor David Ingleby, Department of Clinical Psychology, University of Utrecht and Professor Ch. J. Enschedé, formerly of the University of Amsterdam. I should also like to thank the numerous judges, prosecutors, police, prison staff and administrators, and the prisoners who gave great help in the course of the inquiry into the criminal justice and penal system of the Netherlands.

For the chapter on drug use and social policy, I am especially indebted to Dr Jack Derks, of the Jellinek Clinic, Amsterdam; Dr Ernst Buning, and Dr Astrid de Rojj-Motshagen, of the Amsterdam Municipal Health Organization; Mr G. van Stijgeren, Press Office, Amsterdam Town Hall; Dr O. Janssen, Department of Criminology, University of Groningen; and Richard Hartnoll, Drugs Indicators Project, Birkbeck College, University of London. I should like to thank the BBC for the use of background materials to one programme's coverage of the issues involved.

My thanks also to Professor Eryl Hall Williams, Department of Law, London School of Economics; Andrew Rutherford, Centre for Criminology, University of Southampton; Jon Vagg, Centre for Criminological Research, University of Oxford; Professor Roy King, Department of Social Theory and Institutions, University of Wales at Bangor, and Rod Morgan, Department of Social Administration, University of Bath, for much-needed criticism and encouragement.

The first phase of the research was supported by the Home Office, the second by the Economic and Social Research Council. Roy Walmsley and Paul Softley, of the Home Office Research and Planning Unit, gave constructive advice at crucial stages of the project. I also benefited greatly from discussions in seminars both there and at the National Association for the Care and Resettlement of Offenders, whose information service under Paul Cavadino proved indispensable on several occasions. Without two terms' sabbatical leave from the School in 1981, and a term's leave of absence in 1985, however, that most crucial pre-condition for research—time—would not have been available. I should like to express my appreciation to all concerned for the backing they gave to the research. My thanks also to Jon Whittle for producing superb copy from successive drafts.

Much of Chapters 2–4 is based on the analysis developed in an article published in the British Journal of Criminology in October 1982. I am grateful to the publishers and owners of the journal for permission to draw fully upon it.

Warmest thanks to Hannah Downes for compiling the index and, finally, I should like to thank Connie Wilsack for her formidable powers of copy-editing. After such a wealth of constructive criticism, any faults that remain are undeniably my own.

D. D.

Department of Social Administration
London School of Economics
July 1987

List of Tables

List of Figures

List of Appendices

1 The Criminal Justice Systems of The Netherlands and England [1]

Comparative criminology is nothing new. In their broadest sense, of contrasting institutional arrangements and/or forms of conduct between whole societies, comparative studies have long been an invaluable, though under-used, resource in historical and socio-economic studies. Travels abroad can be as influential as journeyings at home in the realm of criminal and penal policies. It is difficult otherwise to account for such phenomena as the rapid rise of the penitentiary across the continents of Europe and North America in the first few decades of the nineteenth century. More recently, the appeal of victim-related measures has, from relatively small beginnings in the United States in the late 1960s, fanned out to most liberal democratic societies around the globe. From time to time, Britain has attracted streams of enquirers into the workings of the latest penal or reformative innovation. The Borstal system in the interwar period was much admired abroad. Latterly, the Barlinnie Special Unit offered a ray of hope to those who aim to open up greater possibilities of freedom within walls. In the late 1940s, the Henderson Hospital was one source of inspiration for those embarking on the planning of a new wave of mental hospitals for offenders designated mentally ill in The Netherlands. Reformers naturally look for different things at different times. In the late eighteenth century, the spartan regimentation of the penitentiary was seen as infinitely preferable to the chaos of the old 'clinks', where prisoners in chains could be visited or pestered by passers-by in the foul yards that adjoined the prison. In a different vein, *Jane Eyre* offers a grim parody of community care. Custodians would travel in search of different objectives from those of the reformers: more effective security devices, systems of surveillance and control. With air travel,

---

[1] 'England' is used throughout to denote 'England and Wales', unless otherwise stated. Scotland and N. Ireland are specifically excluded because their criminal justice and penal system differ in crucial respects from those of England and Wales—'Britain' is thus used only in the context of comments of a more general nature that can apply to Scotland and N. Ireland as well.

regular conference circuits, and the internationalization of much deviance and control, currently at its most prominent in the terrorism and drugs fields, it is not surprising that criminologists have begun to talk of 'import–export' models in the exchange of systems and ideas. (For an acerbic view of the imbalance in the terms of trade on this front, see S Cohen 1982.)

Much, perhaps most, of the exchanges that occur on the subject of crime and its control emanate not from academic criminology but from journalistic work, and often from the *ad hoc* concerns of professionals and administrators in such fields as police or probation work to learn about the doings of their colleagues overseas. They may derive from short-term governmental agendas regarding pressing social problems, such as soccer hooliganism or drug-trafficking. Criminology has in general been strikingly uncomparative. At the time of its publication, Hermann Mannheim's *Comparative Criminology* (1965) made curiously little impact[2]. A few comparative works have attained classic status, Rusche and Kirchheimers's *Punishment and Social Structure* (1939) being the most notable. There are many possible reasons for this state of affairs. The legendary insulation of criminology from mainstream sociology for most of its history meant that the significance which the comparative method held for the latter simply passed the former by. Moreover, even when sociology impinged most influentially on the study of deviance, in the 1960s and 1970s, it did so from interactionism and phenomenalist perspectives, both of which tended to stress the primacy of the local context and to avoid large-scale comparative projects which rested flimsily on notions such as 'culture' and 'structure' (Robertson and Taylor 1973). Yet phenomenology produced, in Schutz's (1967) essay on the 'stranger', what could be taken as a directive for sociological travel. The stranger may be vouchsafed confidences withheld from fellow-members of the host community (they may also be cast as deviant, ignored, or peddled convenient clichés: there are presumably limits to the tolerance accorded strangers). One does not have to travel abroad to be a stranger: that is possible on the next street. But to be a foreigner may confer certain privileges, in particular a licence to naïveté. In short, there

---

[2]   Nor did Eric Stockdale's *The Court and the Offender*, Gollancz, 1967, a stimulating comparison of the systems of justice in England, Holland, Denmark, and Sweden.

is an affinity between the role of stranger and comparative sociology which render its dearth in many fields of the subject surprising. Anthropology is a different story.

The inhibitions of administratively based social researchers perhaps stem from different sources. The overwhelming requirement for the allocation of state resources to a project is salience (cf. Banting 1979). If the field were military, economic, or environmental, comparative work would be relatively easy to justify in such terms. But in the social or cultural fields, salience is almost monopolized by domestic horizons. The problem with 'abroad' is that the demand of governments for precise answers to limited questions—for example, how to deal with 'soccer hooliganism'—rarely shows more than the broad correspondence of other societies' concerns with our own, and limited forays which simply reveal greater complexity become difficult to justify. For the complexities of a methodological character in comparative work are formidable. Categories and definitions of seriousness and specific crimes may vary; what counts as a 'penal' institution in one country may be labelled differently in another; and persons diverted from the criminal justice system at various stages may be regarded for some purposes as 'sentenced', for others not. The process of attempting to ensure that like is being compared with like is protracted and often imprecise.

The dearth of work in comparative criminology and the sociology of control may or may not derive from the above considerations. But it is ceasing to be so in the fields of deviance and control, despite the strength of the constraints. Relative economic decline may be leading to dissatisfaction, often exaggeratedly so, with all aspects of institutional life that were previously taken for granted or left out of account as grounds for failure.

In the case of the English penal system, no one could rationally suppose that its state was the cause of national economic decline. But its condition parodies it fairly representatively: 'high-cost squalor' is Rutherford's cogent phrase for a system that combines great costs with enormous waste and considerable inhumanity, where staff and prisoners alike, though in contrasting ways, suffer a measure of indignity and oppressiveness that shows every sign of increasing rather than waning. It embodies undue variations of discomfort and privation, with some jails being relatively humane—by and large the training prisons into which proportionally more resources are sunk (King and Morgan 1980)—while others invite metaphors such as pressure-cookers, 'cattle-pens', and the like to capture the reek of overcrowding and subjugation endemic in the local prisons. Reforms are tried and found wanting—parole, suspended sentences, community service orders—in the pursuit of a reduced prison population. Its continuing rise is then declared something akin to a natural law, beyond the realms of political choice or informed decision-making. Crime, after all, has continued to rise. Reducing the prison population, as occurred in the late nineteenth century at a time of falling crime rates, is hardly to be expected or induced. This logic leads inexorably to penal expansion, since building more prisons is the only course that remains unless overcrowding is to be left to take its course, a course that risks ultimate loss of control within the jails: riots, staff resistance, and a visible breakdown of 'law and order' in its major institutional buttress.

The question 'Does it have to be so?' entails comparative study. First, the question invites a straightforward empirical search for negative cases. Examples abound, and tend to defy a simple relationship between crime rates and trends in penal populations. States as diverse as The Netherlands, Australia, and Ontario reduced their prison populations in the context of rising crime rates, as indeed did England in the 1920s and 1930s. Japan did so over a prolonged period of falling crime rates, but the reduction greatly exceeded that fall proportionately. (Rutherford 1986: 122) With the exception of Rutherford's coverage of England, The Netherlands, and Japan, however, data on trends in crime and imprisonment are scattered and highly variable in quality. Enough is known, however, to cast the most serious doubt on the notion that some invariable law dictates a rising recourse to custody in the context of rising crime.

The second set of questions arising from the above concerns the consequences of deviating from meeting crime with custody on a *pro rata* basis. It is commonly assumed that were this to happen for an appreciable length of time, the adverse consequences would be dire—involving at the least a sharp spurt in the crime rate, and more generally a pervasive anomie, a breadown of regulatory norms across the entire range of social and institutional life. Those who adhere to a more or less deterministic view of the relations between crime, custody, and anomie would logically also hold (to use Rutherford's terms) expansionist or, at best, 'standstill' views about penal policy. They would be joined by many holding 'reductionist' views, however, in relation to a third question: 'Would a falling prison population at a time of rising crime be politically feasible?' Few would venture a positive answer to that question in contemporary Britain, but again comparative evidence suggests that it has been possible both here and elsewhere.

Drawn to The Netherlands in what began as a cursory attempt to explore these questions, and fully expecting to find that they had already been largely dealt with, I learnt that post-war criminal justice and penal policy had not been the subject of much analytical interest. In retrospect, this should not have been surprising. We still lack a comprehensive analysis of post-war policies in these fields in Britain, though one is now under way at Cambridge, under the Economic and Social Research Council's 'Crime and the Criminal Justice System' initiative. There is every sign, however, that this period of neglect is over, and that in both countries the key questions of how best to account for sentencing trends and policy process are being actively pursued (Rutherford 1984, Bottomley 1986, van Dijk *et al.* 1986).

This study makes no claim to provide a comprehensive analysis of post-war criminal justice policy in The Netherlands, or a comparative study of such policy in The Netherlands and England. Its main objective is to ascertain why the prison population of The Netherlands has been progressively reduced over virtually the whole of the post-war period, to the point where it has become very nearly the lowest in the world. The origins, character, and consequences of so substantial a process of decarceration remain the focus throughout. There is, of course, nothing even remotely startling about the view that the Dutch penal estate is more humane and relatively milder than elsewhere. From the *rasphuis* of the late sixteenth century on, which is usually credited as the first penal site to offer prisoners work and reformation as distinct from sheer captivity and the infliction of pain (cf. Garland 1986*a* and *b*), the Dutch have in general been compared favourably with the rest of Europe on this score. John Howard was by no means the first to do so, though his accolade (1784) was based upon the most comprehensive survey of contrasting countries, and carried the most weight. The trajectory of Dutch penal policy for a century or more (van Ruller 1981, Blom-Cooper 1986) has been towards decarceration. But history is made, not simply reproduced, and the problem of accounting for the continuation of these trends even after the crime rate began to rise discernibly in the 1960s and 1970s in The Netherlands still seems to resist reduction to the rubric of tradition. There is the related problem of explaining the recent rise in the Dutch prison population, a tendency previously confined in general to periods of war-induced crises.

It is germane to note, in view of this weight of opinion, that for much of the period between the late 1870s and the mid-1950s, the daily prison population rate in England was lower than that in The Netherlands, dramatically so if the Dutch penal labour colonies are counted as constituting 'prisons' (see Fig. 1). The average length of stay in custody in 1913 in England was six weeks, largely because the great majority of receptions into prison were for non-indictable offences or defaulting on fines (Rutherford 1986a p.124). On this basis, it appears as if the historic mission of the English penal system was to be even milder than that of the Dutch. The great British decarceration began in 1877 with the centralization of the local prisons under Edmund Du Cane, the first head of the newly created Prison Board, a man usually cast as a thoroughgoing reactionary. Du Cane actively promoted the case for reducing the prison population by shortening sentences (for a fascinating account of the 1870–1914 period of British penal policy, see Radzinowicz and Hood 1986). In the inter-war years, despite a rising crime rate, the prison population rate actually fell slightly. Again, only negligible research has been conducted on this period of penal policy, which was associated strongly with the liberal character of the Prison Commission under Sir Lionel Fox and with one of its commissioners, Alexander Paterson, providing much of the thinking for a reduction in the resort to custody (see the succinct account of trends in Rutherford 1986: 121–31). The kind of rehabilitative policies favoured in those years suggests they were quite compatible with a lowering of the penal population despite a rising crime rate. Probation clearly acted as a major alternative to custody, with the proportionate resort to imprisonment more than halving and that to probation quadrupling between 1908 and 1938. The belief in the post-World War II period that rehabilitative policies would lower the prison population rested on these foundations. That they did not prove secure in the post-war context perhaps may suggest the deviant case to be that of England rather than The Netherlands from the

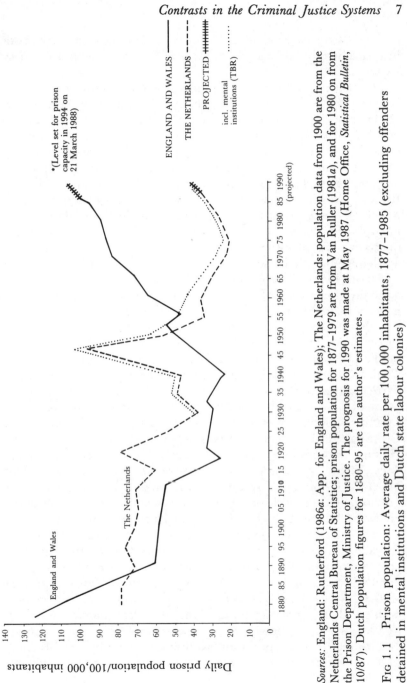

Sources: England: Rutherford (1986*a*: App. for England and Wales); The Netherlands: population data from 1900 are from the Netherlands Central Bureau of Statistics; prison population for 1877–1979 are from Van Ruller (1981*a*), and for 1980 on from the Prison Department, Ministry of Justice. The prognosis for 1990 was made at May 1987 (Home Office, *Statistical Bulletin,* 10/87). Dutch population figures for 1880–95 are the author's estimates.

FIG 1.1   Prison population: Average daily rate per 100,000 inhabitants, 1877–1985 (excluding offenders detained in mental institutions and Dutch state labour colonies)

mid-1950s onwards. The importance of comparative work, both historically and between societies, is certainly borne out by these variations.

The methods used here to address the question of the contrast between the two penal policies mainly focused, however, on the Dutch case. The basic aim was to gather as systematically as possible views and information about how and why Dutch penal trends had developed so distinctively in the post-war period. Deviant or not, The Netherlands has proved the most striking and durable example of a trend markedly different from that in Britain, France, Germany, and most other European societies. My main concern was to interview criminologists, administrators, judges, and public prosecutors about their knowledge of these questions, and to gather materials on crime and penal trends from academic and official sources. From late 1980, in the course of 12 research visits to The Netherlands, mostly in 1981 and otherwise annually, for a total of some 150 days, some hundred interviews have been more or less formally conducted on various aspects of this theme. No claims to representativeness or all-inclusiveness can be laid, but an attempt was made to select 25 judges and public prosecutors from different areas and of varying seniority. Their willingness to be interviewed was in itself noteworthy, particularly when compared with the refusal, at roughly the same point in time, of certain senior English judges to take part in a carefully piloted research project by the Oxford Centre for Criminological Research. Visits were made to prisons at The Hague, Veenhuisen, and the Over-Amstel penitentiary in Amsterdam, the main closed prisons for adult males; to the Mesdags Clinic at Groningen, the maximum security clinic providing treatment for indeterminate periods; and to the Van der Hoeven Clinic at Utrecht. In the course of interviewing prisoners, visits were also made to remand prisons at Utrecht and Rotterdam (see Ch. 6). It was typically the case that fluency in English of people interviewed approached near-mastery of the language, or that their command of the language was sufficient for the purposes of the interview, so that communication was little more of a problem than between people of the same language community. In a few instances, however, interviews would have been impossible without the interpretation skilfully provided by Pia Mitchell, who also summarized documents and written materials available only in Dutch.

Salient differences between the two systems

Comparisons between crime, sentencing, and penal trends in two different societies can be confounded at every point by differences in the legal frameworks, the categories employed in defining and measuring crimes of different kinds, the modes of procedure and classification governing the manner of crime reporting and recording by the police, the structure and procedures of prosecution, the character and powers of the courts, the range and variety of sanctions available to the courts, the modalities of induction, detention, and movement into and from the penal system, and the allied institutional disposals which may be available as alternatives to custody. What follows is a summary of the major problems that arise in any comparison of the Dutch and English data rather than an itemized contrast of all points of difference, which are far too numerous for ease of inventory. The analysis could not proceed, however, without a sketch of three key peculiarities of the Dutch system relating to the system of public prosecution, probation, and the treatment of mentally disordered offenders.

The legal frameworks of the two countries have been contrasted in an exhaustive fashion by Sharples (1972), though signal developments have occurred since 1970 which need to be taken into account. Despite considerable historical differences in their manner of development, the substantive criminal laws of the two countries are broadly comparable with regard to the nature of the standard offences and the sanctions made available to the courts for dealing with them. The Dutch Penal Code of 1886, whose centenary was recently celebrated by a Penal Congress held in Amsterdam (see Van Dijk *et al.* 1986), laid the foundations for the current legal order and represented the culmination of the impulse towards codification which stemmed from the Napoleonic period. Despite the great accretion of special regulatory offences created in the intervening century, particularly concerning traffic and offences of an economic kind involving the revenue and social security systems, the broad range of offences in the Code—against public authorities; against life and the person; against property; sexual offences; and malicious damage—corresponds very broadly with 'standard list' offences in England and Wales (cf. Peters 1986) and petty categories. *Misdrijven* in Holland are the broad equivalent of 'indictable' offences in England, *overtredingen* of 'non-indictable'. *Misdrijven* alone are imprisonable offences in The Netherlands, 'indictable' alone are triable either only before a jury or 'either way', before a jury in a Crown Court or summarily by magistrates. *Overtredingen* are non-imprisonable, though subject to the rarely used *hechtenis* (detention); 'non-indictable' offences are triable only summarily. In addition to Penal Code offences, five kinds of offence categories are also *misdrijven* in The Netherlands: those against the Military Code; more serious road traffic offences (a few of which would be non-indictable in England, e.g. driving under the influence of drink or drugs); economic offences (some of which are fiscal but which mainly include industrial pollution and other non-fiscal economic offences); offences against the Drug Act (mostly narcotic trafficking); and against the Firearms Act. Another similarity is that, in both countries, an attempt (*poging*) is treated similarly to, though usually more leniently than, a completed offence, provided that 'the offence (i.e. the attempt) has progressed to a certain degree' (Sharples 1972: 163). The offence of 'going equipped for burglary' is non-indictable in Dutch law. Interestingly, its prevalence as part of all burglary convictions in England has dropped from 2.0 per cent to 0.5 per cent between 1974 and 1984.

Comparing serious crime rates is not, therefore, fraught with too much difficulty, providing that certain adjustments are made to ensure that like is being compared with like. Thus, in comparing total serious crime rates, traffic offences (except for causing death or serious injury by reckless driving) should not be added to the total of penal code offences known to the police. 'Joy-riding', equivalent to our 'unauthorized taking', should be added along with offences against the Drug and Firearms Acts. These, however, affect gross totals only at the margins. In comparing specific offence rates more difficulties arise. Even now, it is not possible to obtain a time-series for murder and manslaughter for The Netherlands which separates completed from attempted offences. The Netherlands Central Bureau of Statistics (CBS) still on occasion provides a figure for murder and manslaughter which, by including attempts and certain categories of grievous bodily harm, inflates the actual rate of 1 per 100,000 to almost double (Netherlands CBS 1986: 24, Table 6.2; see also Table 4.1 below) and which can be mistaken for an eight-fold increase in the murder rate since the 1956/60 period. On this count data have been cited which erroneously show the Dutch murder rate as eight times its incidence in actuality (Waller 1982: Table 4). A small proportion of burglaries involving violence are inextricably included in the robbery figures for The Netherlands, thus slightly deflating the former and inflating the latter. Crimes known to the police and other indicators of control trends tend to be calculated in Dutch statistics in terms of the population aged 12–79, which needs adjustment for comparative purposes. Broad official offence categories are in general reasonably comparable.

The range and character of sanctions are more diverse in The Netherlands for most of the period in terms of the combinations of unconditional, partly conditional and partly unconditional, and wholly suspended imprisonment, the last of which may be combined with fines. Since 1968 and 1982, respectively, suspended and partially suspended imprisonment have, within not too dissimilar limits, been available to English courts. Community Service Orders originated in England, were first used in 1974 and were introduced in The Netherlands six years later. Formal sanctions of a non-custodial sort are more varied in England: The Netherlands has no counterpart to attendance centres, which have existed in a few areas in England since 1948 and have recently been expanded in scope. There is no strict counterpart to absolute or conditional discharge in The Netherlands. Probation is not a disposal in The Netherlands in the same way as in England: it is a recommended accompaniment to conditional dismissal, a suspended sentence or parole. In reality, the public prosecutor has a range of measures at his disposal which range from fines to restitution of varying kinds, and these exceed in flexibility the penalties available to an English court. Forfeiture of criminally obtained assets is also employed in The Netherlands on a scale not yet permissible in England[3] (Hulsman *et al.* 1978: 321). In general, it is possible to compare proportional use of various sanctions only by combining the extrajudicial settlements of the public prosecutor (see below), which always rest on the defendant's consent, with those of the court, which are imposed. Trend comparisons for sentencing for specific offences are, however, vitiated for the pre-1978 period by the lack of data in The Netherlands distinguishing between two types of waiver: 'technical' (evidential and/or procedural grounds) and 'policy' (social and/or restitutive

---

[3] Similar measures are now framed in the current Criminal Justice Bill now before Parliament.

grounds), (see below, and Ch. 2). Much ground-clearing is therefore needed before sentencing trends can be adequately compared.

Police forces in both countries are the major agency for controlling 'input' into the criminal justice system. If their recording practices vary greatly, if the norms governing public reportage of offences to them change at all markedly, then the possibilities of precise comparisons both within and between societies are substantially reduced. In the 1960s and early 1970s, grave doubts were expressed, and some empirical support was adduced, for the view that police statistics were of negligible validity as indicators of crime trends. From the mid-1970s, however, victim surveys at both national and local levels in a number of countries tend to suggest a broad correspondence of official and victim-based crime trends (Hough and Mayhew 1983, 1985; van Dijk and Steinmetz 1980; Mawby 1979; Bottoms *et al* 1987). To the extent that police work is reactive (Reiss 1971; Manning 1977), and most studies indicate that is predominantly so, the character of police recorded crime is largely shaped by those reported by the public. No obvious disparity emerges between Dutch and English victim survey data to suggest that Dutch police recording of crimes differs at all substantially from that in England (Block 1986). It is possible that Dutch police pay less attention to subsidiary as compared with principal crimes (i.e. crimes 'taken into consideration') at the stage of charge and prosecution, but that would affect the clear-up rate rather than the number of crimes known to the police. In both countries, the police 'cuff' a great many offences, particularly of the minor variety—that is, ignore or deal with them informally (Punch 1979*a*, Chatterton 1983). There are no signs, however, that such practices are sufficiently different in The Netherlands to affect comparative work unduly.

The major difference between the forms of discretionary powers available to the police concerns cautioning. In The Netherlands, despite some informal cautioning, this power—the police *trasactie*—is mainly limited to dealing with minor traffic offenders. In England it extends in principle to all except motoring offences. Official police cautions in practice are overwhelmingly reserved for minor offences committed by juveniles under the age of 17. It is, however, the closest approximation in England to the Dutch 'policy' waiver, since it should be administered only where guilt is admitted *and* the evidence is sufficiently strong for prosecution to be mounted (Walker 1985: 221 ff.). Adding caution to convicted offenders for England would obviously reduce the proportions sentenced to custody, since cautions account for roughly 1 in 5 of all offenders found guilty or cautioned. The rate of cautioning falls, however, from 3 in 4 males aged 10–14 to 1 in 20 for males aged 17 and over. The rate for females is rather higher. Since the age of criminal responsibility in The Netherlands is 12 and not 10, the overlap is reduced somewhat. Overall, cautioning is unlikely to make more than a marginal impact on youth custody and adult imprisonment rates for comparative purposes. Though its impact on diverting even the younger age-groups from prosecution and custody has been seriously questioned (Pratt 1986), it remains an interesting parallel with the Dutch prosecutors' power to waive prosecution. It provides a precedent capable of great extension in the light of the new system of Crown Prosecution in England and Wales (see Ch. 7 below).

It is difficult to exaggerate the importance of the public prosecution service in The Netherlands to the shaping of judicial sentencing policy. 'The cardinal procedural difference between the administration of penal justice in The Netherlands and in England centres upon the organization of the prosecution' (Sharples 1972: 289). Van Dijk has aptly termed the public prosecutor 'the spider in the web' of the criminal justice system in The Netherlands. The prosecutors are empowered to act as the catalysts of policy, with roles that connect them with the judges on one side, the police on another, and the Ministry of Justice and Parliament on a third. The following ten points convey something of their pivotal role.

1. They alone determine which cases should be prosecuted in court.

2. The principle of expediency (*opportuniteitsbesingel*) empowers the prosecutor to waive prosecution on 'policy' grounds (*beleidssepot*) as well as on 'technical' grounds (*bevoegdheidssepot*). 'Unlike the Federal Republic of Germany and Italy, the Dutch criminal process recognises this principle for all offences and makes ample use of it' (Hulsman *et al.* 1978: 311; see also Hall Williams and Leigh 1981). In 1971, the principle of expediency was reinterpreted to mean that prosecution should be waived unless public interest demanded it, the reverse of the previous position which insisted on prosecution *unless* the public interest

demanded it be waived. The change took account of a development that was already substantially realized.

3. They make recommendations about the sentence which the judges are bound to take into account in arriving at a penalty, though they are not bound by it.

4. Though rarely involved in the detail, they both set priorities for and supervise police investigations.

5. Senior police officers can detain suspects in custody for two days. Prosecutors may extend detention for another two days. Further prolongations of detention, up to a maximum of 110 days, need a court order. Release of suspects is at the prosecutor's discretion. This power was the basis for the priority scheme introduced in 1983, whereby a top category detainee would displace a lower category suspect if no cell was available to hold sufficient numbers on the one-to-a-cell basis. (See Appendix 1.2)

6. The Ministry of Justice has since the early 1970s sought to promote the greater harmonization of sentencing by the drafting of guidelines for different types of offence and offender regarding the waiving of prosecution and the sentencing recommendations to be made in court. The senior prosecutors, in collaboration with the Ministry and the Research and Documentation Centre, have gradually adjusted the guidelines on the basis of local prosecutors' views (van Dijk 1983). (See Appendix 1.1) For relatively common crimes such as shoplifting, the guidelines also lay down recommendations for sentence (see 3 above).

7. The five senior prosecutors meet fortnightly to discuss guidelines for specific offences and to review criminal justice policy. This practice began in 1939 to meet the need that was felt to have arisen for joint consultation on civil order (in the wake of the street-fighting started by the Dutch fascist party), and until 1965 these five attorney-generals met fortnightly, presided over by the minister's deputy, the secretary-general, mainly to discuss policing policy. After 1965, on the initiative of A. Mulder, the then newly appointed secretary-general, their purpose was broadened to include criminal justice policy.

8. The minister of justice is thus responsible to Parliament for policy guidelines whose delineation is delegated to the senior prosecutors. The strictly judicial hierarchy of advocates-general, whose apex is the Supreme Court, remains quite distinct.

9. The prosecutor also has the duty to undertake 'proper investigation', which has been the basis for the so-called

'triangular' relationship between the prosecutors, the police, and the local authorities to meet regularly for joint consultation on policing policy.

10. The *transactie*, whereby the offender can consent to pay what in effect is a fine without conviction, has since 1983 been extended from *overtredingen* to *misdrijven* that carry maximum penalties of six years' imprisonment or less (i.e. the majority). At the same time, *Society and Crime* (1985) recommended that the rate of unconditional waivers, which had been growing steadily for the past two decades, be much reduced. (Netherlands, Ministry of Justice, 1985a).

These are formidable powers, and they by no means exhaust the range of prosecutorial discretion. They are wielded by a relatively small number of people, some 239 in all, in 1987, a veritable cadre of thoroughly professional decision-makers. 'Means have been devised to regulate the prosecutor's monopoly' (Hulsman *et al.* 1978: 311)—for example, non-prosecution can be tested by judicial review activated by the victim—but they are rarely invoked. The most important check is that pre-trial detention is usually accompanied by a preliminary judicial inquiry by the 'judge of instruction', i.e. the judge charged with responsibility for the judicial inquiry in its preliminary stages (Sharples 1972: 177, 180–2). In such cases, the judge of instruction effectively takes over the investigation; however, the decision to prosecute still rests with the public prosecutors.

The English criminal justice system has no genuine counterpart to the Dutch public prosecution system. Though prosecution (1 above) has traditionally been the preserve of the police or—in certain cases, especially of a political character—the director of public prosecutions, that role has now been taken over by the Crown Prosecution service. Even so, the role of the Crown prosecutor in England is far more restricted than that of the Dutch public prosecutor, since the former reviews the case for prosecution only after it has been prepared by the police. The supervisory role (4 above) is outside their remit. Apart from its limited expression in police cautioning, the principle of expediency (2 above) has no institutional expression in the English system. Nor has the prosecution any right to make any suggestions about appropriate sentence (though until 1966 the Court of Appeal had the power to *increase* a sentence on appeal). Remand in custody in England is the prerogative of the court, though police requests for bail (which is rarely used in The Netherlands)[4] to be withheld or set at a certain level are usually upheld by the courts. Nor, apart from the limited number of on-the-spot fines which can be levied by the police in traffic cases of a minor sort, is there any equivalent to the prosecutorial *transactie* (10 above).

In the case of judicial sentencing policy (6, 7, and 8 above), the nearest equivalents are the forms of guidance offered by judgments of the Court of Appeal (Thomas 1979, Ashworth 1983) and Home Office Circulars. 'The philosophy followed by English courts when interpreting penal legislation can be and frequently is guided by means of Practice Directions issued by the Court of Appeal, and also by Home Office Circulars' (Sharples 1972: 6–7). In this passage, Sharples understates the constraints against the implementation of such guidance by the courts, and overstates the degree of coherence that they embody. Indeed, he goes on to comment: '. . . a characteristic feature of English criminal law consists in its unmethodical nature and great fragmentation of offences' (p. 7). Much of the burden of David Thomas's work (1970, 1979) is that coherence in sentencing policy can be seen to flow from the judgments of the Court of Appeal. But even Thomas is critical of the loss of coherence in the 1980s, in the wake of innovations such as partially suspended sentences of imprisonment, and the extension of parole (D.A. Thomas 1982, 1986). Ashworth is doubtful of the existence of a coherent 'tariff' (i.e. a coherent hierarchy of sentence severity), and the burden of his critique is that not only does a consistent and defensible criminal justice policy not exist in England, but also that it *cannot* exist in the current constitutional framework:

co-ordination of policy, from prosecution through to parole . . . is essential if the criminal justice system is to be shaped so as to achieve agreed policy objectives . . . The Lord Chancellor, Lord Hailsham, has stated that he 'would not desire to have either the prosecuting process or the penal treatment process under his responsibility', because they are incompatible with the judicial function . . . The Lord Chancellor seems to fear that the independence and impartiality of the judiciary would be put in danger by such a change, but that does not follow . . . What is most important is that a far wider range of groups within the criminal

---

[4] Courts in The Netherlands *may* ask for sureties, but rarely do. Breaking bail is not a criminal offence there, but any defendant failing to respect it will not be released again before trial when caught.

justice system are brought into the formal process of the creation and implementation of penal policy. (Ashworth 1983: 137–8)

The Home Office transformed into a Ministry of Justice might assist in this process: but the change may be more nominal than real.

The very diversity of departmental responsibilities makes co-ordination of policy difficult, and clearly the independence enjoyed by some agencies increases the problems of fashioning an integrated criminal justice policy. Whatever the policy initiatives within the Home Office, the fact remains that the Home Secretary cannot exert sufficient control over certain vital aspects of the system. For example, 'Constitutional considerations put policy-making in the areas of prosecution and sentencing remote from the influence of central government, save through changes in law. (Moriarty 1977, quoted in Ashworth 1983: 102)

The law, however, can never be framed so precisely as to do more than suggest very broad ranges of penalties for relatively diffuse types of offence. Both in England and The Netherlands, judicial discretion is very wide, and necessarily so. No *minima* exist in English criminal law, with a few exceptions, such as the mandatory life sentence for murder, and disqualification from driving for drunken driving. The minimum prison sentence in The Netherlands for *all* offences is one day. *Maxima* are very high in England, well above the general run of sentences (see ACPS 1978), and though lower in The Netherlands (see Appendix 4.1, p. 122) the same disparity occurs with actual sentencing. Short of mandatory sentencing (which in the United States led to the doubling of the prison population within the space of a decade), it is difficult to see how an integrated criminal justice policy could be activated, let alone devised, without some equivalent body to the Dutch prosecutorial system. The new Crown prosecutors may provide the embryo for such a system; a Sentencing Council may, as Ashworth suggests, supply the appropriate forum for practice directions. But the difference between the two systems is at this point extremely wide.

The strength of the Dutch prosecutorial system should not lead one to suppose that the courts simply rubber-stamp the prosecutor's recommendations. The latter are framed with the views and attitudes of the judges in mind, just as the sentence takes account of the prosecutor's recommendation. Since 1983, courts may impose higher penalties only by giving explicit written reasons, a further encouragement to stay within the prosecutor's recommendation. The convention that the latter sets a 'ceiling' (in all but some 3 per cent of cases) to the sentence is derived from the obligation on the prosecutor to take account of the 'public interest' in framing the recommendation. The judges are thus relatively more inclined to take into account the needs of the offender, once a conviction has been decided upon.

The sitting judiciary is independent: this means that the judges are not subordinate to the Government. Judges owe obedience only to the law, and their duty to account for judicial decisions extends no further than an obligation to motivate these decisions which is anchored in the law. They are nominated for life (with an age limit of 70 years) in a specific court, their salaries are fixed by law, and they are irremovable and non-transferable without their consent . . .. (Sharples 1972: 175)

The judges on the criminal panel are also a relatively small, wholly professional body, with no lay element equivalent to English magistrates or jury. Roughly one-third of the 917 judges in 1986 worked in the criminal, as distinct from the civil, courts, much the same number as in 1981. There are additionally part-time judges, who are largely unpaid although they too have legal qualifications, who serve for perhaps a day a week in court. Their numbers have *expanded* from 230 in 1970, to 400 in 1980, and 700 in 1986 (Netherlands, Ministry of Justice 1986); again, roughly one-third work in the criminal courts. Even by continental standards, The Netherlands is unusually professionalized in its system of criminal justice. Belgium has a jury system, for example, though in many other respects its criminal justice system resembles that of The Netherlands.

A far more fundamental difference between the two systems than the independence or otherwise of the judiciary is the form of the judicial division of labour, and the whole character of the procedural frameworks. As Sharples (1972) has put it, 'English penal procedure—based on the presumption of innocence, albeit there is a natural tendency to assume that a person committed for trial after an examination before magistrates is probably guilty—is distinctly *accusatorial* in character. The prosecution and defence (who have equivalent status) are in conflict with each other in the presence of the passive judge, who exercises a supervisory role in seeing that the parties observe the procedural rules.' In magistrates' courts, a lay bench (stipendiaries are the minority) performs the judicial function. 'Under *inquisitorial* procedure, the court (including the judge) is active in the search for truth. There appear before the court not so much a prosecutor and a defendant, as rather a prosecutor and an accused. The accused is not an equal party in the proceedings, but an object of inquiry . . . The core of the distinction between the two systems would seem to lie mainly in the differing functions of the judge: thus in an English criminal trial he acts in the capacity of an umpire until the defendant's conviction (cf. Dutch civil procedure), but acquires the power actively to participate in the proceedings from conviction to sentence. On the other hand, the Dutch penal judge has to take part actively in the actual trail from its outset' (Sharples 1972: 173–4). 'Because the judge is an independent, active seeker of the truth, the prosecutor is relatively passive during the trial, in contrast to the Anglo-American model . . .' (Hulsman, *et al.* 1978: 311).

There are perhaps more similarities between the two systems than the above might suggest. In both systems, there is provision for legal defence and usually for legal aid. In both the process of establishing mitigating and aggravating circumstances can form the real business of the trial (Shapland 1981). Yet there is undoubtedly a real difference in the experience of being a defendant in the contrasting courts. In the English adversarial system, the focus is mainly on the elicitation of the facts germane to guilt or innocence, so that even where, as in the great majority of cases, guilt is admitted, the facts must still be heard in open court, within rules of evidence of a highly structured, often ornate character. Of course, the precise nature of the facts as proof of the charge is of great importance in the Dutch procedure. But it is mainly established at the investigating stage, so that in this respect the Dutch public trial is mainly a check on whether the investigations have been properly carried out. For this reason, a relatively larger part of the trial can be devoted to personal circumstances and to an understanding of why the offence occurred. In the Dutch trial, therefore, the precise nature of the facts is less of a priority, the degree of culpability more of a real concern. 'We wish to know the person not the facts' rings, to English ears, very oddly from a judge: but it was repeated in several interviews as the key to the distinctive character of Dutch sentencing and trial procedure. The case dossier has been assembled for the court, and this 'written report plays a crucial role in criminal proceedings in the Netherlands, especially in those cases in which no preliminary judical inquiry takes place, comprising the vast majority of cases' (Hulsman *et al.* 1978: 348). This does not necessarily stem from some peculiarity of doctrine. Both the English and Dutch systems are compromises, philosophically speaking, between the various objectives of retribution, deterrence, incapacitation, and rehabilitation (Sharples 1972: 286). Both the 1948 Criminal Justice Act and the Statutory Rules of 1949 in England, which gave rise to the distinction between local and training prisons, may be compared to the 1951 Principles of Imprisonment Act in The Netherlands, Art. 26 of which stresses the need to prepare 'for the return of the detainees to life in free society'. Both stress the principle of rehabilitation: though, as we shall see, with markedly different effects.

In many respects, there is a close parallel between probation work in both countries. In each, they respond to requests from the judiciary (both prosecutors and judges) for social inquiry reports on the personal, family, social, and economic background and future prospects of the defendants awaiting trial and sentence; they offer a 'throughcare' supportive role in connection with those remanded in custody and serving prison sentences, especially in the period before release; they play a supervisory role in connection with community service orders; they advise, assist, and support those consenting to a probation order (England) or those who have been conditionally sentenced to prison (The Netherlands), and those who have been released on parole (both). Both probation services can claim origins in the early nineteenth-century work of the charitable societies assisting discharged prisoners and inspired by the work of John Howard, though the Dutch Society for the Moral Reformation of Prisoners, founded in 1823, perhaps paid more attention to 'after-care' than Elizabeth Fry's Prison Discipline Society of 1817, whose main concern was the condition of the jails. The major difference between the two systems, however, relates to the greater degree to which the Dutch probation service has maintained a functional autonomy in its relations to the court. *Reclasseringstoezicht* (probation order) is a measure which Dutch courts cannot impose in its own right, but only in combination with a suspended prison sentence. However, though the Ministry of Justice has sought to exercise greater control over the *reclassering* in recent years, 'the probation service has made it plain that it no longer wishes to perform supervisory duties and that it does not intend to report breaches of special conditions'. Its supportive role is client-centred and even in the case of pre-sentence reports, the client's assent is sought both for its content and its submission to the court (Hulsman *et al.* 1978: 318, 315). The 1970s saw the development of radical strategies (e.g. client refusal) in probation work in England (Simpkin 1979). But these moves occurred within a system historically less detached from the state and the courts than was the case in The Netherlands, where a voluntary tradition and private organization persist despite professionalization and total subsidization by the state.

At both local and national level, the probation service in The Netherlands has more scope for exerting an influence on policy than is the case in England. The insulation of the probation service in England is partly self-induced, born of the fear of loss of identity in the generic social work framework. Under the Dutch system, probation boards for every district court combine representatives from probation agencies locally and community representatives, as well as a judge, a prosecutor, a psychiatrist, and a prison officer or official. These boards have 'a general supervisory and co-ordinating task and serve as a forum for discussion and consultation for the local authorities and agencies involved in probation work and allied activities' (Hulsman *et al.* 1978: 316). They have their national counterpart in the Central Advisory Board for Corrections, Treatment of Mentally Disordered Offenders and Probation. These bodies, which have no real counterpart in England, may play a role in policy making: but the real impact of *reclassering* was usually claimed to lie at the court level. Thus, for example, one senior prosecutor interviewed saw the probation service as the key mediating link between research and the judiciary. 'The ideas of the criminologists about the penal system reach the judges via the probation. And probation has a very great influence on the judges,' though its influence had declined with the radicalism of the 1970s. The difficulties of evaluating that notion are expanded upon later (Ch. 3). It is difficult, however, to conceive of so heady a claim being made by a senior English judge or magistrate. Clearly, 'the situation in The Netherlands (regarding probation) differs profoundly from what is customary in most of the neighbouring countries and in the United States' (Hulsman *et al.* 1978: 331).

The prison systems of England and The Netherlands, are not

entirely dissimilar. A point-by-point comparison would prove unwieldy but some principal similarities are:

1.   Both systems are differentiated to some degree: prisons in this country between local and training prisons, the former for remand and short-sentence prisoners, the latter for longer term prisoners. Specific prisons may be run on specialist lines (e.g. Grendon Underwood's psychiatric regime). In The Netherlands, prisons are broadly divided into closed, semi-closed, and open. A similar distinction exists between prisons (for convicted prisoners) and houses of detention (for unconvicted), with the latter also used for prisoners serving sentences of three months or less, and for longer-term prisoners awaiting allocation to prison. The security spectrum is more developed in English prisons, with the most secure prisons holding prisoners designated Category A, the least secure 'open' prisons Category D prisoners. No formal categorization system obtains in The Netherlands.

2.   Comparable forms of age and gender grading are employed in both countries. Women are held in separate prisons, though in The Netherlands only one such prison exists. Some 23 per cent of Dutch prisoners are under 23 years of age, some 29 per cent of English prisoners are under 21, making the English prisoners relatively, though not dramatically, younger (Nijboer and Ploeg 1985: 230; Home Office Prison Statistics (1985), Tables 1.4 and 3.12; English figures relate to males under sentence). Youth prisons in The Netherlands for the 18–23 age range correspond to youth custody centres in England. *Tuchtschools* (reformatories) are similar to detention centres, though the regime is less militaristic.

3.   In terms of sheer material environment, the age range of Dutch prisons is similar to that in England, with a number of nineteenth-century establishments of panopticon design (e.g. The Hague, Haarlem) paralleling those of Pentonville, Wandsworth, and similar establishments. As Vinson (1985) has noted, two-thirds of the cells in the closed prisons in The Netherlands remain un-sewered, though the figure for England is almost 90 per cent. Even so, ready access to toilet facilities is the norm in Dutch prisons.

The differences between the two systems are far more notable than the similarities, and form much of the substance of Chapter 6 and some of the material in Chapters 2 and 4. Some striking dissimilarities are:

1.   One prisoner to a cell is the almost invariable rule in Dutch

prisons, the only exception being the open prison at Heerhugowaard, where two prisoners occupy rooms formerly occupied by four migrant workers. No such constraint on the use of capacity exists in England. In 1982, for example, some 16,000 prisoners were sharing cells designed for one prisoner—11,000 sharing two to a cell, 5,000 three to a cell. Prison overcrowding has become the single most potent issue in penal policy over the past two decades (for the most comprehensive analysis see Rutherford 1986; but see also King and Morgan 1980, and successive reports of H M Prison Inspectorate). This difference between the ratios of prison population to prison capacity is the most striking surface constrast between the Dutch and English systems. Yet the real contrast is between the principles underlying those ratios: English prisons are obliged to accept immediately those remanded in or sentenced to custody by the courts; Dutch prisons are obliged *not* to accept those for whom a place is not available. Although Dutch prisons must make a place available for those sentenced to imprisonment for a range of the most serious offences, this is not the case for either remand detainees (the majority of the daily prison population in The Netherlands) or those (e.g. motoring offenders) eligible for the 'call-up' system (see Ch. 2).

2. The proportion of remand (unconvicted and unsentenced) prisoners to the total is far higher in The Netherlands than in England in 1980, over 60 per cent and 15 per cent respectively. In 1985 the disparity was somewhat less, that for The Netherlands being closer to 50 per cent and that for England being 21 per cent, but the magnitude of the difference remains most striking. The flexibility of the Dutch penal administration is in part attributable to the discretionary release of remand prisoners (subject to recall) if numbers exceed capacity. In both countries, time spent on remand in custody is offset against sentence. As van Hofer (1975: 117) comments, 'to a considerable extent, Dutch prisons function as pre-trial centres of detention', though the reverse is also true: Dutch 'houses of detention' function much as prisons. It is therefore important to combine remand and sentenced prisoners for comparative purposes, and not to focus on sentenced prisoners only, though the average sentence of two months or so in The Netherlands is much the same as time spent on remand in custody.

3. The size of Dutch prisons is much smaller on average than

those in England. In The Netherlands in 1985, some 4,500 prisoners were held in 45 institutions with an average capacity of 100, ranging in capacity from 20 to some 150 (Brand-Koolen, p. 9). In England, some 150 establishments held roughly 46,000 prisoners in 1985 (a peak of 48,111 was reached in mid-July of that year), an average of 300 or so in each institution, with a range from under 50 in a few juvenile remand centres to over a thousand in nine local prisons, one or two exceeding 1,500 on occasion (e.g. Liverpool, Manchester). Thus, the average English prison establishment holds three times as many prisoners as those in The Netherlands, and some hold ten times as many as the largest Dutch prison. Such different orders of magnitude have immense implications for social relations within prison (see Ch. 6).

4.   In one major respect, English prisons are less militaristic. In closed prisons in The Netherlands perimeter guards are armed. British prison officers remain wholly (and British police largely) unarmed by comparison with those in The Netherlands, and indeed the rest of the world.

5.   Automatic remission of part of the sentence was abolished in The Netherlands in 1951. Remission of one-third of any sentence of over five days is automatic in England, except for those forfeiting some part of the time remitted as penalty for offences committed in prison, and for those serving life sentences. Far more extensive use is made in The Netherlands than in England of the 'pardon'. For example, in 1983, of 6,176 requests for pardon, 1,793 (29 per cent) were entirely or partially granted. From 1915 until 1987, conditional release by means of parole has applied to those at the point of serving nine months or more, or two-thirds of their sentence. The system has now been modified to allow prisoners serving sentences of one year or less to be released on parole after six months plus one-third of the remainder of their sentence; for those serving sentences of over a year, the rule remains two-thirds of the sentence, but without the nine-month threshold. Parole in England was first introduced in this century in 1967, (its nineteenth century precursor was the 'ticket of leave' system) and applied to those at the point of serving one-third of their sentence, or one year, whichever was the longer. Under the Criminal Justice Act of 1982, that threshold was in 1983 reduced to six months for all prisoners except those serving sentences of five years or more for violence or drug-trafficking. In July 1987, Douglas Hurd, the British home secretary, announced the setting-

up of a committee to review the parole system in England, under the chairmanship of Mark Carlisle, a former home secretary. Pending its outcome, an interim measure to relieve the pressure on penal capacity was also announced, introducing half, instead of one-third, remission for prisoners serving sentences of 12 months or less. This measure had the immediate effect of reducing the prison population, which had been climbing steeply since the previous autumn, from 51,000 to 48,000: its longer-term effects remain uncertain. In sum, therefore, in comparisons of sentencing trends, time actually served is therefore the best indicator of the use made of imprisonment, wherever possible, rather than sheer length of sentence.

6.   A final major difference between the two systems concerns the disposals available to offenders deemed mentally ill, disordered or psychopathic. In both countries, the use of special hospitals for such offenders has the character of a semi-indeterminate sentence, though in The Netherlands it is termed a 'measure' and those so detained are not commonly counted as part of the prison population. In The Netherlands, the measure was introduced in the so-called Psychopaths Acts which became operative in 1928, and by the 1950s a substantial proportion of the institutional population of offenders were dealt with by such treatment orders: roughly a third, though the proportion had dropped to nearer a tenth by the late 1970s. *Terbeschikkingstelling van der Regering* (TBR) or 'placement at the disposal of the government' is not, however, equivalent to 'detention at Her Majesty's pleasure' or life imprisonment, since the case is reviewed judicially every two years (a long-standing issue is the case for annual reviews) unless the order is terminated either conditionally or unconditionally by the minister of justice. TBR corresponds in essentials with detention in the special hospitals such as Broadmoor and Rampton in England under the terms of the 1959 Mental Health Act, though the numbers involved are far lower in England proportionally to the prison population, though not in terms of the population as a whole. In 1979, for example, 1,897 patients were detained under the provisions of the Mental Health Act. The equivalent figure for The Netherlands was 449 (on 15 Jan. 1980). In 1985, the number so detained in England stood at 1,626, a slight decline; that for The Netherlands was much the same, 440 (DHSS 1987: 14, Table 7; Netherlands Ministry of Justice 1985*e*).

In the context of the much smaller prison population of The Netherlands however, TBR looms large as a measure:

The special hospital is one of the distinctive aspects of the Dutch criminal justice system . . . From the point of view of facilities as well as manpower, the special hospitals are extremely well-equipped by comparison with other countries. A very individualised regime is possible in these hospitals, which facilitates considerable contact with the outside community. (Hulsman *et al.* 1978: 328).

A TBR order can be made either alone or in combination with a prison sentence; and prisoners whose mental state is thought to warrant such action may be transferred to such hospitals. Though the numbers involved are small, in relation to the relatively few (though growing) numbers of long-term prisoners in The Netherlands they assume increasing significance (Koenradt 1983). Clearly, for most comparative purposes, such 'total institution' populations should be added to those in penal establishments.

Conclusion

Problems in comparing sentencing and penal trends in The Netherlands and England vary at different stages of the sentencing process; the extent to which such trends have been or are the result of policy, or are largely independent of policy-making, will figure in much of what follows. Initially, however, it does appear that the distinctive role of the public prosecutor in The Netherlands makes possible a degree of overall integration in sentencing policy which has no equivalent in England, both in terms of its formulation and implementation.

APPENDIX 1.1.   Example of a numerical guideline for the prosecution of thefts in The Netherlands based on an analysis of current policies.

Factors to be considered	Score
OFFENCE-RELATED	
Damage	
Nil	0
Under 50 guilders	1
50–100 guilders	2
100–250 guilders	3
Over 250 guilders	4
Victim	
Large firm	0
Not a large firm	2
OFFENDER-RELATED	
Previous convictions	
None	0
One	1
Two	2
Three or more	3
Age	
65 +	0
30–65	1
22–30	2
18–22	3

Source: Van Dijk (1983: 12).

Note: The recommendation to prosecute would be based on consideration of the total score on all factors, as follows:
0–2   very strong indication not to prosecute (i.e. definitely drop case)
3–5   strong indication not to prosecute
6–8   indication to prosecute
9–12   strong indication to prosecute.

APPENDIX 1.2.   Prosecutors' priority scale for remand in custody
(January 1984)

I   Offences carrying a maximum of 12 years or more
      imprisonment (including attempts and accessory)   A
II   Offences against the drugs law:
      1.   Danger of flight or collusion   A
      2.   Offences of 6 years or more imprisonment (hard
           drug trafficking)   A
      3.   Offences of under 6 years imprisonment
           (possession of hard drugs/all soft drugs offences)   C
III   Other offences:
      1.   Any 2 of the following 3 criteria: A
           a)   More than 5 crimes on this occasion; and/or
                involving over 100,000 guilders' property;
                and/or serious injuries.
           b)   Ten or more previous convictions, including
                waivers and suspended sentences.
           c)   Serious danger of flight and/or collusion.
      2.   If the following criteria are met: C
           a)   Less than 5 offences on this occasion;
           b)   Loss and/or damage of under 1,000
                guilders;
           c)   Injuries light or none;
           d)   Three or less previous convictions;
           e)   No suspended sentences;
           f)   No danger of flight and/or collusion.
      3.   Neither A nor C   B

Source: Berghuis and Essers (1985: 8).

2 Post-war Penal Trends in The Netherlands and England

THE broad picture of contrasting trends in penal populations in Britain and The Netherlands is by now familiar to many who have even a passing interest in such matters. Over the past few years, not only have a number of sources dealt explicitly with the contrast in some detail (some of which compare the situation in The Netherlands with societies other than Britain, e.g. Rutherford 1984; Steenhuis *et al*. 1983), but also the theme has emerged quite distinctly in a number of television documentary series about penal policy in Britain (e.g. London Weekend Television's '*Once a Thief . . .?* in 1986). As a result the contrast between the penal estates of the two societies in terms of a central and indisputable feature—that over a lengthy period there has emerged a sharp and growing divergence in the relative size of their respective prison populations—has gained widespread currency. What remains more problematic, however, are the origins, character, and consequences of that divergence and their implications for penal policy in the future.

In the years immediately after the Second World War, The Netherlands actually exceeded Britain in reliance on custodial penalties. In 1950, the average population of prisons and borstals in England was 20,474. In The Netherlands the equivalent figure (excluding political prisoners who were still held in custody following sentences for war-time collaboration) was 5,848. Rates per 100,000 of the population at risk (aged over 15 in England and over 18 in The Netherlands) were 64 and 82 respectively. The fall in the Dutch prison population began in 1947, the year that the findings of the Fick Commission on the prison system were published. Yet even a dramatic reduction of the prison population from 8,577 in 1947 to 5,858 in 1950 still left The Netherlands with a higher average number in custody than England. By 1957, however, the rates of imprisonment (daily average population) converged, and from that point onwards the rate for The Netherlands became progressively lower than that for England. By 1975, the situation had been transformed. The daily average prison population in England had *doubled* to almost 40,000, while that in The Netherlands had *more than halved,* to 2,526. What had been a ratio of 4 : 5 had become a ratio of 4 : 1 in terms of average daily prison population relative to populations at risk. In short, while England had pursued a mixture of expansionist and 'standstill' policies in the penal sphere, The Netherlands had followed a consistently reductionist policy (Rutherford 1984). In the decade after 1975, The Netherlands tended to converge with rather than continue to diverge from the penal trend in England, but the ratio remains roughly 3 : 1, a remarkable reversal of the situation that obtained in 1950.

The striking change is generally attributed almost wholly to reductions in the *length* of sentences passed and served in The Netherlands, and to increases in those in England. Changes in the relative use of sentences of imprisonment compared with non-custodial sentences are seen as contributing little to the trend. Hans Tulkens, former director of the Prisons Department in The Netherlands summarized this position succinctly:

Over the past 25 years the length of prison terms in The Netherlands has shown a trend which contrasts with the trend in Britain. Around 1950 the situation in The Netherlands was much the same as in England and Wales. However, by 1975 the situation had changed completely. The percentage of very short sentences, *viz.* those of less than one month, had doubled in The Netherlands, and amounted to 57 per cent of the total. In England and Wales this category of very short sentences has decreased by one-third to 18 per cent of the total. At the other extreme, long prison sentences (12 months and over) in The Netherlands have decreased by almost two-thirds, from close to 12 per cent to just over 4 per cent, whilst in England and Wales this category has increased from 16 per cent to 28 per cent. (Tulkens 1979: 4)

Tulkens also made the point that there was, in 1975, a 'remarkable correspondence of percentages of cases which did and did not lead to a prison sentence'—14 per cent in England, 15 per cent in The Netherlands (pp. 3–4). Whilst this correspondence existed for the period about which he was writing, the picture has changed somewhat over the past decade, with The Netherlands resorting to imprisonment relatively less than was then the case: in 1983, 15 per cent of offenders in England were sentenced to some form of custody, compared with 10 per cent in The Netherlands. It is no longer the case, therefore, that length of sentence alone accounts for the contrast.

The problem defined

It is one thing to describe and document contrasting trends, quite another to account for them. Some ways of addressing the problem, which will be analyzed more fully in Chapter 3, in effect explain the differences *away*. First, it has been argued that The Netherlands has always maintained much the same penal capacity (e.g. van Ruller 1981; 1985), so that the post-war situation is in reality a continuation of historic tendencies. This argument has much to commend it, but ignores the 'remarkable correspondence' to which Tulkens referred in the immediate post-war period, as well as the extent to which many other societies shrugged off, in the post-war period, the historic tendencies they had displayed pre-war in the penal sphere (e.g. England, where between 1923 and 1938 the prison population held steady at roughly 30 per 100,000 population). Secondly, it was put to me on several occasions during interviews with members of the Dutch judiciary that The Netherlands possessed a quite different system of criminal justice to that of England, and that this system allowed for more rational penal policy making. Again, though this view captures a crucial aspect of the problem, it does not resolve it. Throughout continental Europe, the prosecutorial system clearly differs very substantially from that in England, but variations in policy are often as acute as those between England and The Netherlands (e.g. between The Netherlands and West Germany; see Steenhuis *et al.* 1983). The existence of the administrative apparatus to facilitate a particular policy formation does not mean that one policy has to be followed. Thirdly, there are ways of explaining the problem away by reducing it to other terms. These are in principle quite valid, but they raise empirical questions to be dealt with in their own right. For example, if the crime trends in The Netherlands are markedly less serious than those in England, a correspondingly less severe penal policy could be accounted for in those terms. Similarly, if a set of 'hidden' sanctions are operated in The Netherlands which serve as the functional equivalent of custodial sanctions, then again the problem would be dissolved into one of accounting for institutional rather than non-institutional differences. The recourse to mental hospitals as distinct from prisons as a form of deviance control would be such an instance. These issues are taken up below, but to anticipate the evidence on these issues, they affect the nature of the trends only marginally.

The nature of the problem is perhaps best disclosed by a study of the process of sentencing carried out in The Netherlands in the late 1970s. Jan van Dijk summarized the results of an analysis of sentencing in some 3,000 criminal cases as follows: 'Most judicial decisions appear to be influenced foremost by the material seriousness of the crime. Offender characteristics seem to be an important point of consideration only with the less serious crimes' (van Dijk 1980: 4). Variations naturally occurred, but the material seriousness of the offence(s) committed emerged as the predominant influence at all stages of the sentencing process: the decision whether or not to prosecute; the decision whether or not to order pre-trial detention; and the severity of the final sentence. He also conducted observational studies of the sentencers at work, in some of which prosecutors spoke their thoughts into a tape-recorder. The results suggested that sentencing was too rushed a process to allow each case to be considered afresh in the light of competing philosophical arguments. 'Sentencing in practice is *not* a process of relating the facts about the case and the offender to the aims of punishment. In most cases it consists of relating these facts to a scheme, that is based on former decisions . . . Consistency in relating sentences to culpability could very well be the working goal of the majority of the sentencers' (pp. 7–8). On the basis of what is clearly a major study, with few, if any, precedents in its scope and methodology, it is concluded that *material seriousness* and a concern for *consistency* are the predominant elements in sentencing, from which in all but the most exceptional cases the judiciary will resist too great a deviation. 'It is only with such exceptional cases that the sentencer finds himself reasoning at length about the various conflicting aims of punishment [such as rehabilitation, deterrence, retribution, and incapacitation] as the textbooks on penal law expect him to do routinely' (p. 9).

What happens when we apply this model (as van Dijk did not aim to do) to *trends* in sentencing practice? How well does it help to account for changes in observed outcomes over time? It seems to account quite well for developments in England over the past 30 years. As the crime rate has risen, and with it the flow of offenders through the criminal justice system, so the prison population has risen also. The parallel is by no means exact, for attempts have been made, with some partial success, to divert certain groups of offenders from prison and to reduce the amount of time served by suspended sentences, parole, decriminalization and the adumbration of such alternatives to custody as Community Service Orders, attendance centres, and the like. But the correspondence btween the rise in crime and the rise in the prison population has been far closer than in The Netherlands where, for two decades at least, from 1955–75, precisely the reverse situation obtained. Whether or not we accept the finding that seriousness and consistency are the overriding guidelines for sentencing practice, it is clear that, in The Netherlands, something *other* than the pursuit of these guidelines has also been going on. Indeed, it is difficult to square the finding that these guidelines have been the foremost touchstones of sentencing process in The Netherlands with the actual downward trend in the prison population for this period. If we are to account for trends in sentencing which are inconsistent with the predictions we might logically make from such guidelines, it seems in order to assess the reality of the trends, to compare contrasting theories which might account for them, and to speculate about possible ways in which sentencing process and sentencing outcomes may be discrete yet related phenomena.

The reality of the trends

Crime trends

Crime trends in the two societies between 1950 and 1985 were broadly parallel, with the rate of serious offences fractionally lower in The Netherlands both in 1950 and 1985. Within that broad picture, however, there are substantial differences in the *pace* of overall increases in crime rates (see Fig. 2.1). By 1965, the crime rate in England had more than doubled since 1950, rising from about 1,000 to some 2,300 per 100,000 population. In The Netherlands the rise had been far milder, from about 975 to roughly 1,250. The scope for reducing lengths of prison sentences in the Dutch context was somewhat greater, if we assume that anxieties about rising crime are a major obstacle to such a policy. However, perhaps the most remarkable feature of the Dutch situation is that lengths of sentence, and the overall daily prison population, continued to decline over the next decade, 1966–75, when the crime rate more than doubled, from about 1,250 to almost 3,000. From that point onwards, the period of 'reductionism', in an absolute sense, came to an end, and the prison population began to climb, roughly matching the crime rate in the decade from 1976–85, with both

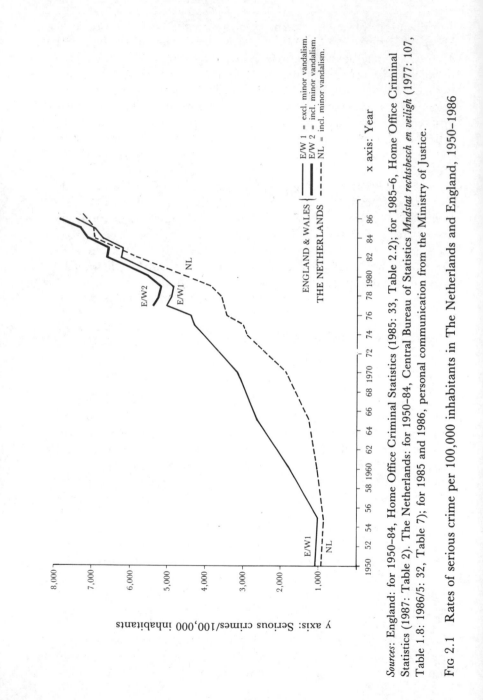

Sources: England: for 1950–84, Home Office Criminal Statistics (1985: 33, Table 2.2); for 1985–6, Home Office Criminal Statistics (1987: Table 2). The Netherlands: for 1950–84, Central Bureau of Statistics *Mndstat rechtsbesch en veiligh* (1977: 107, Table 1.8: 1986/5: 32, Table 7); for 1985 and 1986, personal communication from the Ministry of Justice.

FIG 2.1   Rates of serious crime per 100,000 inhabitants in The Netherlands and England, 1950–1986

more than doubling in the course of ten years. Even so, the ending of the period of sentence shortening and falling prison populations in The Netherlands has not, as yet, done much to reduce the formidable contrast outlined above.

Within these overall trends, the nature and seriousness of the crimes also differed between the two societies. In 1979, for example, crimes against property in both societies constituted over 90 per cent of 'serious' crimes. But over the period 1950–75, the rate of increase of crimes against the person was more marked in England than in The Netherlands: in England it rose tenfold whereas in The Netherlands it remained roughly constant. Only since 1975 have the rates of offences involving violence against the person risen at much the same pace in both countries. Rates of sexual offences as a whole remained roughly the same in both countries over the period, though rape increased somewhat in both. In sum, the overall tendency up till 1975 for the rise in crime to be limited to property offences may have been a factor which facilitated the reductions in sentence lengths in The Netherlands.

Neither the slower pace with which the crime rate rose in The Netherlands nor the absence of crimes of violence within that rise can arguably account for more than a fraction of the disparities between the penal trends in the two countries. For the fact remains that crime did rise in The Netherlands, albeit more gradually than in England, so that a small rise, rather than a large drop in the prison population, would have been the logical expectation. And although crimes of violence did not rise proportionately, most people in prison, at least in England, are there for offences against property and not for crimes of violence. However, if the crime situation in The Netherlands was much less serious overall than in England, one might infer that like offences would attract like sentences, but that the smaller number of really serious offences would create a far smaller 'core' of offenders predestined for long periods of imprisonment, which would create a more favourable climate for a reductionist policy with reference to the far larger numbers of relatively petty offenders.

A crucial test of that proposition is the extent to which the two societies reacted similarly to the more serious offences. To that end, three of the most serious offences in both societies—rape, robbery, and burglary—were examined in terms of sentencing trends. Surprisingly, perhaps, it appears that differences in the resort to imprisonment by sentencers have affected all kinds of offence, not only the less serious. Sentencing trends show consistent and even growing differences between the two societies in this regard (see Table 2.1.)

The figures in Table 2.1 confirm the 'reality' of the trends even for the more serious offences in The Netherlands. By contrast, the pattern for England is much more in line with the notion that consistency and seriousness are the touchstones of sentencing, particularly in the case of rape and robbery. What seems to emerge is that Dutch sentencers at all stages of the judicial process exercised far more resistance against prosecution and imprisonment. Though the trend is not uniform—for example, institutional sentences for rape were much the same proportionately in 1981 as 1960—it appears that the proportion of cases waived increased, the proportion sent to prison decreased, and shorter sentences were imposed on those imprisoned. A principal reason for the paradox that, until very recently, the Dutch imprisoned roughly the same proportion of offenders as the English, though for far shorter periods of time, is that The Netherlands employs very short sentences of imprisonment far more frequently for motoring offenders, particularly in cases of drunken driving. In 1960, motoring offenders accounted for almost a fifth, in 1981 almost a third, of all sentences of imprisonment, the great majority being for less than one month. In the case of England in 1979, motoring offenders accounted for perhaps 3 per cent of those imprisoned. This disparity remains virtually the same today. As a result, the explanation for the much lower rate of imprisonment in The Netherlands in non-motoring cases rests on more than the simple difference between the lengths of sentence imposed: a variety of other strategies are employed to accomplish that result.

Table 2.1 shows that over the 1960–81 period the tendency to waive prosecution increased markedly for burglary, returned to its 1960 level for rape (perhaps reflecting a response to campaigns by women's groups for less leniency to be shown in these cases—though the mean length of sentence has not returned to its former level), and increased also for robbery, despite a relative drop in waiving since 1970. However, this table makes no differentiation between waiving on 'technical' grounds and for 'policy' reasons. The former corresponds to grounds such as the adequacy of the evidence which in England would probably mean that a case would not be brought. Such grounds loom larger for rape than for burglary, where policy waivers are relatively more important. These waivers are made on primarily non-legal grounds, for example, the willingness of the offender to admit guilt, profess reasons for future compliance, and perhaps offer restitution. If we exclude technical waivers, the disparities between sentencing in the two countries is somewhat reduced. Even when 'technical' waivers are eliminated from the disposals, the disparities in sentencing by no means disappear (Table 2.2). It is interesting to see, however, how late in the day it was before sentencing in The Netherlands for burglary began to diverge at all significantly from that in England: until 1970, both the proportions sentenced to institutions and the length of sentence (allowing for remission in the case of England) was much the same. Until 1967, however, there was no system of parole in England to further mitigate the duration of a prison sentence, whereas in The Netherlands parole operated throughout the period with virtually all prisoners being granted parole after nine months or two-thirds of their sentence, whichever is the greater. In around 90 per cent of cases, the prisoner is paroled at the earliest possible date. (Hulsman *et al.* 1978: 327). Even after 1967, no such assumption could be made about the operation of parole in England where it has been much more stringently used. Even after 1983, when the parole eligibility period was reduced from 12 to 6 months, an even tougher exercise of parole was introduced for offenders convicted of violence or drug-trafficking, which effectively, and even retrospectively, removed their right of parole (Bottomley 1984). Another device employed by the Dutch which has no real counterpart in England, is the pardon. 'About a third of the 6,000 requests for pardon considered annually are granted. Pardon may be full or partial, conditional or unconditional and a detention or a prison sentence may be commuted to a fine' (Hulsman *et al.* 1978: 319). In short, a veritable armoury of devices have been evolved by the Dutch to review sentences, and these provide a variety of means whereby the size of the prison population can be calibrated to fit the available capacity. That is not to say, however, that such flexibility is infinitely elastic, or that such devices will inevitably be used for 'reductionist' ends, to use Rutherford's term. In England, for example, the length of custodial sentences for robbery increased after the introduction of parole, which may reflect a judicial desire to offset its effects by longer sentences at the outset. And in The Netherlands a 'mass' pardon in 1977, of very short-term offenders (mainly motoring), expressly

TABLE 2.1   Sentencing in relation to three 'serious' offences, 1950–1981

| | The Netherlands | | | | England | | |
| | Waived by prosecutor (%) | Custodial sentence | | Mean sentence (months) | Prison (%) | Sentence (months) | |
		Prison (%)	All (%)			Total	Less remission
Burglary							
1950	*	*	*	13		15	10
1955	*	*	*	12		16	11
1960	34	38	40	11	42	14	10
1965	50	31	32	11	36	17	11
1970	54	28	29	7	29	15[a]	10[a]
1981[b]	57	18	22	5	31	13[a]	9[a]
Rape							
1950	*	*	*	16	78	36	24
1955	*	*	*	14	82	39	26
1960	46	43	47	16	76	32	21
1965	38	50	57	15	84	42	28
1970	52	36	41	11	83	39	26
1981[b]	46	41	47	11	88	47	32

Robbery

1950	*	*	29	*	77	32	21
1955	*	*	24	*	77	26	18
1960	22	59	23	65	77	27	18
1965	39	53	16	57	78	30	20
1970	52	36	17	41	73	36	24
1981[b]	37	39	11	49	78	43	28

* = no data available for waiving (non-prosecution) therefore no estimate can be given for per centage imprisoned.

[a] = mean of data for burglary in a dwelling and other burglary.

[b] Data for England are for 1979.

Sources: Rates for the Netherlands derived from figures supplied to the Public Prosecutors by the Central Bureau of Statistics; for England, figures for 1970–9, Home Office Criminal Statistics, (1979: 137); for 1950–65, from the same source, relevant years. Mean sentence length was calculated by taking the mid-point of each category, and multiplying by the appropriate number. The total of sentence months was then divided by the total under sentence for the offence.

Notes: 'Prison' = wholly unsuspended and partly suspended for The Netherlands and for England and Wales for 1981. 'All institutions' include TBR (secure mental institutional confinement) and *tuchtschool* (reformatories).

TABLE 2.2   Sentencing adjusted in relation to three 'serious' offences, 1981–1983

| | The Netherlands | | | | England | | |
| | Policy waivers by prosecutor (%) | Custodial sentence | | Mean sentence (months) | Prison (%) | Sentence (months) | |
		Prison (%)	All (%)			Total	Less remission
Burglary[a]							
1981[a]	50	21	26	5	31	13	9
1983	49	21	*	3	32	10	7
Rape[a]							
1981[a]	18	61	71	11	88	47	32
1983	21	53	*	10	91	51	34
Robbery[a]							
1981[a]	21	49	62	11	78	43	28
1983	27	47	*	10	76	32	21

Sources: For The Netherlands, raw CBS data provided for the Public Prosecutors; for England, *Home Office Criminal Statistics* (1983), 148–9: Table 7.2, and *Supplementary Tables*, vols. 1 and 2.
[a] Data for England are for 1979.
* = not available

designed to relieve pressure on penal capacity, brought strong protests from the judiciary, and it is unlikely that such a measure will be repeated. Such acts of clemency are not, however, unknown in England. In 1910, Winston Churchill as home secretary initiated the release of large numbers of short-term prisoners (Rutherford 1984: 124–6 n. 10; 148–9).

Despite these measures, the rising crime rate in The Netherlands has led to an increase in the numbers of offenders processed through the criminal justice system, from some 120,000 in 1975 to almost 220,000 in 1983, and the increase in final custodial sentences has led the Dutch authorities to plan to expand their penal capacity by 1990 to roughly double its 1975 level—up from 3,127 places to some 6,000. (In England, an even larger increase in penal capacity is now (21.3.88) planned for 1994, with some 26 new prisons to provide a notional 21,200 extra places, an increase of 55 per cent or so in penal capacity since 1983). To what extent is the change attributable to an abandonment of reductionist aims, as reflected in sentencing, in the 1978 period onwards? It would appear from detailed breakdown of the figures for selected serious offences, that the principal reason is the increased number of offenders, rather than an abandonment of relatively sparing resort to imprisonment—which has increased since the mid-1970s—or longer sentences, which have been employed selectively, mainly in cases of hard drug-trafficking (Table 2.3).

Over a five-year period with the steepest increases in serious crime rates in The Netherlands since the war, the sentencing pattern either showed a proportionately reduced use of imprisonment or remained much the same. The proportionate use of policy waivers rose in every case; the proportion of policy waivers to all waivers increased for offences against life and hard drugs, but remained unchanged for the other offences; and although some long prison sentences of over five years were passed in cases of drug-trafficking, their overall length rose by only two months. In the case of offences against life, it should be stressed that the great majority (about 80–85 per cent) are attempts. The figures do, however, provide striking confirmation of the resistance of the Dutch judiciary to penal measures at every stage of the criminal justice process.

It should be noted that the nominal length of sentence is in all cases an over-estimate of the actual *time served* in prison (other than

TABLE 2.3   *Sentencing of serious offences in The Netherlands, 1978 and 1983*

Offence and year	Total 1: all cases	Total 2: Excluding technical waivers	Of Total 2		Mean sentence (months)	Policy waivers as % of policy and technical waivers
			Policy waivers (%)	Prison (%)		
Opiumweg[a]						
1978	2,906	1,904	42	34	11	74
1983	5,672	4,059	55	32	13	79
Offences[b] against life						
1978	360	241	17	63	26	31
1983	950	568	41	44	27	51
Burglary						
1978	14,066	9,374	41	25	3	79
1983	24,298	14,586	49	21	3	79
Rape						
1978	381	245	17	53	10	27
1983	591	351	21	54	10	26
Robbery						
1978	1,044	694	22	54	11	46
1983	2,350	1,494	27	48	10	49

Source: Raw CBS figures supplied to the Public Prosecutors.

Total 1:   All cases before the court, including those subsequently found Not Guilty, not available for processing, under appeal, etc.
Total 2:   All cases before the court excluding the above categories, and also excluding those cases where prosecution was waived on technical grounds.

[a]   Hard drugs.
[b]   Murder and manslaughter (including attempts).

for the small number of prisoners who commit a serious offence within jail). The figures for mean sentence length in Table 2.3 are very precise, since they have been calculated by The Netherlands Central Bureau of Statistics (CBS) on the basis of the number of days of each individual sentence. Such figures are not available before 1978, and for this period we have to rely on averaging out sentence categories, a far cruder exercise. Time actually served in prison can in principle be measured much more exactly, since the number of receptions annually can be related to the daily average population, and expressed as an average in days, months, or years (Pease 1980). Difficulties arise with the problem of double-or triple-counting of receptions into prison, as when a single person is counted once as a remand in custody, once as a reception awaiting sentence, and once as a convicted prisoner. The Dutch figures purportedly avoid this problem by counting each individual reception once only. Only for 1978 and 1979 are data available for England which avoid the problem. On this basis, the Dutch figures show that mean time served amounted to between 1.3 and 2.0 months in the period from 1965 to 1981; in England the mean time served for all prisoners in 1979 was 5.0 months. These differences are roughly in line with the differences in the prison populations of the two countries. The disparity is far greater for sentenced prisoners only, since prisons in The Netherlands to a considerable extent function as pre-trial centres of detention (van Hofer 1975: 117). In 1972, for example the mean time served by sentenced prisoners (excluding fine-defaulters) in The Netherlands was 1.4 months; in England, 10.0 months. The average time served by pre-trial detainees in The Netherlands was 2.1 months, longer than that served by sentenced prisoners. Again, however, some part of that disparity must be due to the large numbers of motoring offenders in The Netherlands who are sentenced to extremely short periods of imprisonment. Differences in length of sentence or time served are not, therefore, the whole story.

Another factor possibly accounting for the differences in the prison populations of the two countries is the so-called 'clear-up rate'—the proportion of crimes known to the police which actually result in the apprehension of those responsible, whatever subsequently happens to them by way of sentencing or prosecution. By definition, if nobody is arrested for crimes, the criminal justice system lacks its raw material: suspects. The rate of crimes cleared up can vary quite independently of the actual level of crimes known to the police, which is also a different matter from the unknown quantum of crimes committed. If these variables were stable over time and only the prison population varied, there would be every reason to focus exclusively on the sentencing stage as the key stage at which custodial populations are determined. But this cannot be so when the trend in clear-up rates varies over time, which is more apparent in The Netherlands than in England.

For most of the post-war period until the late 1970s, the clear-up rate in England hovered around 44 per cent, though by 1986 it fell to 32 per cent. In The Netherlands, by contrast, it has fallen consistently, from some 60 per cent in 1960 to around 25 per cent in the late 1970s. The logical implication of these trends is that, but for the fall in the clear-up rate in The Netherlands, the input into the criminal justice system would have been at least doubled if clear-up had stayed as high as 60 per cent throughout the period, and some 50 per cent greater if the Dutch clear-up rate had stabilized at the level achieved in England in most of this period. This variable is given great weight by Steenhuis *et al.* (1983), who argue that the Dutch system emerges as far less lenient, by comparison with Sweden and West Germany, if the ratio of sentences of imprisonment to defendants is used rather than that of sentences of imprisonment to the whole population: 'ideally, comparison of the penal climate in various countries should mean investigating, for each crime and with due regard to the average gravity of each crimes, the percentage of known suspects who receive unconditional prison sentences, and the average length of such sentences' (Steenhuis *et al.* 1983: 3–4).

The clear-up rate, however, is only variably connected with the number of defendants processed by the system, and is not necessarily a valid guide to police effectiveness and efficiency (Bottomley and Coleman 1981). First, for comparative purposes, police organizations may differ in the degree of importance they attach to clear-up rates in review and promotion or for resource-allocation purposes. It appears that the Dutch police pay much less attention to a crucial component of clear-ups, offences 'taken into consideration'. If the Dutch police apprehend a suspect for a principal offence, they are not particularly concerned to write off other offences which the same defendant may have committed in the past (van Dijk, interview, 18 June 1985). By contrast, so intense is the pressure in England for clear-up rates to be improved that considerable sleight-of-hand seems to have become institutionalized in many forces to manufacture spurious write-offs, (Davies 1986*b*). Secondly, it is unwise to attempt to equate the relative extent of the fall in the Dutch clear-up rate with a corresponding fall in the prison population in The Netherlands. In both countries, the more serious offences against the person have a higher clear-up rate than those against property. It is the clear-up rate for the latter which has fallen most sharply in The

Netherlands, but it is the former which are more likely to attract prison sentences. Moreover, within the broad crimes against property category, hard-pressed police likewise focus on the more serious cases.

Arguably, however, *some* significance must attach to the fall in the clear-up rate. It is most unlikely that it equals the contribution to the fall in the prison population in The Netherlands of declines in the length of sentence, particularly in the late 1940s and 1950s when the most dramatic reduction in their prison population occurred. From 1965 onwards, however, the fall in the clear-up rate assumes growing importance as a variable shielding the criminal justice system from the effects of the rising crime rate. An attempt is made below to estimate the impact of that shielding effect, but it must be stressed that such an exercise is problematic in the extreme, for these reasons.

'Hidden' sanctions

'Hidden' sanctions provide the second possible basis for questioning the reality of the trends. If the Dutch system can be shown to employ sanctions other than but equivalent to imprisonment, then the disparity between the average levels of imprisonment and those of England might be reduced or eliminated. The three principal forms that such masking might take are: (*a*) the nature of the 'policy' dismissals by public prosecutors; (*b*) the time those sentenced to custody spend waiting for a prison place; and (*c*) other institutional measures, in particular TBR (placement in a secure clinic for an indeterminate period).

The first of these sanctions includes such diversionary measures as a directive to pay or make reparation to the victim. Technically, the great majority of waivers (some two-thirds in 1980) are unconditional dismissals without warning; most of the remainder are unconditional with a written warning, which may involve attendance at the office of the prosecutor; only some 6 per cent in 1980 were conditional in a formal sense. However, although the formal practice of restitution is very infrequent, informally it is much more widely practiced, with large area variations. In the past few years, attempts are being made to formalize such practices to even out such variations. The scale of the build-up over two decades of unconditional waivers prompted a directive that their use should be reduced by 50 per cent. (Netherlands Ministry of Justice 1985b: 30) in the period to 1990. Conditional waivers or prosecution should take their place. Overall, however, these sanctions remain non-institutional, though the consequence of reducing the proportion of unconditional waivers may hold implications for penal measures in the event of non-compliance.

Prosecutorial decisions may have an institutional outcome, but only with the agreement of the defendant and in only a very small number of cases. Prosecutors can waive if the defendant agrees to seek psychiatric advice, and in 22 cases in 1980 offenders were directed to a non-TBR clinic. More indirectly, the figures for pre-trial detention include some 300 defendants a year who are in actuality freed from custody on condition that psychiatric treatment is sought, 200 of which cases involved treatment in non-TBR mental institutions. If anything, however, this practice serves to inflate the overall institutional population figures, since it is not clear how many in practice become subject to in-hospital treatment, and for how long. What seems clear, however, is that the nature of dismissals by the public prosecutors does not add at all significantly to the overall penal or institutional population in The Netherlands.

The second of these sanctions affects several thousand people a year—those who are not remanded in custody, who are usually those sentenced to very short spells of imprisonment. At times, the queue of potential prisoners waiting to be called up has risen to excessive proportions, but the opening of a large open prison in 1983 at Heerhugowaard reduced the number from just over 7,000 in 1982 to just over 3,500 in January 1985. Of these 'waiting' prisoners, about a fifth do not come forward of their own volition when called up and have to be arrested. Though no research has yet been conducted on how far the offenders who receive such sentences welcome the chance to put their affairs in order, it seems that both costs and benefits attach to this arrangement: it is by no means seen as an extra penalty; it may even have elements of advantage for the prisoner, although there are costs in the uncertainty involved in waiting for several months, or more on occasion, for a prison place. Moving house, changing jobs, even taking a holiday or an unauthorized trip could be consequential, for not arriving at a certain prison on a specific day could spell a substantial loss of privilege. The state retains throughout its power to dispose as its agents think fit, one index of Foucault's (1977) 'carceral society'. Nor is it plausible to regard the people awaiting a prison place as a 'hidden' institutional population. For this common continental practice has some advantages for the prisoner. What might appear a prolongation of sentence does clearly allow much scope for negotiation on the prisoners' part over the actual timing of self-delivery to prison. It is arguably a more dignified process to present oneself at the prison than to be rushed straight from the dock to the cells and into a prison van, irrespective of the extent of over-crowding in the awaiting jail. The Dutch send prisoners home again if a cell is not available. I have heard it said, by a former director of the Prison Department of the Home Office, that if these waiting prisoners are added to those actually in prison in The Netherlands, their prison population is as great as that in England. It is more appropriate to see the call-up system as, in Rutherfords's phrase, 'locating the pressure point outside rather than inside the prison system' (1984: 143). The average time spent awaiting call-up—for those not involved in appeals, requests for pardon, or other procedural matters—is about three months. In short, it may be possible to conceive of ways in which the call-up could be used as a sanction, but that does not seem appropriate in the case of The Netherlands.

The third sanction—other institutional disposals—has been a factor of some significance in the 1950s and 1960s, though decreasingly so in the 1970s and 1980s. As van Hofer (1975) correctly notes:

the Dutch system does not 'hide' a large proportion of offenders in other institutions as does Sweden. Certainly, the total number of persons institutionalized increases (i.e. if we follow a 'total institution' approach in relation to offenders) but not to any considerable extent. The total figure (including prisons, etc., reformatories, TBR, special treatment institutions, and mental hospitals) remains much lower than 'pure' Swedish prison figures (25 as against 59 persons per 100,000 population, 1972).

The same conclusion can be reached if the comparison is made with England, where proportionately far fewer offenders have been and are directed to mental institutions. In 1979, for example, persons detained in mental institutions under the 1959 Mental Health Act constituted 4.3 per cent of the average daily populations in custody and mental institutions combined.

It remains the case that TBR had played a particularly important role in connection with long-term 'prisoners' (in a legal sense, people assigned to TBR are not 'prisoners', and are therefore not included in Dutch prison population figures). In 1955, TBR accounted for over a third (36 per cent) of adult offenders deprived of their liberty for over a year. As late as 1970, that figure remained as high as 29 per cent, largely because, although fewer people were assigned to TBR institutions, there were also fewer being sentenced to prison for long periods. Because long-term prisoners bulk large in the daily average population, the decline in the overall proportion held in TBR institutions was protracted until the mid-1970s. In 1955, TBR accounted for 31 per cent of the total daily institutional population, a proportion which remained as high as 23 per cent in 1970. Its salience has diminished in the 1970s, as the long-term prison population started to rise and the numbers assigned to TBR continued to decline. Its role was reviewed by the Mulder Committee (Netherlands Ministry of Justice, 1983), which sought to regularize procedures for the transfer of mentally disturbed prisoners to TBR institutions. Around one in ten of the institutional population seem likely to continue to be assigned, by a variety of routes, to TBR institutions, and the pressure on penal capacity means that its role, along with that of other mental hospitals, may even be somewhat enlarged—though it is extremely unlikely that the pendulum will swing back to anything like the degree of 'psychiatrization' that prevailed from the early 1950s until the early 1970s (see Table 2.4). During the 1950s in particular, the rise in the influence of treatment policies in The Netherlands, mirrored in the prominence accorded TBR, played a significant part in the growth of resistance to imprisonment of a long-term nature during that and subsequent periods.

The complexity of the differences between two systems of criminal justice makes it difficult to assign precise weighting to specific variables in accounting for the much smaller prison population in The Netherlands. As Steenhuis *et al.* (1983) have pointed out, daily average prison population is only one aspect of the penality of a society. In the same vein, taking only the use of imprisonment and lengths of sentences to custody leaves too much out of the comparative picture. What might the impact be of the Dutch crime rate rising to that of England? What if the clear-up rate also matched that of England? These and other variables need to be brought into the picture if we are to assess more fully the role of prison sentences and their length in contributing to the

TABLE 2.4   *Trends in the use of TBR for adults, 1950–1983*

	1950[a]	1955	1960	1965	1970	1975	1980	1983
TBR detainees as % adults deprived of liberty for over one year[b]	24	36	23	21	29	13	9	6
TBR detainees as % of overall institutional population[c]	11	31	20	24	23	16	11	11

Source: CBS annual statistics; and *6e. Follow-up van het onderzoek van de Werkgroep Capaciteit TBR-Inrichtingen,* Directie TBR en Reclassering, 1985.)

[a]   excluding political prisoners.
[b]   excludes transfers from within the prison population.
[c]   includes b above and also those on conditional release, escapees, etc.

substantial disparity in the prison population. The answers may not be without policy implications, for if shorter sentences are seen as the overriding reason for the differences, as has tended to be the case (Hulsman *et al.* 1978, Tulkens 1979, Downes 1982, Rutherford 1984), then those seeking to reduce the prison population in England may emphasize the need to shorten sentences to custody to the exclusion of other important aspects of the sentencing process.

On the basis of what, it should be stressed, are somewhat crude and hypothetical assumptions about the effect on the prison population of The Netherlands of varying sources of 'input' into the system, one may assign a proportionate influence to each element in the system to the size of the prison population. It is necessary to do so in relation to some alternative state of affairs, in this case the comparison with the same variables in England. The exercise is purely additive, and likely interaction effects between one variable and another are not allowed for. For example, the crime rate rising by 20 per cent would hypothetically add 20 per cent to the prison population. The clear-up rate rising by 20 per cent would achieve the same result. Together, however, a combination of the two would—by the same logic—produce a rise of 24 per cent in the prison population, since the rise in clear-up would apply to a greater volume of crime. In this model, each variable is changed in isolation, and the results then expressed in terms of their proportionate influence. The results obtained on the basis of data for 1980 are shown in Table 2.5; data for other years would of course yield some differences.

The variables entered were (*a*) the crime rate; (*b*) the clear-up rate; (*c*) the rate of policy waivers; (*d*) sentences *to* prison (both unsuspended and partly suspended); (*e*) the system of waiting to be called up for a prison place; (*f*) time served in prison, which incorporates the effects of sentence length, parole and other variables, such as pardons, which may mitigate the duration of sentence; and (*g*) TBR. Each variable was manipulated to show the effect it would have on the Dutch prison population if it alone were brought into line with the situation in England. On that assumption, the crime rate is seen as producing an increase in the prison population of 23 per cent, since in 1980 the crime rate in England per 100,000 population (5,459) was 23 per cent higher than that of The Netherlands (4,423). Minor criminal damage is included in both cases. Increasing the Dutch clear-up rate from some 26 to 27 per cent in non-motoring cases in 1980 to 40 per cent, as in England, would increase the volume of crimes processed on a *pro rata* basis by just over 50 per cent. It is assumed that the points made above about the greater attention paid in England to offences 'taken into consideration' exaggerate the impact such a change would make, hence halving that increase to 26 per cent is more appropriate. Policy waivers were in 1980 some 70 per cent of the total cases waived, which were 54 per cent of the total, hence an increase of 38 per cent in the numbers in prison is assumed to flow from eliminating this measure. Of *all* cases dealt with, some 8.5 per cent in The Netherlands resulted in prison sentences, compared with some 14 per cent in England, a shortfall of 65 per cent. However, this measure is the most problematic of all, since in England only guilty cases constitute the total, whereas that for The Netherlands also includes technical and policy waivers (the effect of which is already included in the model) as well as cases dismissed by the court. Indeed, if only guilty cases before the judge are considered, some 20.5 per cent were imprisoned, roughly 50 per cent *more* than in England. The filtering process involved in the whole public prosecution stage does, however, almost certainly mean that the cases reaching Dutch judges are relatively more serious than those before the

TABLE 2.5   *Variables reducing The Netherlands' prison population relative to that of England in 1980*

	% difference if level aligned to that of England	Cumulative total	% contribution to reduction	Level in England
Daily average prison population	100	100	—	370
Crime rate	+23	123	8	
Clear-up rate	+26	149	9	
Policy waivers	+38	187	13	
Use of prison	+65	252	23	
Call-up system	+15	267	5	
Time served	+108	375	38	
TBR	+11	386	4	16[a]
TOTAL	386	386	100	386

Source: See Appendix A.

[a] In closed mental institutions.

courts in England. Undeniably, however, some double-counting is entailed in the 'use of prison' index employed here. The call-up system is estimated to have affected 9,000 prisoners waiting for a place in 1980. If they served on average a short sentence of 0.65 months, eliminating the system would have increased the Dutch prison population by some 15 per cent. 'Time served' is based upon mean sentence lengths calculated for 1979 for The Netherlands by the Prison Department, and for England on the basis of sentenced receptions and daily average prison populations (see Appendix 2.1): mean days served amounted to 83 and 173 days respectively. Finally, the elimination of TBR is estimated to add 11 per cent to the prison population in The Netherlands.

Ideally, to give a comprehensive picture of changing trends in sentencing in the two countries since the war, a similar set of estimates would be given for five-yearly intervals throughout the period. Ideally also, the model would be applied to particular offences, or combinations of offences—to allow for the different patterns of sentencing in motoring offences, for example. Such a model for the 1950s would show much greater weight to attach to the use of TBR (see Table 2.4). Crime rate differences would be at their largest in the 1960s, and so on, (see Fig. 2.1). But it is still likely that the predominant factor would remain the influence of shorter sentences in The Netherlands. Adding in the other variables clearly reduces the contribution of length of sentence, but it remains the most powerful.

Conclusions

In a review of the kinds of measures that would be needed to reduce the prison population of England at all substantially, Pease (1982) commented that the usual run of proposals, such as making prostitution, the possession of cannabis, and the like, unimprisonable offences, would make scarcely a dent on the prison population. What is entailed, he argues, is little short of a set of revolutionary changes in sentencing practice, since the pressures making for a continuing rise in the prison population, in the context of a rising crime rate, are so strongly entrenched in the normal run of sentences for the normal run of crimes. What is so remarkable about the post-war developments in The Netherlands is that they amount to a silent revolution along those lines. In the next chapter, we take up the question of how so substantial a series of changes was originated and carried through.

Perhaps the principal inference to be drawn from the model outlined above is that an array of devices are necessary if the prison population is to be stabilized, let alone reduced, in a period of rising crime. In the crucial period from 1952–65, for example, The Netherlands was undoubtedly fortunate in experiencing a slight fall (as was the case in England) followed by a shallow rise in the crime rate (that in England rose more sharply) as the context within which to accomplish a reduction in the prison population. From that point on, however, a variety of shielding devices came to be consciously employed to resist recourse to prosecution and imprisonment wherever possible. Co-ordination to that end was given increasingly high priority throughout the criminal justice system. Again, therefore, the problem is to account for differences in the sentencing trends and penal policies of The Netherlands and England which are not reducible to the initial input into the criminal justice system.

Appendix 2.1.   Bases for comparison of Sentencing in The Netherlands and England

Basis for calculation of mean actual sentence length, The Netherlands 1979

Length	Assumed mean length (days)[a]	No. of sentences	Assumed mean man-days[a]	Total man-days
1 week	3	2,122	9.14	19,395
1–2 weeks	10			
2 weeks	14	6,490	16.35	105,463
2–4 weeks	22			
1–2 months	45	2,666	56.25	149,963
2–3 months	75			
3–4 months	105	1,959	130.06	254,788
4–6 months	150			
6 months	180	973	230.50	224,277
6–12 months	270			
1 year	270	816	609.96	497,727
1–3 years	480			
3–5 years	963			
5–10 years	1,807[b]			
10–15 years	3,011[c]			
15–20 years	4,215[c]			
20 years	4,818[d]			
Life	—[e]			
TOTAL		15,026	83.3	1,252,613

Source: Prison Department, Ministry of Justice, The Hague.

[a] Taking into account conditional release.
[b] Forty-seven sentences in 1978.
[c] Three sentences in 1978.
[d] One sentence in 1978.
[e] No life sentences in 1978.

Basis for calculation of mean time served, England, 1980

		Population in custody		
		Male	Female	Total
1.	Average daily population (ADP)	34,783	1,198	35,981
2.	Receptions into custody (R)	72,290	3,606	75,986
3.	Mean time served, months (ADP ÷ Rx12)	5.8	4.0	5.7
4.	Mean time served, days (Item 3 × 365)	175.6	121.3	173.0

Source: Home Office Prison Statistics (1981), Tables 1.3, 1.4, 7*b* and 7*c*.

Calculation of difference in mean sentence length

English mean sentence length: 173.0 days
Dutch mean sentence length: 83.3 days

Difference   89.7 days

$$\frac{89.7}{83.3} \times 100 = 108\%$$

3 Theories of Decarceration: Problems of Accounting for Sentencing Trends in The Netherlands

On the assumption that the reality of the trends dealt with in Chapter 2 have been established, and that they cannot be explained away in terms of crime rates, clear-up rates, or hidden sanctions, the problem remains of accounting for them at all adequately. The problems are particularly acute in the Dutch case, since the rough parallelism between crime rates and rates of custodial sentencing in England are more in line with the canons of consistency and seriousness imputed to sentencers by research into sentencing process. That is not to say that the levels at which consistency and seriousness have come to operate in England are not in themselves problematic. It is that the problems of explanation in the Dutch case are compounded by their evident departure from such canons, despite an operational commitment to them. Nor is it readily apparent that commonsense accounts (which social scientists, if we can use such a pejorative term, are exhorted by politicians to emulate) do the job for us. Both English and Dutch sentencers tend to say alike that they use prison as a 'last resort', avoid it in 'trivial' or 'first offences' wherever possible, and disregard the availability of prison places as a factor in their sentencing. Such affirmations would predict similarity in sentencing trends, rather than the distinct differences that have obtained in the post-war period.

Several theories, or broad ways of explaining the trends, have been derived, either from the criminological literature on penal changes, or from interviews with members of the Dutch judiciary and specialists in allied fields. They are by no means mutually exclusive but, in assessing their merits, it seems essential to ask of each in turn not only how well they fit the facts of the case in The Netherlands, but also how well they do so for England and other comparable societies. A good explanation would also suggest the processes whereby so-called 'causes' are mediated through the human agencies, in this case primarily the judiciary, who accomplish their apparent effects. Having reviewed the strengths and weaknesses of each theory, the somewhat artificial process of separating out the elements of each in isolation can be abandoned, and the best possible combination sought.

The economics of decarceration

In his book *Decarceration: Community Treatment and the Deviant*, Scull (1977) argues that trends towards the de-institutionalization of both punishment and treatment (i.e. of responses to the 'bad' and the 'mad') are increasingly marked in capitalist societies, mainly for reasons of gathering economic stringency rather than from any substantial humanitarian concern or profound therapeutic breakthrough. In the same vein as O'Connor (1973), he sees 'welfare capitalism' as increasingly beset by fiscal crises, as the costs of manning burgeoning welfare institutions outpace economic growth. Morever, the labour-intensive character of welfare institutions forbids more than marginal gains in productivity to offset these costs. Hence the new-found enthusiasm of governments for the panacea of 'community care', though the cheapskate, cost-cutting versions they espouse bear little resemblance to the model of heavily subsidized community support promulgated by the earlier critics of institutions (see, e.g. Townsend 1963, Morris 1969).

Scull's case was based chiefly upon trends in the United States and England, in both of which prison populations had fallen relative to the growth of crime rates in the two decades before the mid-1970s. This definition is the weakest of the relative measures of decarceration, which in stronger form can be based on the proportion of the sentenced population which is imprisoned. An absolute definition would pivot on actual falls in the prison population, unless such reductions were less than falls in either the crime rate or the proportions receiving other disposals. Some critics of Scull's thesis (e.g. Chan and Ericson 1981) have seen decarceration only in absolute terms. However, even in its weakest sense the thesis was quickly overtaken by events in the United States, where the overall prison population doubled in the decade 1975—85, far outstripping growth in the crime rate. In England too, the proportion of offenders[1] sentenced to immediate custody rose steadily from 15 per cent in 1974 to 20 per cent in 1984, though historically, as Bottoms (1983) has reminded us, this remains well below the 29.1 per cent imprisoned in 1959 and the

---

[1]   The reference is to adult offenders.

33.3 per cent in 1938. On the other hand, his argument retains much force in relation to the mentally ill. The rates of mental illness are perhaps considerably higher than they were in the 1950's, notably in connection with the greater numbers surviving to the age of onset of psycho-geriatric illnesses: but mental institution populations have plummeted in both England and the United States. In relation to offenders, the most striking example remains the case of Massachusetts, where juvenile reformatories were closed down virtually overnight (Rutherford 1986).

By any definition, The Netherlands is a classic example of decarceration in the penal sphere. It does not appear, however, to have conformed to the theory of fiscal crisis. If anything, it has conformed to the reverse. The major reductions in the prison population, both in terms of average daily populations and in relation to the rise in crime rates, came from the mid-1950s to the early 1970s, when The Netherlands was experiencing an unprecedented growth in prosperity and a relative absence of fiscal crisis. Conversely, plans are now in train for a doubling of penal capacity from its 1975 level by 1990, at a time of considerable economic anxiety. 'Between 1950 and 1960 public expenditure accounted for about a third of the national product, rising to about half in 1970. It now accounts for about 70%. All growth in the national product during the seventies went into public spending, the greatest rise in expenditure being on social security' (SCPB 1984: 28). Morever, even in relation to the mentally ill, the predictions one might make from fiscal crisis theory have not been fulfilled. Mental institutional care has survived in The Netherlands to a much greater extent than in either England or the United States. 'The present Social and Cultural Report is again forced to note that the desired shift from institutional to non-institutional care has not taken place. The proportion of costs accounted for by the latter even dropped from 31% in 1972 to 28% in 1982' (*ibid* 28). However, the desire was correctly predicted, and with public sector expenditure at 70 per cent of national product, it may be simply a matter of time before some shift towards its fulfilment is discernible.

It may be worth noting in passing that some rough correspondence does seem to hold, in at least the three cases mentioned, between trends in penal and mental institutions. In the United States and, more sluggishly, England, the decanting of very large numbers of patients from institutions to the community has been followed by rising prison populations. In The Netherlands, the relative stability of the mental hospital population has accompanied a fall in that of the prisons. It is, however, unlikely that these two populations are substantially interchangeable, though at the margins there is undoubtedly some possibility of substitution. It would not account at all significantly for the trends, important as the issues involved undoubtedly are. For example, on 30 June 1977 some 769 prisoners in England were defined as potentially transferable to mental hospitals under the terms of the 1959 Mental Health Act, a figure which had fallen to 240 in 1987 (Hansard Col. 1, 25.1.88). (See also pp. 77–81.).

The carceral society and the dispersal of social control

There is one sense in which Scull's approach, with its emphasis on the tilting of control away from the prison and the asylum to the spurious blessing of community corrections or care, chimes with that of theorists who, in the last two decades, have discerned the lineaments of the 'carceral' society in new forms of penality (Garland and Young 1983). In particular, Foucault (1977) and Stanley Cohen (1979, 1985) view the prison as likely to become less prominent (though still held in reserve for the dangerous and recalcitrant) as a focus for formal control in advanced capitalist societies. Instead, a web of control institutions will permeate civil society in an ever-tightening mesh of state regulations. People in general, not only those designated deviant, will come under systematic surveillance. The ideal of the 'carceral society' would in principal render the prison superfluous, achieving perfect social control by other means: Foucault's 'hundreds of tiny theatres of punishment', each a 'perfect arithmetical representation of the bourgeois social contract' (Cohen 1985: 85). In a notable metaphor, Cohen (1979) viewed contemporary trends in social control as subject to processes of 'blurring', 'net-widening', 'mesh-thinning', and 'penetration'. With the best of intentions, penal reformers have contrived to blur the distinctions between what is, and what is not, regarded/defined as punishment (e.g. creative definitions and extensions of licence, conditions, half-way houses, etc.) The scope of the control nets have consequently been widened (e.g. those previously defined as non-deviant may be recast as 'at risk'; those previously informally warned may now be brought into the control system by a formal caution — see e.g.

Pratt 1986). The mesh becomes finer to control more intensively the greater number who are hauled in, e.g. by more searching inventories of their personalities. Finally, the whole system of formal control thus refined and enlarged penetrates more deeply and extensively into the public and private realms of civil society. The ultimate irony is that, despite the origins of these developments in the attack on the prison as outdated and inhumane, these measures come to supplement and not replace it. We end up with the worst of both worlds: an unreconstructed *ancien régime pénal* and a new-style carceral society.

This undeniably gloomy view of modern developments in social control is not without its critics. Bottoms (1983) has made the fundamental point that the post-war growth in the use of the fine, an essentially non-disciplinary penalty in Foucault's sense, is the reverse of what one would have logically expected from a 'carceral society' standpoint. It is of course the case that, before World War I, the majority of prisoners were in custody for the non-payment of fines, and in the past five years the use of fines has fallen relative to other measures of a non-custodial but penal character (i.e. entailing the supervision of a 'penal agent') such as community service. But the fact remains that it is the fine and not probation or community service which has displaced imprisonment over the past two to three decades most significantly. The same holds to a lesser extent for The Netherlands. Garland (1985) has questioned the whole basis of Foucault's case, and implicitly that of Cohen, by conceptualizing modern developments in the individualized treatment of the offender as no simple outgrowth of the disciplinary framework of the prison in its Victorian form, but as requiring a 'discursive' transformation of penality, a transformation that was wrought in the period 1890 to 1914. Garland takes much the same view as Cohen about the character and implications for control of these changes, but sees them as fundamentally discontinuous with the carceral discipline of Foucault.

The problem in evaluating these visions of social control is that they each have considerable merit, not least that of lifting the debate above sheer administrative reformism of the one hand and blanket condemnation of capitalist society on the other. The difficulty lies in finding indicators of what might constitute 'carcerality' or disciplinary forms of penality that are relatively uncontentious. What interests us here is how far this approach may account for the differences in sentencing trends in The Netherlands and England. If The Netherlands is simply 30 years ahead of England in some key respects connected with the dispersal of social control, or if it always was a more 'carceral' society than England in the above sense, then that could account for the disparities we have documented. Take a notion such as 'regulation of whole groups and classes of persons', on which practically everyone agrees as a regulatory trend of a non-penal sort (Mathiesen 1983, Cohen 1985, Bottoms 1983), such as the use of TV monitors in large stores and supermarkets. Short of an inventory of such devices in both countries, it is impossible to say which bristles with them the more. They are about the same in this respect, but it is difficult to see what would be proved by showing that one or the other had more or less, except perhaps that shoplifting and the like were viewed as more of a problem. Another example might be traffic regulations. The typical Amsterdam street is festooned with signs and symbols concerning traffic (of the wheeled variety), but that is largely due to the cycling phenomenon in The Netherlands. The cyclists, a formidable lobby, have gained certain rights which are upheld by large amounts of street markings and furniture. Clearly, regulation in this sense — the by-products of consumer rights and technological developments — need to be distinguished from regulation in the interests of the extension of state control. Absence of regulation may be more detrimental than its presence, as the power of the road lobby in this country shows.

In the penal sphere proper, it may be the case that the Dutch were more advanced for a time on the road to the dispersal of social control. Probation was in embryo in The Netherlands by the early nineteenth century, in England only by the late Victorian era. But probation in The Netherlands was never a servant of the court in the sense that came to prevail with its formal establishment in England in 1907 (Garland 1985). Dutch judges had the choice of suspended and partially suspended prison sentences, the former in combination with the fine, which itself could be partially or wholly suspended, from the early 1920s. But the introduction of some of these variations in England in the 1960s and 1970s hardly staunched the use of immediate imprisonment. Indeed, it is a by-word among penal reformers that non-custodial sentences in English courts are used interchangeably rather as alternatives to custody. In other respects, attendance centres were introduced in some areas in England following the 1948 Criminal Justice Act; and community serice was introduced — indeed originated — in England in 1973, in The Netherlands only in the 1980s . In short, it is difficult to see The Netherlands as a *prima facie* carceral society in contradistinction to England. The waiving of prosecution has been consciously developed by the Dutch in major diversionary ways for filtering out the more routine cases. But, with a few exceptions, that process lacks a continuing penal element, and other countries which share the formal system, such as West Germany, do not use it in a way that helps to shape a reductionist penal policy.

There are some pointers to possible sources of differences in penality between the two societies in the work of Garland. The emphasis in England on the principle of 'less eligibility' (i.e. that institutional life should be less preferable than that of the poorest in the community) is seen by him as crucial for the entire character of the prison, not only in its Victorian form, but also in the transformation which allegedly occured in the 1890–1914 period as a major obstacle to the full implementation of educational and welfare programmes in prisons. 'In the face of recommendations that suggested reformative and educational regimes for offenders, the customary arguments for deterrence and less eligibility presented a strong line of opposition, which was deployed by men such as Anderson, Tallack, and Du Cane, as well as a variety of official reports' (Garland 1985: 164). Writing in 1939, Hermann Mannheim saw the principle of less eligibility as *the* major obstacle to penal reform. It is possible that Garland understates its all-pervasive miasmic grip on the prison system even today. No trace of such a principle survives in the attitudes or policies of contemporary Dutch prisons or welfare institutions in general, and it is difficult to see how its influence would have disappeared so completely if it has been institutionalized in the past. Here the periodization of the industrial revolution seems a crucial factor. Nineteenth-century Dutch society lacked so developed an industrial working class. However, the response to beggars and vagrants seems to have been just as, if not more repressive, in The Netherlands than in England. Penal labour colonies took the place of the English workhouse, for those not provided for by the denominations or voluntary aid. Whether conditions in these 'colonies' were better or worse than in the prisons is difficult to ascertain. Howard had praised the late eighteenth-century prisons in The Netherlands in quite fulsome terms: 'Prisons in the United Provinces are so quiet and most of them so clean, that a visitor can hardly believe he is in a gaol' (1784: 44). The numbers in the penal colonies, however, exceeded those in the jails, and as late as 1905 held some 75 inmates per 100,000 inhabitants, compared with rates of 35–40 in prisons and 20 in the houses of detention. They were phased out as late as the 1970s; in Belgium they continue to account for about a third of the daily institutional population, though in The Netherlands after 1955 their daily average population barely exceeded 100. The variation in continental practice may have lacked the clear formulation of 'less eligibility' that was institutionalized in the English workhouse, but marginal populations were nevertheless clearly subject to punitive treatment (Spierenburg 1986). Hence, one can hardly alight on 'less eligibility' as the crucial differentiating factor in accounting for the greater humanity of the Dutch in post-war policies of imprisonment and penal administration.

Drawing on the work of Donzelot (1979), Garland has also stressed the power of 'welfare state' agencies to exercise a form of sanction which 'takes as its object not a citizen but a client, activated not by guilt but by abnormality, establishing a relation which is not punitive but normalising' (Garland 1981: 40). In at least two major respects, the Dutch welfare system differs from that in England: first, the levels of income maintenance and social security are set at much more generous levels in relation to average incomes: and secondly, the psychological testing and profiling of children is far more comprehensively developed. There is not, however, any indication that this 'soft machine' has developed, in its regulatory mode, any further or faster in The Netherlands than in other societies with a far greater investment in more traditional carceral establishments. The field of welfare sanctions is little explored in contemporary comparative research, but France and West Germany, both societies with relatively high prison populations, are reported to deploy them relatively punitively, reacting to often minor infractions by, for example, the sequestration of goods and the cutting of benefits at source. Such sanctions offer perhaps the clearest indicators of 'carceral' control techniques.

In sum, there is an all too apparent sense in which the 'punitive city', 'carceral society', or 'dispersal of control' model fits The Netherlands. But as it fits other advanced industrial societies equally well, of both capitalist and state socialist varieties, it does not appear to offer an adequate basis for explaining decarceration in The Netherlands. Indeed, much of the theorizing rests on an assumption that the rhetorics and labels of so many of the agencies concerned are translated into practice. What one wants to know is whether the pedlars of 'social control talk' so tellingly catalogued by Cohen (1985: Ch.5 and App.) make the same sort of impact on people's lives as the 'cruelty man' (officers of the National Society for the Prevention of Cruelty to Children) in late Victorian and Edwardian England. In many respects, however, the growth of the machinery of regulation is real enough: the growth of both public and private security, the proliferation of quasi-judicial state agencies in the sectors of economic and administrative control, and the tendencies to substitute executive for judicial power in a growing number of respects even in the criminal justice system: in these kinds of ways, the 'carceral' society has taken quite substantial hold. There are, however, many respects in which this awesome machinery of control limps behind the growth of phenomena which it can barely chart, let alone constrain: the informal economy, tax evasion, corporate crime and occupational deviance are tolerated more because of the dispersal of their victimization than its magnitude (Ditton 1977, Box 1983). It sometimes seems as if the only people in gaol, apart from the occasional spectacular gangster, are those unemployed or marginal workers who lack routinized access to occupational crime. But it is hardly to The Netherlands' discredit to have acted on that insight more than other comparably developed societies. It is difficult to impute to the Dutch, in other words, a more developed 'carceral' society than that in other countries with far higher prison populations.

The limits of penal capacity

Broadly stated, this theory maintains that it is penal capacity which determines penal population levels in any given society, rather than the reverse. A general statement of this view is contained in Blumstein and Cohen's (1973) theory of the 'stability of punishment'. Drawing on the axioms of the functionalist tradition of Durkheim (1895) and Erikson (1966), they maintain that societies exert formidable constraints against undue variations in the amount and type of resource they are prepared to employ on formal social control. This rather deterministic view of societal self-regulation in the penal sphere is subject to the endemic problems of functional theorizing in general, not least a circularity of argument which accounts for changes in penality with reference to rather poorly specified changes in social structure. It is difficult to see how the approach can adequately account for the doubling of the American prison population in the space of ten years. Nor is it entirely clear what is being explained: the amount of punishment, the rate of punishment, or its forms.

If the amount of punishment is the problem, then The Netherlands certainly provides a startlingly durable example. Van Ruller (1981), has provided a well-documented basis for the examination of this approach: 'The suggestion implicit in the rates is that the existing penitentiary infrastructure strongly determines the degree to which the prison sentence is used in The Netherlands.' Van Ruller shows the astonishing longevity of the trend towards a reduction in the average prison population relative to that of the population as a whole in The Netherlands. The reduction is traceable back virtually to the 1840's and is broken only by short-term increases during the crisis periods of the two world wars and their immediate aftermaths, after which the progressive decrease is resumed. By contrast, the penal capacity (excluding the nineteeth-century beggar colonies and their successors, the state labour colonies, which retained separate but diminishing populations until their abolition in the 1950s) rcmained relatively stable over the entire period at 4,000–6,000 places. Its decline to below that figure in the early 1970s produced a crisis of sorts over penal capacity which was only temporarily resolved by the mass pardons of 1975. Recent plans to increase the capacity to 7,000 by 1990 have of late been pruned by the government to some 6,000 places. In short, if penal capacity is assumed to be constant, then the reduction of the prison population relative to that of the population as a whole is inevitable, given the steady growth of the latter (the size of the Dutch population has quintupled since 1840), irrespective of the crime rate. So marked a trend does indeed call out for explanation.

The main question which this approach begs is just *why* a certain level of penal capacity should come to be adopted by a society over so extensive a period of time. The solution is almost a restatement of the problem: penal capacity is the way it is because it has always been so. Van Ruller (1981) essays an answer to this problem, but in terms which raise a fresh set of issues of quite different character: 'The opinion that prison does not solve social problems, and that prison is rather such a social problem itself, and that it should be repudiated, is rather widely propagated in The Netherlands.' The assertion that what has occurred is not so much a passive acceptance of the *status quo* but an active repudiation of the penal sanction, implies that policy choices have been made all along the line. Other societies, England and the United States in particular, have found other remedies for limited penal capacity: building more prisons. And where the resources for such building cannot be found or politically justified, though the courts continue to send more people to prison regardless of capacity, the English have evolved another remedy: over-crowding. In short, to view penal capacity as the major determin-ant of penal policy is to reify that capacity as the major phenomenon *sui generis* that somehow transcends the will to change, expand or transform institutional infrastructures. If, on the other hand, the problem is put in Van Ruller's second form, — 'What is it that leads the Dutch to treat penal capacity as a constant, as a key element in penal policy?' — then we move onto a different terrain.

Even in these terms, however, there are difficulties in placing such an emphasis on penal capacity alone. Not only does it fail to address the issue of why some societies and not others seem to stabilize that capacity: it also leaves unexamined the mediation of cause and effect. It is, in a sense, the criminological equivalent of monetarism: a fixed resource somehow promotes desired ends. But the question of why those ends should be sought in the first place, and how they are in practice accomplished, is left unanalysed. This is also a problem for those who, like Andrew Rutherford (1984) favour reductionist policies in which the limitation or reduction of penal capacity is viewed as a fundamental precursor to reductions in the prison population. As he acknowledges, limiting change to that one variable alone would arguably lead to such unwanted side-effects as even greater overcrowding, unless other related strategies were pursued to divert people from prison or equivalent institutional disposals. For the links between penal capacity and policy are far from clear. For example, one would expect Dutch judges to pay marked attention to penal capacity in their sentencing. However, in interviews, they almost all denied that they often do so on strong grounds of principle.

Nevertheless, it may operate as a background factor to which they pay some regard. If so, there is a far from exact fit between sentences of imprisonment and actual capacity, as the build-up of waiting prisoners in the 1970s testified. Also in the early 1970s, a situation of overcapacity developed, in which penal closures were effected. A strict theory of penal capacity would entail the filling of all available places. Such anomalies point to the inadequacy of this theory as it stands, even for The Netherlands.

If we regard the second of the two approaches as the more fruitful (*i.e.* 'What is it that leads the Dutch to treat penal capacity as a constant?'), the post-1945 period presents a particularly interesting context in which to attempt an answer. First, the progressive fall after 1955 in the penal population was even greater if we include those detained in state labour colonies. Secondly, concern about the crime rate could take numerical form only after 'crimes known to the police' were published after 1950, so that reductionist effects were wrought within the context of a known rising crime rate. Thirdly, the most striking differences between England and The Netherlands only emerged in the period from the mid-1950s onwards. In the inter-war period, the prison population in England was relatively low and stable. In the pre-World War I era, it had fallen, with some fluctuations, from the 1870s , so that in terms of penal trends England in the period from 1870 until the early 1950s was in parallel with rather than divergent from The Netherlands. Yet from the mid-1950s, the rise in the prison population in England was so marked that proportionate increases in the penal budget came to exceed those in the fields of health and education. (King and Morgan 1980)

In both societies, therefore, penal capacity was a constraint, but it was a constraint overcome in England by progressive overcrowding and fresh prison building. The increase in overcrowding was particularly pronounced, but this has been little explored by penal analysts. 'During the first forty years of this century, placing more than one prisoner in a cell designed for one person was virtually unknown. In 1950 some 2,500 prisoners, 12 per cent of the prison population, were sharing cells and by 1980 the number of prisoners sharing cells exceeded 17,000, 40 per cent of the prison population' (Rutherford 1984: 53). Given that prison overcrowding is the major target of penal reform groups in Britain, particularly when combined with over-flowing chamber pots, this development has remained surprisingly absent from

theories of penal history. It is rare in comparably developed
countries and is only marginally necessary in Britain. 'It is
important to note that 12,000 persons were required to share cells
in 1973, despite the near-equivalence of total capacity of the prison
system and average daily population' (Rutherford, 1984: 100).
King and Morgan have repeatedly drawn attention to the policy
decison that local prisons should bear the brunt of overcrowding,
whilst 'training' prisons should be maintained at or under capacity
(King and Morgan 1980). Hence, two of the elements noted by
Garland as crucial for an understanding of British penal policy
seem to be implicated in the practice: first, the legacy of less
eligibility preserves intact the legitimacy of treating prisoners as
undeserving of standards that obtain in the rest of society. And
secondly, the rhetoric of 'treatment and training' borne of the
post-Gladstone Report era is institutionalized in the double
standards which operate in local and training prisons. The result is
that, lacking any stringent guidelines to govern minimum
standards or prisoners' rights, there is in England no impediment
whatsoever, other than the pragmatic, to limit overcrowding to its
present levels. If three to a cell is possible, why not four? Or five?

By contrast, in The Netherlands, from the Fick Commission of
1947 onwards, far more attention to conditions and amenities has
been based on the stringent proscription against exceeding the
limits of one prisoner to a cell. This is not to say that the physical
environment is basically superior to any marked degree: 'almost
three-quarters of the cells in closed prisons in Holland remain
unsewered and without running water' (Vinson 1985: 6). It is the
social and not the bare physical aspects which distinguish Dutch
prisons so sharply from those in England and many other
countries (see Ch. 6 below). But the strict mandate to accept into
prison only as many as can be accommodated on a one-to-a-cell
basis makes the 'limits of penal capacity' a more compelling
theory for The Netherlands. The sources of that self-imposed
constraint are not, however, at all apparent.

The question of sources becomes even more compelling when
the notion of the 'limits of capacity' is applied to the criminal
justice system as a whole. For the limits of capacity apply not only
to the penal sphere, but also to the judiciary and the police. The
numbers of public prosecutors and judges in the penal chamber in
The Netherlands are relatively small. Although they have doubled
in the past 25 years, most of that increase was in the past five

years, and the number of cases processed by the public prosecutors rose at least fourfold over the period from 1960 (Netherlands Ministry of Justice 1985^c: 130, Table 6). The workload of judges rose far less markedly, largely due to the sharp increase over that period in waiving prosecutions. The point of maximum pressure, therefore, was at the public prosecution stage, and increased waiving was in part at least explicable in terms of overload. The objective of waiving is to filter out the routine and less serious cases: but in the process much time is saved, by the avoidance of dossier production and court appearance by the prosecutor. Policing also doubled in strength over the past 25 years, but again this increase in manpower fell far short of the eightfold increase in recorded crime, the result being a much reduced clear-up rate. (see Ch. 2) The cumulative effect of growing constraints and overload throughout the entire criminal justice system logically operated to facilitate a stabilized prison population. Yet the question remains as to why so high a premium was and is placed on minimizing the resort to prison, not only among the judiciary, but also at governmental and ministry levels, as well as among opinion-makers in the media.

The culture of 'tolerance'

A more straightforward theory is that penal sentencing policy and practice in The Netherlands is a manifestation of Dutch 'tolerance', a term which connotes a long tradition of relative leniency towards, and acceptance of, deviants, minority groups, and religious dissent, and which grants a respectable hearing to views which elsewhere would be dismissed as extreme or eccentric. Evidence of the reality of what amounts, in this view, to a culture of tolerance is a matter of impressive historical record. Indicators are, for example, the low rates of execution in The Netherlands in the eighteenth and nineteenth centuries by comparison with other European societies and in the early abolition of both capital and corporal punishment (1870 in The Netherlands, though the abolition did not extend to Dutch colonies, and was superseded in wartime and for collaborators tried in the immediate post-war period). This is not to say that periodic measures of great harshness were absent: 531 members of the robber bands called 'Bokkenrijders' were tried during the period 1741–78. After the mass trials of the 1770s no less than 243 of them were hanged or broken on the wheel'. (Diederiks 1980: 157). In the early 1730s, at least 75 persons were executed by strangulation for the crime of sodomy, an episode which led the editor of the *Free Briton* to compare the Court of Holland with the Catholic Inquisition. By contrast, however, executions in Amsterdam were far fewer than in London: four a year on average, whereas in London, in an admittedly unusually savage phase, some '348 personss died on the gallows in the five years after 1783' (Ignatieff 1978:87). Diederiks argues (1981), *contra* Ignatieff, Rothman, (1971), and Foucault (1977), that the use of custody in The Netherlands as a penalty, rather as a transit camp for those awaiting execution, transportation or for debt, predated the end of the eighteenth century and contributed to a humanization of punishments somewhat earlier. Most notable as an acid test of tolerance was the very low number of wartime collaborators who were lynched in The Netherlands after the war: a total of six by comparison with other occupied countries such as Belgium (400-500) and France (3,000–4,000) (Mason 1952). This culture of tolerance can be said to operate on two mutually reinforcing levels to produce a relatively low prison population: first, directly through the judiciary, who make the actual sentencing decisions; secondly, through the relative absence in The Netherlands of authoritarian 'public opinion' which in other countries, both as articulated through the media and as directly expressed in everyday life, plays upon the judiciary to enforce harsh penal sanctions. The interplay between sentencing and public opinion was seen as one of mutual influence by Barbara Wootton:

What ranks as a long sentence . . . is largely a matter of convention. In Holland, for example, sentences have been steadily reduced over a considerable period until 2 years' imprisonment has come to be regarded as a relatively severe sentence. Moreover, these conventions are seen to be based ultimately on public opinion, and that opinion may itself be, and indeed has been, in its turn modified by changes in sentencing practice. (Wootton 1978: 65)

A comparison of attitudes towards the death penalty nevertheless shows striking differences between the two countries. In The Netherlands, 37 per cent in 1970 and 39 per cent in 1983 favoured its reintroduction (it was abolished, as we have seen, as long ago as 1870). In England, over two-thirds of the population continue to favour its reintroduction, a figure virtually unchanged since its abolition 20 years ago (SCPB 1984: 296; and Jowell, *et al.*

1986: 160–1). Clearly, the influence of legislation and sentencing upon public attitudes is highly variable. Abortion, for example, has become less subject to moral disapproval than was the case two decades ago. However, if attitudes towards the death penalty are any guide, the Dutch remain markedly more tolerant in relation to the most heinous crimes than the British, though there has been a marked loss of support for the view that 'criminals should be changed not punished' (down from 73 to 49 per cent between 1970 and 1983) and that 'sexual offenders should be cured not punished' (70 to 40 per cent) over the same period. The grounds of Dutch 'tolerance' in this sphere may therefore by shifting, if not diminishing.

Similarly, maximum sentences for the offences of varying seriousness are sigificantly lower in The Netherlands than in England (Appendix 4.1). Though maxima are usually greatly in excess of normal sentences (see ACPS 1978), the disparities between the two sets of maxima reflect corresponding differences in actual sentencing to some extent. For example, simple theft in The Netherlands carries a maximum sentence of four years' imprisonment, in England ten years. Robbery in England carries the liability of life imprisonment, as does rape: in The Netherlands, the maxima are 9 and 12 years respectively. Although largely symbolic, these marked differences may indicate levels of tolerance which are possibly translated by the judiciary into normal sentencing practices. However, since in The Netherlands they have been in force since the Penal Code of 1886, they are unlikely to explain trends which have occurred in the past 30 to 40 years.

Dutch tolerance is particularly well documented in the sphere of religious and racial 'pluralism'. Bagley's (1973) study of race relations in The Netherlands also provides useful comparative material with British attitudes and practices towards immigrants. The greater tolerance of the Dutch enables them to turn what was in all respects a more difficult situation to better advantage than has been the case in Britain.

The proportion of coloured immigrants in The Netherlands is similar to the proportion in Britain. The Netherlands is a much more crowded country than Britain, and in comparison with this country has an acute housing shortage. Immigrants to The Netherlands arrived, moreover, in much heavier concentrations than immigrants to the United Kingdom. Despite these facts it appears that the Dutch express markedly less prejudice than their English counterparts, and practise markedly less racial discrimination. Social policy on behalf of immigrants has been, moreover, markedly more generous and systematic than social policy in Britain. Such policy was carried through in a country with (then) somewhat less national wealth per head than Britain. (Bagley 1973: 246)

Events since 1973 serve to reinforce Bagley's thesis, in particular his prescience on the likelihood of violent responses to indigenous racism in Britain, and continuing good race relations in The Netherlands, with the stated exception of the Moluccans. Though the Surinamese arrivals of the mid-1970s generated more tensions than earlier migrants and the Indonesians (see Ch. 5), they have not been goaded into such riots as in inner-city Britain since 1979.

Dutch tolerance in not a simple blanket acceptance of all manner of behaviour and opinion. It is rooted in a society 'marked by kindly authoritarianism, deference to one's elders and those in positions of authority, with particular respect for the moral dogmas of Christianity' (Bagley 1973: 171). In this sense, 'Dutch emigrants to South Africa have been deviants from Dutch life, the extreme Protestants for whom any kind of compromise with other religious groups, including reformed Calvinists and Roman Catholics, was unacceptable. It is possible that this emigration of extremists from The Netherlands has indirectly contributed to the stability of Dutch society' (ibid. 173). Moreover, 'tolerance is extended   only to the extent that the minorities conform to the Dutch *verzuiling* rules of restrained and deferential inter-personal behaviour' (ibid. 171). Over the past 15 years perhaps the most formidable and sustained challenge to the tolerant cast of Dutch government and administration has come from the squatters in particular, and youthful radicals in general, groups who explicitly repudiate these rules.

In Bagley's view, the sources of this form of tolerance reside in two major characteristics of Dutch social structure and colonial history. First, drawing on Lijphart's analysis (2nd edn. 1975), the rules for overcoming *verzuiling* (the 'pillarization' of Dutch society) stress decorum, negotiation, accommodation and pragmatic tolerance (by no means the same as sympathy) for the interests and values of other groups. Equality of consideration and the proportional distribution of power mean that minority groups avoid the fate of endless subordination that has so disastrously characterized Northern Ireland's Catholic population, the working class in Britain, or minority groups in Britain more generally. (Bagley perhaps overdoes his thesis here, for autonomous institutions of socialization and communication do exist among Catholics in Northern Ireland, though these have not, of course, brought them any share in effective power. Also, as he acknowledges, some minority groups in Britain, the Jews outstandingly so, have been integrated without any particularly pronounced loss of their identity.) Secondly, colonialism in the Dutch case did not rest, for largely religious reasons as well as by the export of *verzuiling*, on the assumption of racial superiority which has so poisoned the post-war experience of coloured immigrants to Britain, an absence also accounted for by the fact that miscegenation was far more characteristic of Dutch than British colonialism. In Bagley's view, this absence of prejudice, relatively speaking, can be explained in functional terms. Dutch society does not need to cohere around the scapegoating of coloured or any other minority groups, since it has evolved its own institutional devices to promote social integration out of diverse social groupings: the inter-élite 'politics of accommodation' of the different religious and secular blocs. By these means, class conflict (horizontal stratification) is diffused by cross-cutting bloc allegiances (vertical stratification). In other societies, e.g. the United States, this pattern of fragmentation has not minimized conflict, since the blocs have not materialized or become articulated politically.

To the extent that Bagley's theories have substance, much the same analysis could be made in relation to crime. Marxist criminology in Britain has recently focused on the integrative role played by crime and its 'control' in the context of an otherwise class-ridden and structurally divided society (e.g. Hall *et al.* 1978). Lacking the basis for integrative institutions to form on lines of religious allegiance (to Bagley, Britain is a 'non-Christian' society by comparison with The Netherlands), crime has operated as a basis on which the ruling class can impose the legitimacy of its claims to hegemony. The rhetoric of 'law and order' is the justification for punitive sentencing. By contrast, The Netherlands has never engaged at this level in the 'war on crime' around which all can unite; it has not needed to invoke such grounds for a solidarity which it already possesses by other means.

This approach has considerable plausibility. It seems to account for the relative mildness of Dutch reactions to crime, though it allows for occasional outbursts of hostility to groups which either reject or have yet to accept the 'rules of the game'. It is chiefly lacking in a detailed application to the sphere of crime and its control, that is, in the specification of the mediating processes at work whereby 'tolerant' outcomes are accomplished and, in particular, why tolerance as expressed in sentencing has apparently actually increased at a time of rising crime in the post-war period. It also leaves unclear the reasons why 'religion has been so important to the Dutch nation in the first place' (Bagley 1973: 248), though the most obvious explanation seems to lie in the crucial symbolic role played by religion in the very formation of Dutch nationalism in the sixteenth and seventeenth centuries.

The politics of accommodation

Lijphart's ([1967], 1975) concept of the 'politics of accommodation' has been explicity linked with the reduction of the lengths of prison sentences in The Netherlands by Johnson and Heijder (1983). The distinctive quality of the politics of accommodation is that of bargaining and pragmatic compromise between the élites which stand at the apex of the four 'pillars' of Dutch society. The process of inter-élite negotiation turn to advantage a denominational structure which elsewhere, notoriously in Northern Ireland, would be the basis for endless and unproductive conflict. Catholics, Calvinists, secular liberals and secular radicals each form their own constituency, to which their élites are responsive, and which therefore possess by proxy a stake in the system. The major price, so to speak, for such an arrangement is that the élites, both in and outside government and Parliament, are relatively insulated from criticism, unless in exceptional circumstances. As long as they produce results, the negotiations whereby those results are reached are not of immediate public interest. Delays in the post-electoral formation of governments which in Britain would herald a major constitutional crisis are a normal feature of political process in The Netherlands.

Johnson and Heijder's argument is that, in the crucial post-war period, the law and order issue was effectively neutralized politically by the interlocking character of party coalitions. Quoting van Weringh, they assert that:

issue-oriented bargaining among political parties, none of which hold absolute power . . . have been crucial to criminal justice policy . . . because the long-term rejection of prison by the Social Democrats

became politically significant in this bargaining among political parties
. . . The Christian Democrats are inclined towards a 'law and order'
policy in dealing with abortion, homosexuality, pornography, drug
abuse, and similar issues because of religious conviction. The Liberals
share economic conservatism but do not agree with the Christian
Democrats on moral issues. So the Liberals make accommodations with
the Social Democrats in support of tolerant policies. (Johnson and
Heijder 1983; 7–8)

Socialists presided over the major changes in penal policy for 12
years after the war, which ushered in such major reforms as the
1951 Act which contained the principle of rehabilitation.

   Within this setting, the criminal justice system operates, as it
were, its own politics of accommodation. 'The setting of criminal
justice policy operates largely detached from public monitoring
. . . A small professional élite, with a fringe of complementary
groups, dominates practice in the field of criminal justice. Shared
training, position, norms, and values provide an effective
boundary-maintaining system shielding the operations of criminal
justice from public opinion.' (Johnson and Heijder 1983: 10). No
neat consensus prevails, but the system affords a diverse array of
flexible devices for achieving solutions to problems as they arise.
The various pressure groups lock into the politics of penal reform,
and even advocates of extreme positions, such as abolitionism,
take the business of participation seriously, avoiding the
polarization so evident in Britain. Criminologists like Bianchi and
Hulsman, whose views on criminal justice would tend to exclude
them from advisory roles in Britain or the United States, have
served on commissions of enquiry, are quoted by quite orthodox
members of the judiciary as holding views that deserve to be taken
seriously, produce 'green' papers as alternative policy proposals
that are published along with official policy statements by the
government, in short, operate perhaps to shift the axis of debate to
more radical positions of compromise than would otherwise occur.
Informed criticism by the Cornhort-Liga (the radical Dutch penal
reform group) since the early 1970s almost certainly stiffened
resistance to the swing away from reductionist policies. The
flexibility of the system is such that precedents can be invoked for
extensions of such devices as 'waiting' for places in prison; for the
large number of pardons granted (to judicial objections) in 1975; or
the increase in the proportions of cases waived by public
prosecutors in the 1960s and 1970s. Freedom of the professional

judges and prosecutors from the need to work with lay colleagues
or juries was quoted to me many times in explanation of the
direction sentencing policy had taken since the war. It tends to be
assumed as a matter of course that any involvement of the public is
bound to introduce a degree of unwarranted emotionalism into the
process of sentencing and prosecution. The Dutch criminal justice
system approximates to the Fabian ideal of small, highly trained
élites getting on with their jobs without undue public interference
(though with a due regard to public opinion and the public
interest).

There is considerable evidence for the view that the media have
generally exerted a far more restrained stance towards penal policy
in The Netherlands than in Britain or the United States. The
sensationalism of crime reporting so endemic in the latter societies
is, with the generally cited exception of *De Telegraaf*, notably
absent in The Netherlands. Comment tends to be more informed
and more inclined to present liberal policy sympathetically,
though a concern about rising crime is now becoming
commonplace. The police do not act as a pressure group lobbying
for tougher measures along the lines of the Police Federation in
Britain (which indeed is showing every sign of taking the Dutch
example as a threat to English sentencing policy: see, for example,
the strongly critical editorial and article on Trends in Dutch penal
policy in *Police*, March 1981). Police evaluations emerged as quite
close to those of prosecutors concerning the seriousness of offences
in a study by Buikhuisen and van Dijk (1975), with the public
ranking offences generally, through not too markedly, as more
serious than either group. With the media, the police, the
politicians, and the administrators taking much the same line as
the judiciary, a well-entrenched defence of the policy seems guaranteed. Even so, the last decade has seen an upturn in the
proportion and numbers of sentences of over a year in length, and
there are indications that the period of sentence shortening is
finally over. It still seems unlikely, however, that any wholesale
abandonment of the generally lenient tariff is imminent. The recommendation of Van Hiljkema Commission that the penal capacity be increased by 1,300 additional places over the 1981–85
period stimulated prompt and informed criticism (see, e.g.
Soetenhorst 1981). Since that point, a further 2,000 places have
been planned. Pardoxically, reductionist policies can be pursued
yet 'recarceration' eventuates if the crime rate rises sufficiently
steeply.

Whether or not the two trends are at all connected, the last two decades have also seen the undermining, if not collapse, of the 'pillarized' structure, and the accompanying 'politics of accommodation' that Heijder and Johnson regard as the essential context for Dutch leniency in sentencing. Lijphart, in the 1975 edition of his book, views the period of 1965–75 as that of its disintegration. Bryant (1981) asserts the emergence of social class as a more potent source of allegiance in this period than denominational loyalties. Undoubtedly some realignments of a politically crucial nature have been going on: it seems premature, however, to infer the demise of the 'politics of accommodation' from this realignment. What remains lacking in the approach outlined above is as yet any clear analysis of precisely what connections in the political sphere led to the changes in sentencing policy with which we are concerned. After all, sporadic attempts in England on the part of the Home Office to persuade judges and magistrates to reduce the length of sentences to prison have in general met with signal lack of success. Given the independence of the judiciary in both societies, why should judges and prosecutors in The Netherlands either accede to or even initiate more lenient policies in line with ministry thinking, when in England no such alignment occurred?

Confluence

The view that Dutch sentencing trends are the outcome not of any systematic policy but of a confluence of largely unanticipated prior social developments is put most vigorously by Hulsman:

The considerable measure of de-escalation in penal matters during the past decade in The Netherlands and the general situation of the criminal justice system are less the results of deliberate policy (demands for which have only become clear or clamorous in recent years) than of a development evolving more or less fortuitously from the interplay of the factors outlined above. (Below, in this case: Hulsman *et al.* 1978: 377)

After disposing of two previous myths often invoked to explain the relative mildness of Dutch sentencing, i.e. the 'masking' of institutionalization (see above) and the alleged homogeneity of Dutch society (which is not necessarily a synonym for its degree of integration), Hulsman singles out five 'environmental' factors that have combined to produce the situation: (a) the comprehensive range of social services; (b) the extensive network and character of youth centres; (c) the multiplicity and client-orientation of welfare and social service agencies; (d) the mass media as integrative and destigmatizing agencies (could this statement be made of the mass media in any other country?); and (e) the pressure group activities on behalf of penal reform by the social service agencies (including the probation service). Some of these factors extrinsic to the criminal justice system also operate within it (e.g. the probation service) in a 'de-escalating' manner; and some factors alluded to above, e.g. the limited manpower of the judiciary, also serve to promote an economical use of prison. Other factors not mentioned in this context by Hulsman also seem to be most compatible with this approach, e.g. the often-quoted argument that the experience of internment by hundreds of thousands of Dutch people, including members of the élites, during the Second World War, led to a widespread association of prison with oppression and an intense awareness of the costs of the deprivation of liberty.

There is much to be said for this approach, not least because it takes account of the oldest sociological truism that 'social facts are the product of human actions, not human designs'. But it is exceptionally difficult to gauge the extent to which any or all of the above developments are in some way responsible for the mildness of Dutch sentencing, or are themselves products of the same causal matrix. War-time internment, for example, was also the experience of hundreds of thousands of Belgians and French: but their penal policies are relatively harsh. A comprehensive range of social services and youth clubs is available in Britain, albeit perhaps to a less adequate level (or at least was, until the past decade's mounting toll of cut-backs in social service expenditure): again, without a similar pay-off. Nor does there seem to be any marked correlation between the proportion of GDP spent on welfare and the prison population. As Table 3.1 shows, the relatively high spenders on welfare — The Netherlands, Belgium, and West Germany — include both the lowest and highest prison populations. Conversely, the lowest spenders — Ireland, the United Kingdom, and Italy — include one of the lowest, the second highest, and a country intermediate in terms of prison population. The correlation is no stronger when health care or psychiatric personnel as a ratio of the population as a whole are considered (Table 3.2).

It should be stressed that the amount spent on services is not to be equated with their quality, and is but a poor guide to the quality of

TABLE 3.1 *Social expenditures as a percentage of GDP and prison populations per 100,000 inhabitants*

	Health care		Social budget [a]		Prison population	
	%	Rank	%	Rank	Rate	Rank
Belgium	6.4	8	30.2	2	79	3
Denmark	6.9	7	29.3	4	58	7
France	9.3	2	27.2	5	67[a]	5
West Germany	8.2	4	29.5	3	92	1
Ireland	8.2	4	22.0[b]	9	38	8
Italy	7.0	6	24.7	7	60	6
Luxemburg	9.5[b]	1	27.1	6	74	4
Netherlands	9.1	3	31.7	1	25	9
United Kingdom	5.9	7	23.5	8	85[c]	2

Source: Adapted from Mangen (1985: 10, Table 1.1) and Pease (1980: 10, Table 1).

Note: Prison population data are for 1978, health care for 1981, social budget for 1982, expect where indicated. The fact that the social expenditure data do not pre-date the prison population data is of negligible significance given the stability of the rank order of prison populations over the past decade.

[a] The 'social budget' comprises all forms of public services in the fields of health, welfare, housing, education, etc., as well as social insurance and social assistance expenditure and tax concessions.

[b] Data for 1980

[c] England and Wales only.

TABLE 3.2 *Mental health care per 1,000 and prison populations per 100,000 inhabitants*

	Beds in psychiatric hospitals		Psychiatrists[a] per 100,000		Prison population in (1978)	
	Rate	Rank	Rate	Rank	Rate	Rank
Belgium	2.6	3	12.7	1	79	3
Denmark	2.1	5	8.3	2	58	7
England and Wales[b]	1.9	6	7.6[c]	4	85[d]	2
France	2.6[e]	3	5.1	8	67[e]	5
West Germany	1.9	6	8.3	2	92	1
Ireland	4.1	1	5.3	7	38	8
Italy	1.5	9	2.1	9	60	6
Luxemburg[b]	3.6	2	6.6	5	74	4
Netherlands[b]	1.9	6	6.1	6	25	9

Source: Mangen (1985: 21–4. Table 1.2, 1.3); *q.v.* for full details of problems of enumeration and interpretation.

[a] Various dates 1977–84

[b] Including beds in psychiatric units in general hospitals.

[c] England only.

[d] 1980.

[e] 1977.

social relations that pervades them. (The supreme exemplification of this elementary truth remains, and is likely to remain, Richard Titmuss's *The Gift Relationship: From Human Blood to Social Policy*, 1970.) All that can be noted here is the absence of any obvious relationship between the average prison population rate and the level of welfare provision by certain gross indicators. It may be emhasized in passing that, whatever may be held to have caused Britain's economic decline relative to European competitors, the level of expenditure on the social budget can hardly be among them.

Perhaps the most interesting of the above developments is the character of *reclassering* agencies in The Netherlands. Founded in the early nineteenth century, closely allied from the mid-nineteenth century with the judiciary, and fiercely independent of state or court control (despite the total financial dependence on the state), the *reclassering* agencies in The Netherlands do seem to have played a more influential role in penal policymaking and its implementation than the probation service has in England. The most obvious means whereby their agents influence actual sentencing is their recommendation to the court on the social background and situation of the defendant. The balance of opinion among members of the judiciary was that it was a factor, no more, in the trend towards greater mildness. Until the links can be established with greater precision, it seems impossible to say that the developments listed by Hulsman were any more than an accompaniment to sentencing trends rather than in any way causative.

The culture of the judiciary

A pervasive theme in many interviews was that judges and prosecutors in The Netherlands have evolved a distinctive occupational culture, central to which is the strongly negative value placed upon imprisonment, which is viewed as at best a necessary evil, and at least as a process likely to inflict progressive damage on a person's capacity to re-enter the community. It should therefore be minimized as far as possible. The strength of this negative evaluation is a central feature of legal training, in which lawyers are introduced to criminological teaching and research, including that of abolitionists, which expose them to the weight of evidence against prison as a penalty. For example, several members of the judiciary mentioned in interview Rijksen's book (1958) on the psychological damage wrought by prison, a book based on prisoners' accounts, which the Ministry of Justice originally sought to suppress. By contrast, a few also mentioned a more statistical study by Steenhuis (1977), in which a controlled comparison was made of the blood alcohol levels of drivers from areas in west and east Netherlands. In the former custodial, in the latter non-custodial sentencing tended to be the norm for offenders of drunken driving. No significant differences emerged from these spot-checks of blood alcohol concentrations in the two samples, from which it was inferred that fines should replace imprisonment as the standard sentence. It is difficult to imagine a similar degree of awareness of criminological literature among English judges and magistrates. On the other hand, it does not seem to have deflected the extensive use of custody in such cases (Steenhuis, 1986). This core concern is reinforced when judges enter the penal chamber (i.e. when judges assume responsibility for criminal as distinct from civil cases, by a system of rotation), and especially when they act in more serious cases with two other judges. Their professional activities can also involve them in greater and more complex contacts with non-jurists who share an anti-penal view, and their likelihood of actually visiting prisons is far higher than is the case with their counterparts in England. (Almost every prosecutor and judge whom I interviewed had visited prison at least once, and several had made numerous visits in different capacities, to different types of prison and to TBR clinics). The strong commitment of the judiciary to this aspect of their role was exemplified by one instance in Amsterdam. Some 20 judges and prosecutors spent a Saturday morning along with psychiatrists, viewing a film on TBR. A minor event, perhaps, but on top of the heavy judicial workload and outside the run of formal conferences, it testified to the seriousness with which judges in The Netherlands approach their job. It is difficult to conceive of the same event occurring in London.

Another much-quoted element is the reduced social distance between judges and defendants in The Netherlands compared with the situation in England. In The Netherlands some judges questioned whether they were members of the 'upper ten'. Though it seems to me they were too modest on this score, there is no doubt but that in England judges belong to the 'upper one'. (Even England's magistrates, for whom there is no Dutch counterpart, are drawn predominantly from the upper-middle class. This reduced social distance enables judges, so it is said, to establish more rapport with defendants under the relatively straight-forward rules of Dutch court procedure. By contrast, the ritual and ceremonial aspects of the trial are far more pronounced in England. As we have already seen, 'We are judging the person rather than the facts' was a statement made on quite a few occasions in interview. The Dutch trial process is not conducted on the full-blown adversary model of the Anglo-Saxon tradition. It is more a review of evidence gathered before the trial takes place, evidence assembled in dossiers which judges already know. Victims are rarely present, witnesses have already made their depositions. In the report of the *reclassering* officer, the defendant's needs are given full attention. The prosecutor has to recommend a specific sentence, and as it is his function to represent the 'public interest' while nevertheless, taking other parties (victim, defendant, their families, etc.) into account, judges tend to treat his recommendation as an upper limit within which to exercise their own discretion. Consensus is by no means automatic, but the role attributes are firmly drawn, as the following example suggests. One judge recalled the case of a young man who tried to rob a shop by holding a knife at a woman's throat. The judge, who had not tried the case, was actually 'shocked' by the leniency of the sentence, which had been one month's imprisonment and four month's probation. Because the offender had been the son of a professional, she suspected an element of 'class justice'. She felt strongly enough about it to ask the judge why he had given so lenient a sentence. 'Well', he replied, 'the public prosecutor did not ask for more'. She then asked the prosecutor the same question. 'He was very angry that I asked at all, but replied, 'Well, it *was* a five-month sentence and a first offence'.

Data for 1973–76 indicate that the sentence was the same as the requirement in fully one-third of all cases at the district courts, and that the average difference in the remainder amounted to actual sentences of 12–20 per cent less in length than the prosecutors' recommendations in cases of rape, robbery, burglary, manslaughter, and extortion (Zoomer 1979: 45, 51–4). (Actual sentences were higher in cases of murder and attempted extortion.) But the overall concordance is remarkable. In short, a shared community of values does seem to underpin the scheme of sentencing and the adoption of a certain tariff. The directives and guidelines issued by senior prosecutors are by no means capable of yielding a precise set of sentences and though they are adhered to in general, variations obviously exist. Current attempts at a greater degree of co-ordination of sentencing would doubtless iron out some of the extremes, but in the case of some offences these (to an outsider) do not seem to be at all remarkable, being in general a matter of months rather than years. For burglary, for example, the range by district is from 5.3 to 8.1 months imprisonment, though the dispersion is larger for other offences (Zoomer 1979: 41).

The character of the 'culture of the judiciary' in The Netherlands, as elicited by questions about the attitude to imprisonment, is conveyed by such replies as:

I have to tell you that a sentence of a year or more is, in our opinion, in our custom, already a long sentence. (prosecutor)

The police may feel frustrated as they notice a case takes them more time than the offender has to spend in prison, and that is what you are often hearing. I think, however, it is a matter of habituation, for after a while you would hear the complaints, even if we start to punish four times higher than now. The experience of what is long, what short, is very subjective. Those kinds of remarks are not very rational. I do not think that there will change a lot if we would start to follow a completely different policy. For also in much harsher regimes than Holland people are saying: the judges are too mild . . . Nevertheless, we have to take care for extremities . . . the hard core . . . to keep that group as small as possible. (judge)

In a certain way, we think that giving one a prison sentence of several years will not solve the problem of handling the criminality. The only thing you can say if you put someone in prison five years is that in these five years he cannot do anything wrong. But unless you have the death penalty or the life imprisonment, every prisoner will at a certain time return in our society. And I think that is a remark that everyone here in this country has in his head. (senior prosecutor)

If really necessary, I would be able to deviate from the prosecutor's recommendation. On the other hand, I keep in mind that, especially in juvenile cases, the difference between one month and two months is enormous. So, in general, I do not go over the requirement. (Juvenile Court judge)

One of the books that made a great impression on me was the 'green' book of Professor Rijksen . . . For most people, the only time that really counts are the first weeks, the first months in prison, and the first *time* they are in prison, and every other time doesn't make any difference. So why should we do it when it costs so much to put them in prison? (judge)

The problem in making such excerpts from often long and complex interviews, conducted in what for the interviewees, whatever their facility, was a second language, is the danger of ironing out the nuances, qualifications, and genuine ambiguities which inhere in attempts to answer such conundrums as why and how sentencing trends have taken a certain path. For example, in one interview, a judge stated that the changes 'start at the universities where they all come from. I do not think there is one special side of it. It is not only the prosecutor, not only the judge, but also the *reclassering* and people writing about it.' Asked if that amounted to a 'general consensus', the reply was affirmative. Later in the interview, it became evident that any such consensus could not be neatly assigned to criminological training, 'because the training was not really a criminal training. You had a general training and then criminal law was not my main subject. It was more like a subject you were doing and you needed it because of exams. We had a very fine professor, but not really ideological, more the rules. She went to court with us once, but there was not so much attention paid to what prison means, and so on. It was not very much criminological. No, I think more of it came when I was a lawyer. Well, I think then you lived with the people. And you saw what happened to them [defendants]. And you felt with them what it [prison] meant.

A few members of the judiciary spoke in quite analytical terms about the various influences that had helped to shape the trends in criminal justice over the past thirty years or so. One prosecutor, for example, saw a two- or even threefold set of overlapping influences: the concern about the 'human impact of imprisonment' of the Utrecht school; the 'functional' approach of such figures as Enschedé, who stressed the need to formulate a clearer relationship between the goals and means of sentencing policy; and the indirect influence of Hulsman, not so much for the 'abolitionist' view, but in his emphasis on the scope for referring the offender back to the community and the victim in a restitutive sense.

It was more common, however, for responses to stress the importance of 'on the job' factors, the constraints of time, resources and the judicial division of labour. The only real common denominators were a marked antipathy to long-term imprisonment; acceptance of shorter terms as a minimum requirement lest people 'take the law into their own hands'; and a preparedness to accommodate changes that could be justified in justicial as well as system terms.

Whether or not this pragmatic liberalism is sufficiently rooted to withstand the strong pressures for yet tougher measures remains to be seen. The first five years of the 1980s not only produced a sharp rise in crime of over 50 per cent (though it should be stressed that the rise in England was almost as steep), but a rise also in the welter of demands made of the criminal justice system. A senior prosecutor emphasized the rapidity with which the insulation of the judiciary had broken down in the face of such changes as a more vocal and critical media; demands for stiffer sentencing from, *inter alia*, feminist and minority groups in relation to offences involving sexual aggression and racial discrimination; organizations such as the National Association of Shopkeepers publically calling for tougher measures against shoplifters; uprecedented questions in Parliament about judicial recommendations for sentence; newspapers which ten years ago hardly ever named judges or prosecutors now quite commonly doing so. 'The signals from society are cumulatively very strong and impossible to ignore.' English judges, long accustomed if not inured to the buffetings of the media whenever a sentence approaches the lenient end of the spectrum, might be forgiven a wry smile. Stolwijk cites a number of additional developments as undermining the status quo: the rising salience of a politics of law and order; the pruning of the social services; and the loss of faith in rehabilitation. 'The hostility to custodial sentencing is vanishing. The emphasis on alternatives to reduce imprisonment is disappearing . . . It seems that the ideological base of the alternative movement has gone . . . If there is one lesson to be learned from the period of alternative sanctions, it is the lesson that without a convincing ideology, it is impossible to reduce the use of custody' (Stolwijk 1986: 290–1).

Real as many of these tendencies may be, this tone seems too apocalyptic. The same prosecutor who cited the pressures above also said that nevertheless 'what remains is still a feeling of some community within the judiciary, some common background'. It is not so much an ideology, a neat consensus, and it is doubtful if it ever was: it is more a shared outlook, with some considerable resilience, on the futility of inflated penal expectations. As Stolwijk himself admits, 'it should be noted that the insistent calls for heavier sentences as a means of combating crime have failed to produce a response' (Stolwijk 1986: 289). Yet if the Dutch judiciary were no more than pragmatists, they would long before now have revised their penalties upwards for the sake of a quiet life. That they have resisted this course so far suggests both a principled stand against expansionism, and a marked scepticism about where it would lead. On this interpretation, the expansion of penal capacity is neither simply an 'end to decarceration' (in van Ruller's phrase, 1985) nor a capitulation to 'neo-conservative' penal philosophy (de Haan 1986), but a means of pursuing reductionist aims in what, for The Netherlands, is an unprecedentedly expansionist climate.

Hence, this shared outlook does not preclude change, and in recent years sentences to prison have been stiffer, though they remain mild by English standards. There does not seem to be any marked generational effect involved in this development. A reformed system of judicial recruitment and training, introduced in 1971–72 to broaden and systematize these processes, has if anything strengthened the exposure of younger recruits to the anti-penal influences mentioned above. The problem of accounting for the anti-penal character of the culture of the judiciary in terms of these features, however, is that in different circumstances they would equally well support a pro-penal ideology. For example, English magistrates are not necessarily less penally minded than English judges, despite being closer socially to their defendants. In a salutary demonstration that greater professionalism and criminological training do not necessitate milder sentencing, Stanton Wheeler revealed in one American study that the better-trained judges doled out longer sentences, since their acceptance of a rehabilitative ideology led them to accept the need for more exposure to such influences in reformatories (Wheeler *et al* 1968). In that case, the nature of the criminological training was heavily influenced by psychiatric thinking. How has this linkage been avoided in The Netherlands, where perhaps the most influential post-war school of thought was the 'Utrecht School'? The interplay between the theories and institutional outcomes of some of that School's thinkers perhaps supplies a missing element in the explanation of the trends under scrutiny (Bianchi 1975, Moedikdo 1976).

The rise and fall of rehabilitation

For a relatively brief period, from the late 1940s until the mid-1960s, the rehabilitative ideal was accepted in The Netherlands by the judiciary to an extent unknown in England, where its sway (despite the strong rehabilitative emphasis of the 1895 Gladstone Committee) was always more muted among judges and magistrates. The inter-war period in The Netherlands had seen a pronounced move towards the acceptance of psychoanalytical models for the treatment of a small minority of offenders, and the introduction of TBR in 1928 went beyond any equivalent tendency in England. However, in both countries, treatment of the individual offender by casework methods was regarded as progressive in social work and probation circles. After the Second World War, however, there emerged in the work of the so-called 'Utrecht school' a small group of distinguished professors — Baan, Kempe, and Pompe — whose advocacy of rehabilitative measures, and whose opposition to penal measures, went far beyond that of any comparable group in Britain. The establishment of several clinics of a largely non-custodial kind in the 1950s in The Netherlands was matched in England only by the lone establishment of the Henderson Hospital. The fact that by 1955 a third of all 'prisoners' serving over a year, and a third of the average daily population in liberty-depriving institutions, were in TBR, indicates the extent to which judges in The Netherlands were prepared to invest considerable faith in these measures. By contrast, in England compulsory admissions to mental hospitals were a far smaller fraction of the long-term and average daily population. By 1966, the peak of attempted psychiatrization was reached with the Hustinx Committee recommendation in The Netherlands that all defendants facing sentences of one year or more should be subject to psychiatric reports, and that to undertake this task clinics were needed in all five High Court areas. These recommendations were never implemented, and shortly afterwards the reaction against TBR set in. From a number of disparate standpoints — prisoners' rights, the indeterminacy issue, the flaws in clinic security — attacks were mounted, not least by the judges, against the over-use of TBR. Its use was progressively curtailed from that point, though it remains a fairly standard sentence in combination with prison for aggressive offenders. Its status and procedures have been reviewed by the Mulder Committee (Netherlands Ministry of Justice, 1983) and its role for this much-reduced minority of offenders is secure. The proportion of cases in which psychiatric reports were called for fell from 15 per cent to 7 per cent between 1971 and 1981 in the most serious cases (tried by three judges) and from 0.7 to 0.2 per cent in the less serious (SCPB 1985: 225). Nevertheless, the commitment to treatment remains, relatively speaking, substantially higher than in England in the 1980s — though in the 1950s it was remarkably higher.

How can we account for this contrast? First, the energies and evangelistic zeal of the chief members of the Utrecht school were obviously formidable. As Frank Kuitenbrouwer, a journalist specializing in criminal justice policy, put it in an interview: 'They spoke all over Holland, they wrote newspaper articles, they hammered at the Establishment to be more humane. Pompe made the link between the reform of prisons and the reform of sentencing. He had immense moral authority and a very strong personality. And he was teaching lawyers.' Secondly, the talents of the group were complementary: Baan provided psychiatric expertise, Pompe the legal and criminological linkages, and Kempe the concept of the 'dialogue' between therapist and client which lent philosophical lustre to the mental health movement and the professional social workers. *Reclassering* gave strong support to the ideals of the school. Thirdly, the anti-penal critique implicit in their approach reinforced the pre-existing antipathy to imprisonment that had already been fostered by war-time experience. It seems likely that, even when in the 1960s the judiciary abandoned the high hopes that treatment would have discernible positive effects on offenders, they retained their acceptance of the school's rejection of prison for its negative impact on them. This is not to say that the school was the sole source of anti-penal thinking, merely that it reinforced it at a critical period. Nor is it to deny that the school's treatment orientation was strongly opposed from the outset by certain leading criminologists, such as Nagel, who none the less endorsed the anti-penal strand in their thinking.

By contrast, in England, despite the attempted innovations of the 1959 Mental Health Act, judges have never really been swayed from their belief in the need for the fundamentally punitive and deterrent functions of prison, though a minority perhaps placed some faith in the notion of prison as a context within which rehabilitation could occur. The designation of so many establishments in Britain as 'treatment and training' prisons testifies to the lack of serious Establishment opposition to the very compromise that the Utrecht school rejected: that punishment and treatment could be rendered compatible.

There was in some cases sharp disagreement in interviews with the view, expressed most forcibly by Bianchi (1975: 53–4), that the Utrecht school's impact in The Netherlands was 'enormous', and that they 'converted' the authorities to their views. Also, the nature of the commitment of Baan, Kempe and Pompe to the medical model varied considerable (Moedikdo 1976). They did, however, share an anti-penal, anti-retributivist, and in some respects existentialist philosophy of treatment that was unique; and they occupied the plurality of roles necessary for them to mediate their views at all levels of the control system, from the Ministry of Justice and Supreme Court down.

It is difficult to be more assertive than this about the influence of the Utrecht shool. Certain moments stand out as clear indicators of the shift from a relatively strong and clear advocacy of treatment and rehabilitation, in the early and mid-1950s, to the greater stress on the damage wrought by over-long imprisonment of the early 1960s. In the first wave of ministerial and judicial enthusiasm for rehabilitation, a quite remarkable degree of co-ordination prevailed at senior levels. Dr A. M. Roosenburg (in an interview on 27 June 1985, subsequently clarified by personal communication) outlined the twofold role of the Psychiatric Observation Clinic in Utrecht. First, it had to advise courts requesting a psychiatric report before trial. Secondly, it advised the Ministry of Justice on special problems with people serving long-term or life imprisonment, for instance, whether or not it would be safe for society to pardon them.

The essence of Baan's achievement was that he did not restrict the role of the Psychiatric Observation Clinic to advice on statements on imputability. Instead, he tried to conceive constructive ways, within the boundaries of the Dutch legal system, for dealing with people who were under observation because of their 'dangerous' behaviour. Yet his advice could often not be acted upon: first, because of insufficient resources within both prisons and treatment institutions; and secondly, because the practice of the Ministry of Justice was to 'more or less administratively and routinely allocate patients to institutions instead of the reverse: adapting institutions to patients' and community needs'.

A high degree of co-ordination between people at senior level developed *because* of this impasse. Baan, psychiatrist and lawyer, felt the need to discuss such difficulties with everybody involved with policymaking: the head of the Prison system, the head of the TBR system, the head of the Probation Service, the Utrecht University professors of penal law (Pompe) and criminology (Kempe), as well as the directors of the several treatment institutions. 'Every six weeks, Baan called them together and Roosenburg prepared two or three cases for discussion. Then the prisoner or 'patient' was called into the already crowded room and every participant could say and ask what was on his mind. So the files began to live for them'.

These meetings, which testify to the extraordinary sway exerted, by the Utrecht school, went on until 1957, as long as Baan was the head of the Psychiatric Observation Clinic; afterwards they were discontinued. It was in this context that in 1955 some 263 offenders were committed to unsuspended TBR, and 353 to suspended TBR, of whom perhaps 20–30 per cent would have the measure activated due to a subsequent offence. Almost a third of the long-term institutional population (sentences of a year or more) were then detained under TBR regulations: some 1,478 compared with a prison population of just over 3,000. So marked a conversion to the treatment model was never apparent in England, or indeed in Britain as a whole.

This degree of psychiatrization had never been without its critics and, as the problems it entailed became apparent, the judiciary began to question its use for other than the most serious sexual and aggressive offenders. A standard remark in interviews was 'In the 1950s, you could get TBR for bicycle theft'. Its relative decline was most marked in cases against property (see Table 3.3).

In fact the shift is even greater than shown in the above table . . . If account is taken of all violent offences committed before admission (including offences against morality and property including violence) it is found that 22 per cent of the patients admitted in 1955–6 and 84 per cent of those admitted in 1975–7 committed at least one violent offence. (Van Emmerick 1982: 19)

In TBR institutions as a whole, the decline in property offenders,

TABLE 3.3   *Admissions into the Van der Hoeven TBR Clinic by type of offence 1955–1977 (percentages)*

	1955–6	1957–62	1963–69	1970–4	1975–7	Total
Offences against property	75	68	60	46	38	59
Violence	8	9	20	25	42	19
Morality	14	22	19	25	16	20
Other	2	1	1	4	4	2
Total no. of offences	117	142	156	133	79	627

Source: Van Emmerick (1982: 19)

both in numbers and as a proportion of the whole, was even more marked (Netherlands Ministry of Justice 1977: 7).

The case against the view that the Utrecht school influenced the judiciary significantly in the growth of milder sentencing was made most notably by Nagel, Enschedé, and Moedikdo, prominent respectively as criminologist, jurist, and analyst of the school's theory and practice. Interviewed in May 1981, Nagel enumerated three points which he saw as limiting their influence: first, they were too diverse to be a 'school', and did no research to test their approach, a point also made by Enschedé (at an interview in the same year); secondly, he had opposed their teaching concerning rehabilitation, despite liking them personally. In 1951, he had said at a meeting at the Ministry of Justice concerning TBR: 'If I commit a crime, I would stand upon my rights to be punished for it, and not to be cured by you, Baan.' He thought prison for up to two years would be bearable, but to be perpetually 'aroused' by doctors intolerable. Thirdly, Baan's successor as medical director of the Van der Hoeven Clinic, Roosenburg, had been too extreme in rejecting due process of a legal character and propagating indeterminate treatment as an alternative to imprisonment, an approach which 'upset the lawyers in training in her lectures.' Hence he demurred from the idea that TBR had weaned judges from imprisonment, seeing penal capacity as more central to the shortening of sentences. Enschedé put forward a more comprehensive explanation of the capacity argument, viewing the workload of public prosecutors in particular as critical for the sharp increase in the waiving of the prosecutions in the 1960s and 1970s (see pp. 68–9 above). Moedikdo

(1976) has given the most sympathetic distillation of the work of the Utrecht school but later (interview, 23 Apr. 1982) also resisted the view that the 'school' had much influence on trends in penal policy. A more likely source of such influence, in his view, was M. P. Vrij (1895–1955), Professor of Law and Criminology at Groningen University, whose work introduced elements of sociology into the study of criminal law (see, for example, Vrij 1956), and who in 1947 became a member of the Supreme Court. His influence can be discerned in the making of the Economic Offences Act of 1950, which was mainly the creation of A. Mulder, whose doctoral research on the theme of economic criminal law had been conducted under Vrij's aegis. Vrij and his pupils (the latter are still united in the 'colloquium Prof. Mr. M. P. Vrij' that holds conferences once or twice a year) were linked by their interest in criminal law as a just but efficient instrument of criminal justice policy. The more effective integration of the latter was the main interest shared by his ex-students, several of whom attained high office, notably Mulder, who as chairman of the senior prosecutors in the mid-1960s initiated the extension of the subject-matter of their fortnightly meetings from public order to criminal justice policy as a whole (interview, Enschedé, 1982) as well as Van Veen, his successor at Groningen and chairman of the Appeals Council that deals with prisoners' complaints (see also below, pp 97–8). Insofar as 1965 was a crucial year for the 'making of a rational criminal justice system' (Enschedé), of a sort which does not and cannot exist in England (as the constitutional basis for it is lacking), considerable significance must attach to the intellectual formations which made such developments possible.

Taking these points in turn, it is, first, difficult to see the diversity of the Utrecht school as a weakness. Its diversity was its strength, much as that of the so-called 'Chicago school' resists easy assumptions of uniformity of outlook or method (Rock 1979; Bulmer 1985). The research point is most telling for the later period of disenchantment with the more radical psychiatrization of Roosenburg; but even Nagel did not criticize Kempe and Rijksen on this score. The nature of their research was (to employ a perhaps outworn distinction) qualitative rather than quantitative, exploratory rather than evaluative, and of a case study/life history form rather in any way positivistic. Pompe was by no means anti-empirical, but his work was juridical rather than research-oriented. However, the influence of their *form* of research was clearly marked. Their main appeal was philosophical: a form of existentialist and phenomenological reinstatement of the offender as a human being with individual rights, against which the penal system was seen as imposing an authoritarian and often unjust, as well as counter-productive, and unnecessarily oppressive, regime. In the aftermath of the German occupation, one can readily apppreciate a not unreceptive climate of opinion for such an approach, put forward as it was with immense conviction and persuasive power by men who, like Pompe, had emerged from the war with much credit. His Catholicism led him to the notion of requital, or reconciliation, between offender and authority, a notion with a strong confessional element. But a punishment which embitters the punished and disgraces him in the eyes of others not only misses its target but is also unjust. The ideal of requital is the voluntary expiation on the part of the guilty themselves. In 1956, the Criminological Institute of Utrecht organized lectures on the long-term prison sentence. Pompe compared the ruining of people by long-term imprisonment with human sacrifices in honour of Moloch (Moedikdo 1976). He argued for the implementation of the reduction of the parole threshold to one-third of the sentence, a recommendation that was never taken up. But his major theme remained, with subtle shifts over the course of his long career, for the possibilities of requital, undertaken by the offender accepting moral responsibility for his offence, to be as unimpeded as possible by the character of punishment. Indeed, ideally the nature of the penalty would enhance the possibilities of requital, by granting trust to the prisoner and strengthening his legal rights. 'In fact he proposed the juridication of the prison community with clear rights and duties for all participants' (Moedikdo 1976). This position involved much tension with the advocacy of treatment by Baan and Kempe, but their views of rehabilitation took account of similar concerns.

As Moedikdo comments, it is to the credit of the working group behind the Utrecht school that criminology there both broke with traditional (orthodox legalism) ways and yet did not collapse into Social Defence, which considers the criminal as an identifiable type to be institutionalized until cured or for life (Radzinowicz 1966: Ch.2). Kempe's work in the areas of social inquiry reports and *reclassering* led him to formulate the concept of the dialogue between the social worker or psychiatrist and the offender. The main task of the investigator was to accept the act as a meaningful expression which can only be revealed by the offender himself in the dialogue/meeting with the investigator. Whilst the latter should avoid moral judgment, he must not simply empathize with the offender, but somehow situate the act in the context of the latter's existential reality. To do otherwise is either to objectivize the offender as a criminal in the Lombrosian way, or as a social product in the more sociological sense. Both in pre-sentence reports and in after-care, however, without taking the authorities' part, the investigator should, on the basis of his knowledge, mediate the insights gained to them. Baan took a similar view from a more psychiatric standpoint. The two differed in the role they would accord the investigator in sentencing and parole decision-making: for Kempe, that was to be the responsibility of the judge; for Baan, the psychiatrist should have an equal say with the judiciary in those matters. The lines of future conflicts were laid down in these differences, with Roosenburg pushing Baan's views somewhat further, whilst Pompe, Kempe and later the 'new' Utrecht school, of Kelk, Peters, and others adhered to fundamental legal procedures, rights and duties. This later became the entire project of the 'new' Utrecht school, who came to distance themselves somewhat from the world of the clinics: while accepting that they have a role to play with a small minority of seriously disturbed offenders, they have tended to focus on extending and clarifying prisoners' and patients' rights (Kelk 1983, Koenradt 1983).

It would be a great mistake, however, to reduce the project of the 'old' Utrecht school to a purely psychiatric mission, on the one hand, or to a semi-mystical existentialism on the other. (The standard joke about the latter is that guards were to be trained to unlock doors as 'encounteringly' as possible.) The achievement of the Utrecht school was not only to mount a critique and adopt a coherent philosophy: it suggested many practical alternatives, some of which were actually realized. And even in the work of Roosenberg, who is usually cast as the most extreme advocate of psychiatrization, the methods were psychotherapeutic, not behaviouristic. TBR should involve as much contact with the community as possible, both intramurally and via conditional release and extra-mural projects. It was not an advocacy of brain surgery and ECT.

It was only with the work of Rijksen, however, that the Utrecht school made a direct impact on the judiciary. The publication of his *Prisoners Speak Out* in 1958 was clearly an event of major importance in the history of Dutch post-war criminal justice. Thus far, the concern of the members of the school for the human dignity of the offender as a legal subject and a responsible person has always been mediated through their therapeutic and scholarly concern.

In 1958, a collection of letters was published in this spirit. These letters, written on request by prisoners, covered their experiences of the administration of criminal justice. Most contained considerable criticism of judges and public prosecutors, but also of lawyers and probation workers. The result was a storm of public indignation: the different functionaries were, for the first time, confronted with the implications of their own actions and, for a while, their self-confidence seemed to be shaken. What had been achieved in any case, was the first piercing of the hermetically closed prison situation. For the first time, prisoners could let their voices be heard from captivity. (Kelk 1983: 158–9).

The Ministry of Justice first tried to suppress the book, thus perhaps guaranteeing an even greater impact. Even 20 years after its publication in a fresh edition in 1961, judges and prosecutors named this more than any other book as the source of their belief that too long a sentence of imprisonment would embitter and damage prisoners, both socially and psychologically. The attempted suppression, incidentally, seems to qualify the commitment of the Ministry of Justice to taking the initiative in reducing the prison population, though its opposition to the book's publication may have been due more to a fear of such issues becoming openly debated issues rather than to any rooted objection to the policy message. However, it is also significant that the author and his colleagues did not 'go public' on the issue of attempted censorship: though critical of the Dutch 'Establishment', they were also very much in and of it. It is also significant that, faced with perhaps the closest English equivalent some ten years later, Cohen and Taylor's *Psychological Survival* (1972), published in strict breach of the Official Secrets Act, the Home Office decided against prosecution, prompted no doubt by the publicity it would have stirred. Judges and magistrates are not known to have led the rush for copies, though the message was much the same as Rijksen's, albeit in more sociological terms.

As a result, the pre-war work of Pompe on requital, and the

impediments to it embodied in the criminal justice and penal system, and the post-war work of Kempe and Baan on the need for dialogue with a fully human subject found perfect expression in Rijksen's elicitation of prisoners' experiences of such barriers. It completed the paradigm. By comparison, it is difficult to see so coherent a philosophy in reductionist terms emerging from the work of Vrij (as discussed in Sharples 1972: 172–3) who *inter alia* argued for sterner measures against prostitution and a notion of 'subsociality', which entailed a measure of account being paid analytically to public opinion in the criminal justice process. Such views may be expected to have had expansionist implications for the penal system, though it may well be that his influence was felt in other respects, notably in the attempts to promote a more integrated system from 1965 onwards.

Vrij suggested that in addition to guilt and unlawfulness, a third condition for criminal liability or culpability should be what he termed 'subsociality'. An act should not count as an offence unless some damage or disturbance to the social order could be established. Four levels at which such disturbances might be discerned fanning out from the infraction concerned the victim(s), the witnesses or spectators, the community, and the larger society. The notion of 'subsociality' was later revised by his followers, prominent among whom have been van Veen, A. Mulder, G. E. Mulder, R. de Waard, and Enschedé, to refer not so much to the *offence* as to *prosecution*. Discernible here are criteria for operating the principle of expediency which minimize the recourse to prosecution unless the public interest can be shown to be served by it. 'With this doctrine Vrij carried penal science into the field of social politics, thereby introducing a de-juridicating element into penal law' (Remmelink 1980). The crucial linkage here, however, was also made by Pompe (1959), who 'did not see *het subsociale* as constituting either a third element of the offence or any independent condition for imposing punishment. He considers that its significance consists in providing guidance for operating the expediency principle and for meeting out punishment. From this standpoint, the negative condition of *subsocialiteit* take a place quite different from unlawfulness and guilt' (Sharples 1972: 173; Pompe, 1959: 77–80). While it would be an oversimplification to see the Utrecht school as supplying the direction of reductionist policies, and that of Vrij the functional framework for their accomplishment (their influences holding sway in the 1950s and 60s respectively), it is in their interpenetration that much of the cast of post-war penal policy in The Netherlands must be sought. (See also p. 121 below)

What then can be made of the varying views put forward on the influence of the Utrecht school on reductionist policies? First, it has to be acknowledged that 'many of the milder tendencies in penal practice might just as well have occurred without the Utrecht school' (Moedikdo 1976). For example, the Fick Committee of 1947, which initiated the long-term fall in the prison population in particular and the institutional population in general, recommended a wide-ranging series of humanizing reforms to penal regimes, notably the opening up of prisons to community living and association within walls. They reaffirmed but did not initiate the concept of one prisoner to a cell, which was already standard, albeit in terms which amounted to solitary confinement. 'One-to-a-cell is more constitutional than the Constitution' (Kelk, interview, May 1983). Also, though the war-time experience of several of the Committee members, and of scores of thousands of Dutch people, may have facilitated liberalization, it may have also encouraged rehabilitation even more. Similar experiences of mass internment and occupation in Belgium and France did not lead to reductionist penal policies. But the equation may have been drawn between the pains of imprisonment and mental disturbance: would anyone in their right mind ever risk imprisonment? The 1951 Act codified such tendencies, but again, similar acts of rehabilitative intent in Britain and elsewhere, e.g. the Children and Young Persons Act 1969, have been preludes to increases in the prison population rather than the reverse. It is mainly in the maintenance of the impetus towards reductionism in the 1950s and 1960s that the influence of the Utrecht school should be sought.

One must also pose the question of where the offenders committed to TBR actually were. From the late 1940s through to the early 1970s, with peaks in the mid-1950s and mid-1960s, between several hundred and 1,500 people were assigned to TBR at any one time. But they were not necessarily in the clinics, whose capacity rose to 500 or so only relatively late in the 1950s. So they were either on conditional furlough, home leave, or elsewhere in the mental hospital system, or they were *passanten* in the houses of detention (remand), waiting for a place in the Selection Clinic. Indeed, the opening of the Van der Hoeven Clinic was accelerated by legal steps on the part of a group of *passanten* to activate their TBR orders! Before 1960, that wait could be measured in years, rather than months. Hence, one major effect of rehabilitative policies was to load on to the prison system hundreds of offenders who were indeterminately sentenced, which must have made at times for severe capacity problems even in a prison system which overall was running at a capacity to population ratio low enough to enable prison closures to take place. This could have been one substantial reason for the growing disenchantment with TBR among judges which took several forms: first, the indeterminacy issue, particularly over routine property offences. Though judges had the decisive voice concerning release, they had to pay due attention to psychiatrists' recommendation. Secondly, the process of graduated release was felt to be too risky: several scandals erupted over offences committed by paroled patients. Thirdly, the clinics were thought to be insufficiently secure (with one exception: the Mesdag). And fourthly, the capacity problem put pressure on the staff to release (though only conditionally) even risky cases (de Smit, interview June 1981). The power of the psychiatric experts was too entrenched for any direct challenge. However, as judges could only gradually move away from the psychiatric model, and were indeed still convinced of its value for the most serious cases of sexual and aggressive crimes, they could compensate by becoming even milder for the non-psychiatric cases. The strength of the conversion to rehabilitative policies in the 1950s, partly inspired by anti-penal convictions, may as a result have accelerated sentence-shortening for other cases. De Smit has written of the 'babylonic confusion between psychiatry and criminal law' (1976)—and, by this point, TBR was being used less readily, and with reductions in the average length of 'sentence': though a move to limit TBR to six years, reviewable annually after two, has so far been delayed. The rise and fall of rehabilitation may therefore have contributed to reductionism, both directly—through the work of Pompe, Kempe and Rijksen in particular—to the shortening of prison sentences, and indirectly—through judicial moves to compensate for the unanticipated side-effects of indeterminacy. Such considerations would, however, matter only among groups who were already committed to anti-penal sentiments, and who adhered to high standards of social relations for those in custody.

Conclusion

Adequate tests of theories in the social sciences are in far more parsimonious supply than the theories themselves. Use of the comparative method, however, suggests that the first two approaches have considerable shortcomings in their starkest form. Economic constraints are unlikely to account for reductions in the resort to imprisonment at a period of unprecedented economic prosperity in The Netherlands. Countries similarly placed, or even experiencing greater economic stringencies, failed to match the Dutch example of relative decarceration. For much the same reason, penal capacity does not seem, even allowing for inertia, to account for the trends under scrutiny. What happened pre-war did not prove much of a basis for predicting what occurred post-war in any society except in The Netherlands. Progressive declines in penal population occurred from around the 1880s to around the eve of the Second World War in Britain, France, Germany and Belgium, a trend that Rusche and Kirchheimer (1939: Ch 9) attribute to improvements in economic conditions and falls either in the incidence or the rate of increase of crime from the alarming levels of the early and mid-nineteenth century. If, however, the limits of penal capacity are extended to the criminal justice system in general, then a substantial (though by no means the major) part of the phenomenon can be accounted for by the progressive filtering out of potential inputs by (*a*) the sharp decline in the clear-up rate, (*b*) an increase in the proportion of offences not brought before the prosecutor even though they have been cleared up, and (*c*) an increase in the proportion not passed on to the court by the prosecutor.

Some of these trends can be accounted for by policy considerations. The 'principle of opportunity', whereby the public prosecutor may waive prosecution for reasons of public interest, provides the constitutional imprimatur for considerable flexibility. The progressive waiving of prosecutions may thus be linked with the shortening of prison terms by judges. Explanations in terms of a generalized 'culture of tolerance' operating within the context of a 'politics of accommodation' help explain *how* the élites concerned were enabled to carry their policies through without eliciting fierce opposition and public hostility. The context of an unusually generous welfare state which gave high priority to the assimilation of minority groups would also ease the task of justifying such measures. But the main burden of accounting for the trends seems to fall ultimately on variables closely connected with the actual accomplishment of sentencing by the prosecutors and judges themselves; and here the manner of judicial training and socialization, and the character and timing of the brief ascendancy of rehabilitative policies, seems to be crucial in ways which have yet to be analyzed at all adequately. What is incontestable, however, is that rehabilitative policies, in the Dutch context, were clearly compatible, if not causally connected, with the striking reduction in the prison population.

4   Consequences of Sentencing Trends in The Netherlands

By far the most contentious aspects of the study of sentencing policy are the possible consequences that may be attributed to it. In so far as Dutch sentencing policy has figured in debates about penal policy in Britain, most controversy has centred around the alleged costs and benefits of adopting a similar policy. Those opposed to a more lenient sentencing policy (not least, the Police Federation) have argued that it has led in the Dutch case to a disproportionate rise in the crime rate. Those in favour tend to stress the more tangible benefits that a relatively small prison population can experience in terms of conditions and human rights. Little more can be attempted here than assessment of the difficulties involved in elucidating these issues.

Crime trends

Comparative crime rates in The Netherlands and England have been alluded to above, and there is little point in denying their broad correspondence with lay theories of the interplay between crime and punishment. The relative mildness of prison sentencing in The Netherlands in the 1955–65 period was succeeded by a steepening of the rate of increase in the crime rate thereafter. The reverse scenario does not apply quite so neatly to England, despite a purely temporary slackening in the rate of increase from 1977–79 (see Fig. 2.1). Over the past ten years, the Dutch crime rate has risen more steeply than that in England, to the point at which the broad convergence of 1950–55 in crime rates between the two countries is almost re-established. In 1985–6, however, the crime rate in The Netherlands stabilized, while that in England rose by 10 per cent.

The strong likelihood that these trends have no casual relationship in the sense implied by lay (and some criminological) theory will hardly prevent the equation being drawn between mild prison policies on the one hand and soaring crime rates on the other. Against such an equation, several points can be made.

First, it is ludicrous to draw any causal inference from a surface comparison between only two countries over so limited a period of time. Over a longer period, and in relation to several societies, Rusche and Kirchheimer concluded quite the opposite: ' . . . the policy of punishment and its variations have no effective influence on the rate of crime. Changes in penal praxis cannot seriously interfere with the operation of the social causes for delinquency' (Rusche and Kirchheimer 1939: 294). Though there is much scope for interpretation of their use of the word 'seriously' little has since emerged to warrant a different conclusion.

Secondly, the problems of comparing crime statistics have been greatly elaborated over the past few decades. While their use should by no means be abandoned, they should only be employed in combination with other indicators of the character and distribution of crime. Victim surveys in both England and The Netherlands show a huge disparity between levels of officially registered crime and crime as reported by victims. The level of crime as recorded in a London survey was some 10–11 times as high as the official rate; in The Netherlands, some 4–5 times as high (see Sparks *et al.* 1977, for London; Fiselier 1978: 62, Table 21, and van Dijk and Steinmetz, 1980: 13, Table 2, for The Netherlands). From these sources it should not be concluded that the English police ignore twice as much crime as the Dutch police, but that the hidden economy of crime is several times larger at least than the data on its formal volume suggest. A due caution in monitoring crime rates is therefore essential. Even so, the utility of victim surveys has been to show that, broadly speaking, the rising crime trends which emerge from the official criminal statistics are neither without substance nor largely the product of police manipulation of the raw material. Where victim surveys provide the basis for time-series, they broadly match the rise in official crime rates, though there are some interesting anomalies (Hough and Mayhew 1983, 1985; Van Dijk and Steinmetz 1980). Even at the inter-area level, victim survey rates tend to correspond with those of the police (Mawby 1979; Bottoms *et al.* 1987). On this basis, the burden of crime, as revealed both by victim surveys and the official statistics, is now much the same in The Netherlands and in England. In a carefully monitored comparison of victim surveys in both countries carried out in 1984 (The Netherlands) and 1982 (England) Richard Block (1986) gives a figure of 25.6 per cent of those aged over 15 in The Netherlands as having been the victim of at least one of the main 'standard list' offences. The 1982 figure for England is 21 per cent, which becomes 24.8 per cent if the differences between official crime rates in 1981 and 1984 is allowed for. These data also show the futility of attempting any longer to account for disparities in penal populations by reference only to any substantial differences in crime problems. There are interesting cultural and opportunity differences in the rates of certain offences: bicycle theft and vandalism are higher in The Netherlands, car theft in England. But burglary, robbery, and sexually aggressive offences rate much the same. Sadly, The Netherlands has caught up with her more crime-ridden neighbour across the sea.

Rates for the more serious offences considered in relation to sentencing trends in Chapter 2 show a broad similarity rather than any striking difference. It should be stressed that much more detailed scrutiny is needed of how the offences are constituted by different subcategories before firm conclusions can be drawn about differences in order of magnitude. The figure for 'murder' for The Netherlands, for example, includes euthanasia, aiding and abetting suicide, and unlawful abortion as well as the offences of murder, voluntary manslaughter, and premeditated murder. Involuntary manslaughter is included in a different offence group, which also includes the more serious cases of grievous bodily harm, including attempts. The figure of 278 'murders' in Table 4.1 incorporates the category containing 'involuntary manslaughter' but also grievous bodily harm and attempts.

The figures indicate that the rate for rape is distinctly higher for The Netherlands than for England, but again, without more detailed research on a sample of relevant cases, it could not be held to indicate a 'true' difference, especially in view of the distinct differences in the figures for indecent assault. It may well be, for example, that attempted rape is more likely to be classed as such in The Netherlands, but as indecent assault in England. Such factors may in part account for differences in sentencing for rape. The higher rate of burglary in The Netherlands is not matched by victim survey rates, which show parity (Block 1986). The lower rate of car theft in The Netherlands may reflect more stringent licensing of vehicles, an opportunity variable.

Thirdly, the tendency of the crime rate in The Netherlands to correspond with that in England and in other industrial societies, suggests that parallel rather than divergent trends are at work in

TABLE 4.1   *Current figures for serious crime in The Netherlands and England*

	Year	England	The Netherlands	Ratio[a]
Total rate per 100,000 population	1986	7,803	7,145	1.1:1
Murder, manslaughter, infanticide	1985	616	278[b]	2.2:1
Rape	1985	1,842	1,201	1.5:1
Indecent assault	1985	11,410	2,057	5.5:1
Robbery	1984	24,890	7,608	3.3:1
Burglary	1985	871,261	345,380	2.5:1
Theft or unauthorized taking of motor vehicles	1984	344,806	47,687	7.2:1

Source: Netherlands CBS, *Mndsat rechtsbesch en veilig* (Monthly statistics on justice and security), CBS 86/5, p. 32, Table 7. Home Office, *Criminal Statistics* (1984, 1985).
[a]   The ratio of population in the two countries is 3.5 : 1.
[b]   Including involuntary manslaughter, but also 'grievous bodily harm' and 'attempts'. The figure for 'completed' murders and voluntary manslaughter only is 151.

both societies. The most obvious candidate from the theoretical array is offered by the general phenomenon of economic growth and persistent inequalities. As Hulsman put it, in a slightly different connection: 'The Netherlands, perhaps more than other nations in Western Europe, is closely involved in precisely those processes of change that in the past have led to increased repressiveness [as a result of soaring crime rates] wherever they occurred' (Hulsman *et al.* 1978: 374). A high rate of population growth, particularly in the most 'risk prone' age-group for crime, the 15–24 year-olds; rapid urbanization; a changing occupational structure; ideological values 'undergoing an even swifter and more radical change'; large-scale immigration from Surinam and the Antilles following that from Indonesia; the inflow of foreign workers; and the immense growth of The Netherlands as a centre for youth tourism and as a world traffic centre: these variables have combined to exert intense pressure on the 'pillarized' structure of Dutch society (see Ch. 7). In the sphere of crime, the emergence of drug addiction as a phenomenon by no means confined to Amsterdam's inner city was cited in many interviews as one of the most serious to emerge over the past decade or so, and its scale and complexities are hardly attributable to sentencing policy, but rather to the factors listed by Hulsman. The upsurge of youthful rebellion in The Netherlands took the form of 'making fools of the authorities' and promoting 'alternative life-styles', rather than any routine criminal form. In the 1970s, however, the squatting movement has adopted more extreme strategies that have involved several running battles with the police in Amsterdam, most notably at the ceremony of the royal succession in 1978. Again, the dynamics of this movement, often cited as the most serious challenge to authority in The Netherlands, probably have more to do with the chronic shortage of housing in Amsterdam than with sentencing policy, though the activists have exploited to the full the flexibility of the Dutch criminal justice system.

In sum, it seems more plausible to suggest that the Dutch crime rate has reflected, obliquely and distortedly, the consequences of myriad social and economic changes which have, overall, both weakened social controls and sharpened economic aspirations. Due to the greater investment in post-war reconstruction in The Netherlands, the full impact of economic expansion was subject to a time-lag by comparison with Britain, but that impact was eventually greater in terms of prosperity and change.

In what amounts to a 'control theory' of the rise in crime in The Netherlands, Jan van Dijk, speaking at the 1986 Penal Congress in Amsterdam, argued that over the past two decades 'the pillars have collapsed'. The decline of denominational allegiances (see Lijphart 1975, Bryant 1981) has removed or eroded the three substantial contributions made by 'pillarization' to the criminal justice system. First, the socializing and integrative effects of denominationalism were progressively weakened. Secondly, the denominational structure of institutional life in The Netherlands dissolved in crucial respects, especially among the trade unions, and (significantly for the criminal justice system) in the system of probation. Thirdly, the extent to which the élites were shielded from public opinion by the deference and willingness to 'leave things to the authorities' inherent in pillarization began to evaporate. Popular opinion began to mobilize on a series of fronts, not least that of 'law and order', to demand that the authorities become at least more responsive to their wishes and to the public mood. The first effected an erosion of the major sources of informal social control which had made for a slower rise in crime in The Netherlands than in most other industrial societies, Britain included, in the period up to the mid-1960s. The rise in crime in the 1970s outstripped that of other countries, especially with regard to property crime. The second weakened the forces that made for a milder penal climate in The Netherlands than elsewhere: probation played a pivotal role in mediating anti-punitive attitudes to the judiciary in particular and the larger society in general. The third meant that the judiciary came to be exposed, as did both local and central governments, to popular demands for tougher measures against drug-related crime in particular. It cannot be denied, according to van Dijk that, as a result, the Dutch criminal justice system is in serious trouble. The Roethof Committee set up in 1983, the policy plan spelt out in *Society and Crime* in 1985, and the projected expansion of the prison capacity by 30 per cent by 1990 are measures best understood in this context. They are an orchestrated policy of 'damage limitation' which seek to shield the core elements of Dutch liberalism in the criminal justice and penal sphere from undue slippage towards greater repressiveness. Some response was required for, if there is an 'iron law' of criminology, it is that losses of informal social control are eventually converted into demands for formal regulatory measures. A kind of regulatory inflation can all too easily result, in which the debasement of the penal currency leads to prison populations outstripping the available supplies of serious crime (see Pratt 1985). This escalation has occurred most markedly in the United States, where three minor frauds can now entail mandatory life imprisonment (Hood and Radzinowicz 1980: 1305, n. *b*).

The evidence for progressive depillarization is certainly strong. It is evident not only in the non-denominational way in which such important institutions as labour unions and the probation service are now organized, but also in the trend of opinions held both generally and by church members in The Netherlands (see Table 4.2).

Two points can be made about the opinion trends culled from the surveys of the SCPB (which contain a wealth of material and commentary far outstripping the British equivalent, *Social Trends*). First, the opinion shifts had been most dramatic between 1966 and 1970, since when the trends have flattened out somewhat. Secondly, denominationalism holds up most strongly in non-

TABLE 4.2   *Indicators of depillarization: Opinions about the relationship between religion and social organization, 1966–1983 (percentages)*

	Everyone			Church members		
	1966	1970	1983	1966	1970	1983
The relationship between politics and religion is best:						
Separate	58	70	71	46	58	60
it depends	6	7	11	7	9	14
Not separate	36	23	18	47	33	26
The following should be based on religious principles:						
Broadcasting	42	23	20	57	33	31
Trade unions	33	18	14	46	27	23
Political parties	n.k	21	21	n.k	31	32
Sports clubs	23	9	6	33	13	9
Youth clubs	55	33	18	72	46	29
The best primary schools are:						
Private	39	35	37	17	16	15
Doesn't matter	6	24	27	5	25	23
Based on religious principles	55	41	37	78	59	62

Source: SCPB (1984: 294–5, Table 11.24).

recreational fields, such as politics and education. It remains the case that broadcasting continues to be based on 'the respective religious, ideological or political standpoints of the major broadcasting organisations' (SCPB 1986: 194). But it seems, in the wake of the above trends, to be only a matter of time before the denominational basis of the media also becomes depillarized.

Finally, in interpreting these trends in relation to crime, it should be remembered that The Netherlands and England had much the same crime rate in both 1950 and 1985. The implications of depillarization are best seen as contributing towards a steeper rise in crime in The Netherlands than in England in the 1970s, with the much slower rise in the 1955–65 period being attributable to the continuing strength of the 'socializing and integrative' effects of the 'columns': lack of cultural data before 1966 make such inferences hazardous, but that seems the most plausible. There remains the problem of accounting for depillarization. 'Pillars' of the social and cultural sort do not simply collapse: they are eroded or demolished by stronger forces. Sharply increased economic aspirations and strong accompanying demands for greater political and cultural rights and freedom, particularly among the rising post-war generation, should not be left out of account here.

Control trends

In terms of Durkheim's classical functionalist theories of deviance and control, The Netherlands is experiencing increasing anomie (of which rising crime is one manifestation) to which it responds with a remarkably restitutive system of justice, whose distinctive purpose is to restore harmony rather than to exact retribution. The police are located at the interface of these two moral universes, and somehow must wrest a *modus vivendi* from what appear to be irreconcilable demands. Maurice Punch has vividly described how the world looks to police on the front line in Amsterdam's inner city: a battle-weary civil soldiery, lacking authoritative guidelines but retaining allegiance to the authorities, confront a rapidly changing political economy of crime (1979 *a*, 1979*b*). The results are ambivalence, a certain cynicism, a tendency to distance oneself from one's role. Johnson and Heijder capture something of this world-view:

The willingness to forego arrests seems to be less a matter of sentimental leniency and more a desire to avoid unnecessary effort because of policies that drift down from the offices of public prosecutors. The attitudes differ among officers, but, as an example of the effect of previous actions, one officer said: 'When the judge puts them in jail, it is worthwhile to take them off the streets, but, when the judge sends them away as quickly as you can send them, you become tolerant!' (Johnson and Heijder 1983: 10).

The steep decline in the clear-up rate seems to operate both as cause and effect of police demoralization, a sequence that could lead, in time, to police pressure for stiffer sentencing. Police officer training, however, is of a comparable standard to a university degree and ensures some common ground in terms of awareness of the rationale for sentencing policy. Innovations seem more likely in the fields of community policing and technology, as well as calls for more manpower, than in the direction of more punitive sanctions. Comparatively speaking, even the tougher levels of sentencing in Britain have done little to assuage police demands for yet stronger measures, which in 1981 embraced a call for the restoration of the death penalty for the murder of police officers; and in terms of police corruption, experience in England over the last decade is hardly superior to that of The Netherlands (Punch 1979*b*). At ministry level, 'target hardening' and victim compensation are the core of Dutch crime prevention policy, and annual victim surveys are actively promoted in part to draw attention to the high volume of petty offences that do not readily justify an undue 'fear of crime'.[1]

These trends—the immense rise in property crime in the 1970s and early 1980s, the overload of judicial capacity, the bottle-necks in the penal system—culminated in a relatively unprecedented concern about the need for longer-term forward planning. Short-term pragmatic adjustments were no longer enough to meet what was beginning to surface, for the first time in Dutch post-war history, as the political issue of 'law and order'. In the 1980s, capacity problems increasingly gave rise to the adverse publicity of serious offenders, including people charged with manslaughter and hard drug trafficking, being released from pre-trial custody because of lack of cell space. (It should be noted that comparable cases have occurred in Britain, see p 194 below). The introduction of priority grading for pre-trial detainees did not iron out these problems sufficiently quickly or well to staunch both political and public concern about the mismatch between detainees and places in which they could be held. More cell spaces were seen as necessary, on top of those called for by the Inter-Departmental Committee of 1981. In 1983, in the run-up to the general election, the liberal (VVD) party called for a Committee of Inquiry into crime problems. The Roethof Committee, set up with all-party support after the election, in September 1983, was most significantly entitled the *Commissie kleine criminaliteit* (the committee on petty criminality). At a stroke, the main crime

---

[1]   For example, the huge rise in bicycle thefts (an almost undetectable crime) contributed markedly to the overall rise in crime rates and to the fall in the clear-up rate in The Netherlands. The rise in burglary has been a more substantial element in the former, however.

problem was implicitly defined as the great mass of thefts, burglaries, and traffic offences, as well as minor assaults and vandalism, rather than the more potent but statistically far rarer symbols of the 'fear of crime' such as murder, rape, and major drug-trafficking. The latter figured rather more centrally in the subsequent reports on prison capacity and the major amalgamation of the two, *Society and Crime: A Policy Plan for The Netherlands* (Netherlands, Ministry of Justice 1985).

The Roethof Committee produced its 'interim' (in fact, final) report in October 1984. It combined a series of recommendations for crime prevention with a few for greater prosecutorial stringency. The crime prevention measures aimed essentially at a collective form of consciousness-raising as far as petty crime is concerned. The source of the old informal social controls, *verzuiling* (pillarization), could not be reconstituted: but the two main methods of reactivating a higher degree of community awareness of the need for crime control could be actively promoted by both central and local government. The first, termed 'norm traps' by Erhard Blankenberg, one of the committee's academic members, consisted of stepping-up the existing forms of regulation which had become only weakly enforced, such as ticket inspections on public transport. The second, which also had employment implications, was to promote new forms of occupational surveillance, such as employing concierges in apartment houses, providing special incentives for schools to involve pupils in the better maintenance of buildings, and drawing a range of ministries (Traffic, Education, Cultural Affairs, Economic Affairs, and Housing) into negotiating minimal standards for crime control with employers and unions in public transport, schools, sports (especially soccer) clubs, shops (especially department stores), and public housing. Prosecutors were to avoid dropping cases of petty crime on individual grounds, if their scale had become of sufficient concern in geographic areas designated for 'triangular action programmes'. Offering a monetary fine should be the norm in such cases. The triangular co-operation programmes, in which police, prosecution, and the local authority co-ordinate control priorities, were an attempt to extend schemes which had been initiated in the cities for the past decade. Finally, victims should be kept better informed of the progress of their cases, and restitution to the victim by the offender should be more widely pursued, as should the effective implementation of fines. Both the call for restraint in dropping cases and the stiffening of the execution of fines had some implications for custody.

Hard on the heels of the Roethof Committee Report came the setting up of a Project Group on Penal Capacity in November 1984. Its report (Netherlands, Ministry of Justice 1985*c*) spelt out the case for the creation of an extra 2,070 prison places by 1990, two-thirds of which are seen as required for drug-traffickers. Full implementation of the projection would have meant a penal capacity of just over 7,000 in 1990, though it is now more likely that expansion will be limited to an extra 1,000 places or so, giving just over 6,000 places by the end of the decade (see next section). In May 1985, the *Society and Crime* policy plan combined the analyses of these two reports and made a consolidated set of recommendations that go somewhat beyond Roethof, taking account of serious as well as petty crime in the process. The main importance of *Society and Crime* (which will be discussed more fully in Ch. 7) is that it is an attempt to uphold the line of modified reductionism against the growing clamour for tougher policies against rising crime. The liberal 'inner circle' (Rock 1980) of Dutch penal policy makers argue that no fundamental change is involved in the building of five new prisons. That was the price to be paid for maintaining the principle of one to a cell, and the hope is maintained that the extra places will not be filled as long as drug problems 'go out of fashion or at least out of Holland' (van Dijk, interview, 4 June 1985). Van Dijk is a prominent spokesman for the view that there should be no increase in the length of prison sentences except for drug dealers, though again the hope is that even these would remain highly selective: 'It does no good to fill up our prisons with drug traffickers from Pakistan.' This hope is set against the expectation voiced by himself and other leading criminologists, such as Hulsman, that the temptation for the judiciary to pass longer sentences of imprisonment for offenders in general will be difficult to resist. To Haan (1986), for example, 'penal reformers in the Netherlands regard these plans as a historical break from a long tradition of tolerance and lenient criminal justice . . . [and as] showing certain similarities with the neo-conservative penal policy manifested in various Western countries, especially the United States . . .(pp. 163–4). Another reductionist hostage to fortune in '*Society and Crime*' is the recommendation that public prosecutors cut the extent of their unconditional waiving by half. The effect of such a measure may have custodial implications. In short, *Society and Crime*, remarkable as it is as a summation of the best endeavours of liberal policy makers to limit the damage to penal policy wrought by rising crime, shows the loss of room for manoeuvre which has come to afflict the Dutch criminal justice system.

No comparable development has occurred in England, despite the sharp deterioration in the crime rate in the 1980s, and the emergence of a hard drugs problem as serious as that in The Netherlands and elsewhere. The only discernible policy trend is that termed 'bifurcationism' (Bottoms 1977)—the ever-steeper trend in repressiveness towards the more serious offenders being offset, at least in principle, by milder measures in relation to petty criminality. The current Home Secretary, Douglas Hurd, began his tenure of office just before the major riots of Handsworth, Birmingham, and Broadwater Farm, Tottenham, in the summer and autumn of 1985. No distinct reformulation of policy has evolved so far, though his preoccupation with the levels of overtime worked by the prison officers, which led to a major outbreak of riots in several English jails following attempted overtime cuts, may indicate a desire to improve working practices above and beyond cost-cutting. The priority accorded such initiatives as 'Fresh Start'. (Home Office 1986*a*), however, suggest that horizons are limited to 'an expanded, more efficient, managerially less incoherent version of what exists today', rather than set on 'a modern, humane prison system . . . where prisoners are treated decently and staff have satisfying and worthwhile careers' (Stern 1987: 177). The previous Home Secretary, Leon Brittan, balanced the reduction of the parole threshold to six month's custody by withholding it prospectively and retrospectively from prisoners sentenced to five years or more for offences of violence and drug-trafficking. He made the most decisive move in an expansionist direction for over three decades by endorsing the construction of some twenty new prisons over the next ten years. This decision was made in the face of considerable evidence to the effect that much penal capacity in England is over-secure and under-occupied, while over-crowding is concentrated in the local prisons (King and Morgan 1979, 1980). His predecessor, William Whitelaw, showed signs of embracing a mildly reductionist policy but was forced to disavow it after a hostile reception at the 1981 Conservative Party Conference. There is little sign that the political will exists to launch a comprehensive policy review along the lines of the Dutch plan (Bottomley 1986) though certain similarities exist in crime prevention and victim support measures (see Ch. 7).

A further indicator of possible consequences of different sentencing policies is the resort to citizen 'direct action' in the realm of self-policing. Several judges and prosecutors interviewed stressed the fundamental significance of relating penalties to the limits below which 'public opinion' would favour 'taking the law into their own hands'. On this score, despite several incidents in The Netherlands which testify to the potency of this issue, England also has recently experienced a marginal drift towards 'vigilante' self-policing, particularly among black minority groups. Moreover, disaffection from the police seems— particularly in the wake of the recent rioting—no less prevalent in England than in The Netherlands, not only among minority groups but pervasively throughout the most deprived inner city areas.

Finally, it may be one consequence of the very flexibility of the Dutch system that the scope of judicial powers in the legal realm become progressively displaced by executive discretion in the pre-trial and post-sentencing areas. The increase of waiving by the prosecutors, although an acknowledged and historic part of the Dutch judicial system, does involve less direct accountability to the community, since such decisions are based on grounds which are not publicly available in open court (though no judges expressed opposition to this trend). Similarly, the reduction in direct sentencing to TBR has been matched by an increasing trend to send the more troublesome prisoners to clinics from jails under article 47/120 of Prison Rules.

The criterion is whether the prisoner is 'difficult', not whether he needs treatment. As a result, the various institutions are being forced to negotiate with one another in order to get rid of difficult cases, in other words to trade in people, and this is unacceptable. Furthermore, since eight to ten people are involved in any decision, it is unclear precisely who decides what, and the accused lack proper legal protection.' (*SCPB* 1978: 153).

It seems that, the limits of leniency in the present social context having been reached, with stiffer penalties being passed in greater proportions over the past ten years, penal capacity is now the critical variable, and somewhat arbitrary discretionary measures of an executive kind are the consequence. If The Netherlands has a 'penal crisis', it is to be found in this constellation of devices to handle the 'difficult' long-term prisoner. It is on this issue that the recent demand for extra capacity partly rests.

Penal trends

By comparison with the above possible adverse consequences of Dutch sentencing policy, the more beneficial effects on the prison system and on the court processing of defendants seem more definitely attributable to the relative mildness of the sanctions employed. First, Dutch prisons are far less oppressive institutions than all but the best training prisons in England, and their regimes seem to promote a correspondingly less repressive experience of imprisonment. The small scale of the prisons makes administration of a more humane kind inherently possible. More generous staff–prisoner ratios mean less anxiety on the part of staff for their physical safety. Amenities and facilities are nowhere comparable to the squalor and decay evident in far too many local prisons in England. Overcrowding is ruled out, and police cells are no more likely to be used for prisoners remanded in custody than is the case in England. The composition of the prison population is heavily loaded with disproportionate numbers of foreign workers serving relatively long sentences, and the work of Jongman (1981) suggests that the social class composition is disproportionately lower-class, as in England. However, the general expectation of rapid release for the majority of prisoners is in itself a tension-reducing element, and arrangements for leave and 'interruptions' to sentences are far more generous than is the case in England, where longer sentences could make for high rates of absconding. Though by no means unique to The Netherlands, the innovation of ceding responsibility to less serious offenders to ensure their own reception into prison is an imaginative departure which makes sense in the context of short sentences.

In neither country are regimes democratically structured, in the sense that prisoners have the right to participate in decision-making about how prisons should be run. The only notable exception is that of the Barlinnie Special Unit in Scotland (on which, see Boyle 1977 and 1984), though the regular group meetings at Britain's only psychiatric prison, Grendon Underwood, and the Inmate Committees in Dutch prisons deserve mention. In the weaker sense of democracy, however, that of responsiveness to prisoners' needs, and the openness of institutional procedures for the resolution of complaints and disputes, the Dutch system is superior. Since the introduction in 1977 of an Act to regulate grievance procedures (Wet van 21 October 1976, Staatsblad 568), each institution must establish a Grievance Committee, which possesses the requisite legal knowledge, which is independent of the administration, and whose judgments have a legal power. 'This meant that the prison Governors were obliged to accept the decisions of the GC's and to carry them out.' (Nijboer and Ploeg 1985: 233). By contrast, the recommendations of the Prior Committee (1985) in England, that a similarly legal backing be given to grievance procedures in English prisons, has yet to be acted upon by the Government. (See Stern 1987, and Fitzgerald and Sim 1982, for comprehensive accounts of such salient features of the British prison system).

Work training programmes, recreational facilities, and welfare services seem far more generously funded. (A crude calculation indicates that Dutch prison costs per prisoner are some three times as high as in England e.g. in 1979, £18,000 compared with £6,000, respectively; data from Prison Department Ministry of Justice, The Hague, and Shaw 1980: 82, App. C.) A recent comparison of the costs of prison systems on an international basis showed those of The Netherlands to be less than half as costly as those of England, while having roughly twice the number of personnel per prisoner. Measures of cost were estimated per capita of the population as a whole, and as a proportion of GNP. Of 11 European countries studied, England spent a higher proportion of GNP on its prison system than any other country except Ireland, though the latter had over twice the number of personnel per 100 prisoners than England. England stands out in this comparison as having a relatively low ratio of staff to prisoners combined with a relatively high systems cost. 'High-cost squalor', as Rutherford termed it (1984), seems a not inappropriate description of this state of affairs (Netherlands Ministry of Justice 1984*b*: 82, Table 18).

Even so, it would be a mistake to suppose that all problems have now been ironed out of the Dutch prison system. A trend that should worry the authorities more than it appears to is the rising rate of suicide in Dutch prisons (R. Smith 1984). The number of suicides rose from less than two per year in the 1971–74 period to eight per year in that of 1979–82. By contrast, the average for

English prisons was 18 in the 1980–2 period. The *rate* of suicides among prisoners as a whole is therefore now several times higher in Dutch prisons, despite a more humane regime and better medical facilities. Though one member of staff at the Ministry of Justice had been assigned to the task of conducting research into suicides in prison, it had yet to be established which groups are most at risk (interview, June 1985). The far greater proportion of foreign prisoners in Dutch jails, and the possibility that mental abnormality figures more prominently in the far smaller prison population in The Netherlands have yet to be evaluated. Nationally, suicide rates in The Netherland are some 50 per cent higher than in England, but this accounts for only part of the difference. Although it may be tempting to assert that sheer repression plays a role in preventing suicide in English prisons, that would not explain the far lower rate in The Netherlands in the period up to 1975, when regimes were more relaxed than now. Secondly, several of the older Dutch prisons remain physically run-down.

I have been surprised to see that almost three-quarters of the cells in closed prisons in Holland remain unsewered and without running water. If prisoners merely use their cells as a place to sleep or are confined to them for comparatively brief periods of the day then the seriousness of the deficiency is lessened. This is certainly not the case in many institutions visited where the necessity to save money recently has seen prisoners confined to their cells until 1.00 p.m. on Saturdays and Sundays. (Vinson 1985: 6)

Though Vinson goes on to stress that the distinction of the Dutch prison system lies in its social, not its physical, environment (see Ch. 6 below), the recent pruning of the prison budget has met with both resistance and concern on the part of staff, who are aware of the environmental problems that remain and the risks that may be run with regard to the high calibre of the social fabric. Tensions have arisen most fundamentally over the extent to which the decline in cell vacancy levels will erode the differentiation system for allocating prisoners to the most appropriate regime—too few vacancies mean a loss of flexibility on this front.

Other economies entailed by the planned expansion taking place within cost limits are beginning to affect the relatively high standards of humane containment that characterize the Dutch prison system. So far, these effects are marginal, but cumulatively they must make for increased tension and loss of flexibility. For example, work programmes are now more rigid, and no visits can be allowed during working hours. Some 60 chaplains must be paid for by their churches, with a consequent cut-back of 40–60 per cent in some places; and guards must accept more general duties, such as armed perimeter security. Staff tolerance of the transfers basic to the planned expansion may be diminished by such measures. As Vinson remarks:

'The Dutch prison system is about to undergo considerable expansion. There is a danger of underestimating the difficulty of attaining in new institutions, in a relatively short time, the notable but patiently won achievements of the established institutions . . . overfamiliarity with reforms that have eluded most other countries may tempt unproductive short-cuts or bureaucratic tinkering with the existing prison system. (Vinson 1985: 43)

While interviewing prisoners in Veenhuizen, I was aware that a meeting was taking place in the prison between the governor and representatives from the Ministry of Justice about planned expansion of the prison from 140 to 200 places with staff cuts. Such changes are bound to affect some of the major points of strength in the Dutch prison system. Even so, it would need a momentous deterioration to reduce the conditions and standards in Dutch prisons to those all too prevalent in English jails. (see Ch. 6).

How do the two systems fare in terms of reconviction rates? The Dutch system embodies many features of the liberal view that shortness of sentences combined with a humane regime, and the progressive elimination of squalor combined with the minimization of coercion and repression, should both ease the reintegration of prisoners into society after release and reduce their likelihood of reconviction. The British system tends to embody the view, founded in the doctrine of 'less eligibility', that unless prisoners are treated more harshly than the most deprived members of the outside community, high rates of recidivism will result. Unfortunately, the Dutch do not produce reconviction figures on the same model as the British Home Office Prison Department, nor do they routinely assemble reconviction data. Two studies by van der Werff (1978, 1986) provide some basis for comparison, though the contrast is problematic due to a number of differences in the construction of key indicators. For example, the Dutch study includes traffic offences, such as causing death by dangerous driving, but excludes drunken driving. The follow-up period for the British figures is two years, that for the Dutch six, though some allowance can be made for that difference. Thirdly, the Dutch figures combine all ages and both sexes, whereas the British are given in disaggregated form. Within those constraints, comparable figures for England give reconviction rates between 1972 and 81 of 48–52 per cent for adult male prisoners, 59–69 per cent for young male offenders released from institutions, and 33–43 per cent for women so released (Home Office Prison Statistics 1980). As numbers of adult and young males are roughly equal, and far outstrip those for women, an overall rate of 56 per cent seems appropriate. Van der Werff's figures for The Netherlands are 60 per cent for those released from unconditional prison sentences in 1966 and 72 per cent for those released in 1977. Some 62 per cent of the recidivists (which included those receiving non-custodial sentences) had been reconvicted within two years of conviction. Unfortunately, time spent in custody is not allowed for in this analysis, whereas the British follow-up relates to the period after release. Hence, despite the overall shortness of Dutch custodial sentences, a two-year period is not enough to compare like with like, whereas a three-year average is probably too long. Taking 70 per cent as the likely reconviction rate within the ex-prisoner sample after 2.5 years, the recidivism rate is 70 per cent of 72 per cent for the Dutch sample, i.e. 50 per cent, compared with 56 per cent for England. Though inevitably suspect, these comparisons show that the Dutch reconviction rate is almost certainly no higher than that for England, and is probably somewhat lower. They at least contradict the view that a more recidivistic prison population will automatically ensue from relatively humane penal policies.

An ironic consequence of the allegedly greater insulation of the élites from public criticism in The Netherlands than is the case in Britain may be that they are actually more open in crucial respects to outside scrutiny of institutions. The miasma of secrecy that pervades prison (indeed, institutional life in Britain in general), and which is buttressed by the Official Secrets Act, effectively blocks access to representatives of the media, the social sciences, and the public at large. Access to prisons in The Netherlands is more readily negotiable by a wider range of people than is the case in Britain. The rights of prisoners to visits by family and friends, to use the telephone, and to communicate with lawyers free from censorship, are examples of rights which make Dutch prisons relatively relaxed in atmosphere by contrast with the pressure-cooker ethos of so many British jails. In these quite tangible respects, it can be argued that more liberal sentencing policies have indeed paid off.

It may also be the case that Dutch courts are less mystifying than their British counterparts. As I have noted, several judges alluded in interview to their concern to know 'the person not the facts', the precise reverse of the aim in British models of court procedure. These statements are to be read in the context of 'the facts' already having been established at pre-trial stages, but obviously this represents a major difference between the two systems. Whatever the merits of this emphasis, it conceivably makes possible a species of rapport between judge and defendant that is ruled out by the rigid ritual of British courts. At the least, the general absence of the prospect of a lengthy prison sentence in all but the most serious cases must enhance the prospects of defendants approaching the court without so developed an expectation of status degradation as occurs in the British context.

Conclusion

The Netherlands is not Utopia, and the Dutch penal system is clearly under considerable pressure to cope with increasing demands for more humane standards to be adopted, on the one hand, and an increasing proportion of long-term prisoners, on the other, not least due to the diminishing resort to TBR as a direct means of disposal for the most difficult offenders. Comparatively speaking, however, these issues seem relatively tractable against the scale of the problems that beset the British penal system. Though the past few years have seen a considerable tightening-up in the administration of the closed prisons and clinics in The Netherlands, with the resurgence of a more authoritarian model of administration due to a rash of escapes in the mid-1970s, there still seems little reason to dispute Bianchi's statement that the Dutch control system is 'one of the least inhuman control systems in the world' (Bianchi 1975: 151). The relative shortness of the length of prison sentences is surely among the principal reasons for this state of affairs.

Of the possible unintended and generally adverse consequences of sentencing policy, the most serious—the rise in crime—seems more plausibly attributable to more fundamental social and economic developments. Perhaps more closely connected with the pattern of sentencing is the fall in the clear-up rate, though it is difficult to specify how these two phenomena are linked. As yet, however, citizen resort to 'direct action' of a self-policing character and levels of concern about police performance seem no more evident than in Britain.

In sum, three phases can be discerned in post-war sentencing trends in The Netherlands. In the first, ranging from the late 1940s until the mid-1960s, the impact of a rehabilitative anti-penal philosophy seems crucial in explaining the trend towards shorter sentences. In the second, from roughly the mid-1960s until the mid-1970s, constraints on the capacity of the criminal justice system as a whole, and in particular the falling clear-up rate, assume an increasing importance in enabling the judiciary to effect a continuation of these trends. In the third period, from the late 1970s to date, the period of shortening sentences has ended, and pressure to expand the capacity of the system is working through the political processes.

Appendix 4.1:   Statutory maximum sentences of imprisonment (years)

	England	The Netherlands
Murder	Life	20[a]
Rape		
Simple	Life	12
Resulting in death	Life	15
Robbery		
Simple	Life	9
With aggression	Life	12
Resulting in death	Life	15
Burglary		
Simple	14	6
With aggression	Life	9
Hard drugs		
Possession	14	4[b]
Supply	14	8
Import	14	12
Cannabis		
Cultivation	14	*not listed*
Possession	5	*not listed*
Supply	14	2
Import	14	4
Theft	10	4
Joyriding	3	0.5

Source: Walker (1985: App. B); and personal communication from the WODC.
[a] There is theoretically a life sentence but it has never been used.
[b] If for more than own use. If for own use only, the maximum is one year.

5 Drugs: The Limits of Tolerance?

IN recent years, The Netherlands in general and Amsterdam in particular have tended to be viewed as victims of their own tolerance in the sphere of illicit drug consumption. The image usually propagated is of a blinkered liberalism belatedly struggling to cope with the results of its own permissiveness. Thus a *Sunday Times* correspondent, Brian Moynahan, could write in 1984 that 'Amsterdam has a long tradition of free-thinking and of tolerating most things, except law and order . . . But the city's tolerance has been worn thin by crime, drug abuse and militant squatters . . .' His report focused on the attempts of the mayor of Amsterdam to combine a crackdown on drug-traffickers with a plan to distribute free heroin to hard-core addicts (a plan subsequently altered by the refusal of the government to agree to the second aspect). Similarly, a BBC-TV programme in the *Out of Court* series dealt with the Dutch experience of drug abuse and drug-related crime as instances of an ineffectual switch from tolerance to repressiveness:

Amsterdam is one of the principal supply routes for Britain's heroin. Home Office experts and ministers made a special study of Amsterdam in planning Britain's response to the heroin problem. Because the city has tried both approaches, the permissive, and the restrictive, to the drugs plague. Neither seems to have worked. Indeed, the very liberalism of the seventies has yielded a desperate harvest of drug abuse, which authoritarian measures now seem desperately powerless to control. (transcript, 28 Feb. 1985, p. 4)

The latter passage is particularly rich in imputation of the 'looking for Rousseau and finding Hobbes' vein which Ralf Dahrendorf, in his 1985 Hamlyn lecture, identified as the mark of misguided liberalism. Both sweepingly condemn the liberalism of the 1960s and 1970s, in relation to drug abuse in particular or law and order problems in general, as a double failure: first, as ineffective in coping with the problems thus addressed; and secondly, as 'selling the pass' for more authoritarian though equally ineffective measures. Yet liberal measures had worked quite well in England in the 1960s and 1970s to moderate the rise of hard drug addiction. However, the definition of that policy as a failure or as inappropriate to The Netherlands, combined with a rejection of the prohibitionism of the American approach to narcotic addiction, left a policy vacuum that was coherently filled only in the 1980s. By then, the habit-forming tendency to define The Netherlands as the weak link in the mighty chain of international drugs control had already taken hold (cf. Kaplan, 1984).

These views are increasingly propounded by the Dutch themselves: the image is becoming a self-image. As one drugs specialist put it: 'A lot of progressive people have lost their ideals—[the belief that] if you provide a perfect society, you have less crime. Many of the 60s flower power generation are now in positions of more power, but are becoming less progressive, [in favour of] more "law and order" ' (Ernst Buning, interview 9 June 1985). Drugs have tended to become the issue around which 'permissiveness' and 'tolerance' are not simply detached from law and order as desirable objectives, but are set in antithesis to them. The elision between law and order as desirable objectives and 'law and order' measures of an authoritarian kind is then made almost imperceptibly.

Strong domestic pressure for something to be done about drug addiction in The Netherlands has never, as in Britain, the United States, and Germany, centred on soft drugs. Cannabis has never been formally legalized in The Netherlands, but its possession and small-scale distribution have in effect been accepted as legitimate. In the 1970s, however, the sharp increase in the use of hard drugs, particularly heroin, began to fray public and official composure on the drugs issue. Legislation in 1976 to stiffen the penalties for dealing and trafficking in narcotics did little to halt their spread from the major centres of Amsterdam, The Hague, and Rotterdam to most urban areas, and by the 1980s a distinct shift in mood and policy was evident. Though the high visibility of the addict populations in the red-light district of Amsterdam provided the most dramatic symbol of the problem, the major concern of local communities, and subsequently the government, came to focus on drug-related crime rather than the addiction problem itself. In this respect, there were echoes of the American concern, strongly voiced by Richard Nixon in the late 1960s and early 1970s, that hard drug addiction was an exponential factor in crime. The drug-related aspect of crime, although stressed by government and police sources in Britain, has perhaps as yet been less prominent than a more generalized concern about rising crime and rising addiction as somewhat separate problems. In general, and notwithstanding Jay Epstein's (1977) critique of the Nixon administration's handling of the drugs issue in his *Agency of Fear*, there is an undeniable reality to drug-related crime which tempts governments and communities to define hard drugs as *the* major crime problem. Tougher measures to control the spread of the problem become commonplace, and pressure to systematize such controls, internationally as well as domestically, takes institutional form. Kaplan (1984) has analyzed the 'uneasy consensus' which is sustained by the International Narcotics Control Board, and its censure of The Netherlands for its 'permissiveness' towards drugs control. Dutch resistance to this 'consensus' and its pursuit of standardization in the policy sphere, as counter-productive in terms of both the quantity of secondary crimes thus generated, and as diminishing the credibility of the law, is most forcefully expressed by Ruter (1986).

In short, by the mid-1980s, policymakers in The Netherlands have been under severe pressure to adopt tougher measures towards hard drug abuse, both domestically and internationally. In this chapter, it is argued that The Netherlands has, ironically, in one major respect at least, been less 'permissive' towards hard drug abuse than Britain; that the widespread image of The Netherlands as moving from outright permissiveness to belated authoritarianism is badly flawed; and that the drugs problem in The Netherlands is in most respects no worse, and in crucial respects better, than in societies which criticize the Dutch response to the problem. The key question is: how far has the politics of drugs changed the direction of post-war penal policy in The Netherlands?

Narcotic control trends in England and The Netherlands since 1960

In his comparative study of the entire conspectus of narcotic control policies in Britain and America, Arnold Trebach goes far to document the inverse correlation between influence and success or failure in the narcotics policy realm. The most influential control model has been that of the United States, a notably prohibitionist society yet one which has almost totally failed to staunch the rise and spread of narcotic addiction, drug-related crime, organized criminal distribution networks, and attendant policy and political corruption. With the extirpation of the

Shreveport Clinic in Louisiana in 1923, whose morphine maintenance programme for the period from 1919–23 had met with encouraging success in the task of control, the Treasury Department ushered in half a century of rigorous prohibitionism in narcotics policy. Two minor dents in this prohibitionism have been the 1970s decriminalization of cannabis (a soft drug) in several states, since reversed following Reagan's anti-drugs campaign; and the willingness to experiment with methadone maintenance programmes following the work of Dole and Nyswander (see, e.g. 1968). Otherwise, the criminalization of narcotics remains so sweeping and stringent that morphine cannot be prescribed for terminally ill patients in hospital. (Trebach 1982).

By contrast, the British system developed along lines far more consonant with a 'medical' model of narcotics control that, for roughly half a century from the report of the Rolleston Committee in 1926 stood in sharp contrast to the 'crime control' model adopted in America. Once modified in the 1968 restriction of heroin maintenance for registered addicts from general practitioners to designated hospital-based treatment centres, most clinics had by 1970 substituted injectable methadone for injectable heroin. More gradually throughout the 1970s, and especially from 1977–79, the hospitals switched from injectable to oral methadone as the main drug and mode of administration for addicts, a move heavily influenced by practitioners' disillusionment with the experience of heroin maintenance from a curative perspective and the more optimistic assessments made possible by the methadone programmes then in use. However, the steep rise in the prevalence of heroin use from the late 1970s in Britain suggests that the reliance placed upon methadone was unduly optimistic, and the disillusion with heroin maintenance as *one* aspect of narcotic control programmes was unduly pessimistic. Whatever the causal role attributed to the clinics' change of course may be, however, the steep rise in heroin addiction and abuse over most of the past decade in Britain has coincided with the abandonment of heroin maintenance programmes. 'The current estimate is that there are upwards of 60,000 regular users, and many more casual ones.' (Stimson 1985). And although the new conventional wisdom on treatment is beginning to be questioned, along with the greatly increased investment in crime control measures of the government (see e.g. Stimson 1985, Davies 1986*a*) the trajectory of narcotics control in Britain is converging rapidly with that of the United States. The least successful model of narcotics control is proving the most influential.

The Netherlands followed a narcotics control path which differed from those of both Britain and America. Though no detailed history of the emergence of a hard drugs problem in The Netherlands has yet been compiled, a number of specialist sources indicate that the problem arose substantially later there than in the other two countries (Punch 1979b, 1985; Erkelens and Janssen 1979; de Roij-Motshagen 1985; Johnson 1984; Sansone 1984). Until 1972, the use of opiates was more or less confined to the small Chinese enclave of Amsterdam's red-light district policed from the Warmoessraat (Punch 1979b). From 1972, the spread of larger scale heroin use beyond the confines of that district was dealt with pragmatically in crime control terms, with the police in effect making *ad hoc* treaties with the various factions of the ethnic groups most involved in the trade, the Chinese and the Turks, to try to stem the diffusion of narcotics from their localities. In policy terms, little was clear beyond the parameters set by a desire to avoid both the criminalization of the addict of the American model and the heroin maintenance strategies of the British alternative. The first was discerned as in itself criminogenic; the second as too risky in a city with Amsterdam's potential for attracting foreign addicts over The Netherlands' open frontiers with other EEC countries. But the definition of the British model as essentially a failure seems to have been to the fore even in the early 1970s, 'failure' being defined as the inability to resolve or reduce the problem, rather than to dampen the rate of its increasing prevalence.

This early policy vacuum could be termed 'permissive' in the negative sense that, apart from attempts to accommodate the problem in much the same fashion as the Dutch had extended a qualified acceptance to cannabis use, no coherent justification could be made of what was in effect a stance of *laissez faire*. That the model which worked for cannabis, a non-addictive recreational drug of symbolic appeal to a broad cross-section of the young, would not work for heroin, an addictive drug with a particular appeal for the marginal and the dispossessed, became painfully clear with the mass immigration into The Netherlands of a large group of Surinamers from the former Dutch colony in 1975. The build-up to the independence of Surinam in 1975 had seen an estimated one-third of its population emigrating: 'in the last desperate year before the gate was closed, 40,000 people left for The Netherlands.' (Bagley 1983). The equivalent situation in Britain would have been the migration of roughly 150,000 people from Jamaica in a single year. The earlier migrants from Surinam had been absorbed without much difficulty into the growing Dutch economy of the 1960s; but the later arrivals brought 'a less educated group, more prone to unemployment and the vagaries of the Dutch labour market, and with fewer skills both social and technical which would enable them to take advantage of a dispersal policy' (Bagley 1983: 12) into an economy already moving into recession. Thus, 'a major problem which has emerged in the past three years [1976–9] is that of an alienated reaction by young Surinamers to Dutch society which has taken the form of retreat into drug-using subcultures . . . At the present time, indeed, there is a danger of the minority of young Surinamers becoming labelled as "junkies" or "heroin slaves" as the Dutch press is wont to call them. In Amsterdam there are an estimated 3,000 Surinamers using heroin with some regularity.' (Bagley 1983: 13–14). Moreover, 'there is no possibility of obtaining heroin through the health service (as in Britain) and thus Surinamers who do eventually become addicted are forced to obtain their heroin from illegal dealers, at a price of at least £50 a day. This often leads to the growth of secondary crime in order to finance even occasional use. This kind of situation has almost certainly been obviated by the British clinic system (Edwards 1979)' (Bagley 1983: 15). It is yet another irony of the drugs policy world that by the time to which Bagley refers in extolling the British system, it had been practically abandoned. Instead, oral methadone maintenance had been adopted as the appropriate policy in both Britain and The Netherlands.

It thus appears that in the mid-1970s, the Dutch simultaneously bungled both the politics of migration and of provision for narcotic addiction in a way which was both uncharacteristic and unfortunate in its effects. They have not, however, stood still, and in the past several years have developed a strategy for narcotic control which appears to have stabilized the addict population at around 20,000 or so, a figure much in line with Stimson's estimate of 60,000 regular users in Britain, on a per capita basis, though the disparity between Amsterdam and London remains marked. In many respects, the scale and sophistication of Dutch provision for hard drug addiction outstrips that of Britain. For in Britain, the hard-won lessons of the 1960s and early 1970s had given way, by the end of the decade, to a somewhat complacent official provision of pared-down clinical maintenance and a continued reliance on private and voluntary assistance for addicts on the street. As rates of addiction rose sharply in the 1980s, British treatment agencies were hopelessly ill-equipped to cope, and the stepping-up of policing measures was, apart from a campaign to stimulate educational programmes of a preventive nature, the main governmental strategy. An additional £15 million was provided to fund short-term counselling projects from 1984–7, otherwise existing treatment centres were offered only same-level support, despite rapidly increasing demands on their resources. It was a poor basis on which to criticize the Dutch manner of response. For now, instead of having a distinctive policy to offer, the so-called British 'system', we were now simply offering less of the same.

A tale of two Amsterdams

On 28 February 1985, the BBC-2 series *Out of Court* programme concerned the Dutch system of narcotic control, mainly by covering the situation in Amsterdam through a series of filmed interviews with agencies and addicts, and ending with a discussion between David Mellor, the junior minister at the Home Office in London responsible for drugs policy co-ordination, and John Brown, a police studies specialist. The programme appeared in a series with a justifiably high reputation for salient, fair, and unvarnished reportage of issues in the socio-legal sphere. The Dutch authorities, in particular the Public Relations Department of the City of Amsterdam, actively co-operated with the making of the programme by providing information and contacts with the relevant agencies connected with drugs control.

The result was a programme markedly critical of Dutch policy and practice in this field. The tone was established in the presenters' introduction:

COMMENTATOR I Hello. And in this week's live look at the law we examine an epidemic of crime spawned by the trade in hard drugs. As the government announces its publicity drive against heroin abuse, *Out of Court* goes to Amsterdam, a city where the hard drugs nightmare has come true.

COMMENTATOR 2   A city where ninety percent of city centre crime is committed by junkies desperate for cash. Where addicts fix openly under the eyes of powerless police. And where the prisons are so full of drug offenders that any more the police catch have to be released onto the street again. (Transcript, p. 1).

The presenters then went on to convey the relative change in heroin abuse from 'fringe' to 'mainstream' activity in Britain, quoting the figure of 60,000 addicts, and citing the need to pay for the drug on the street as a major aspect of crime, stressing the crime as 'the most serious effect' of heroin abuse (p. 3) and the toughening of the law and its administration here as a response. As we have seen, the example of Amsterdam was considered salient because the city had tried both the permissive and the restrictive approaches. 'Neither seems to have worked'. (p. 4).

Up to this point, there is little to quarrel with about the programme's exposition, apart from the assertion that crime is the 'most serious' effect of heroin abuse, since 'the drug itself won't kill you, except in overdose' (p. 3). The opportunity was missed at that point to raise the most pivotal issue in the hard drugs field: why, if the drug is not lethal, is it illegal? And does the crime stem principally from the drug itself, or from the fact of its legal prohibition?

The next sequence is a filmed interview with Commissioner Winkel, the chief of police in Amsterdam. He estimates that 80 to 90 per cent of the crime in the crucial one square kilometre of Amsterdam is drug-related, and that reported crimes totalled 30,000:

INTERVIEWER   What these are (*sic*) breaks-ins, robberies, cars being smashed open?

COMM. WINKEL.   Everything God has forbidden and the law has forbidden.

INTERVIEWER   You say it with almost a despairing smile on your face.

COMM. WINKEL.   Oh I don't know if it's in despair—it's everything—they do everything, shoplifting, burglary er, even shooting, everything you find here. [Music] (transcript, p. 5)

Later in the programme, a further selection from the interview with Commissioner Winkel concerns his view that the problem was discerned early on by the police but that politicians did not act on their warnings about the growth of the problem; and that the lack of prison capacity involves arrested drugs dealers being released time after time.

The emergence of a somewhat apocalyptic tone in the interview extracts was one which the programme came to stress in both commentary and interviews with others. For example, accompanying two police officers on a tour of duty which took in the drugs scene on the immense Bijlmeer housing complex in the south-west corner of the city, the camera homes in on 'the hut', a makeshift affair which, the commentator tells us, is 'Mr Mayor's latest concession to drug tolerance, paid for by the Council to let drug users fix in peace. And well off the tourist map. It's another world in the hut, and all the police are allowed to do here is pop in, and look' (p. 21).

COMMENTATOR 2.   The odour is overpowering, no-one in uniform or not comes out of this place unaffected. The only justification the police are prepared to utter is that at least they know where the junkies are . . . But it's rather like locking the stable door after the horse has bolted. Because the addicts have outgrown the hut, another unsuccessful attempt to keep the problem in one place. The addicts are everywhere.

POLICEMAN.   This place they have been sleep, slept (*sic*). And they use here their drugs.

INTERVIEWER.   It's grotty.

POLICEMAN.   It is.

INTERVIEWER: Very grotty.

POLICEMAN: It's hopeless.

COMMENTATOR: As hopeless as they always said it would be.
(Transcript, pp. 22–3)

But the apocalyptic tone is interspersed with another innuendo, much jauntier and more knowing, that implies the patently ridiculous character of such attempts to cope with the problem. This interplay between the apocalyptic and the knowing gives the programme a distinctly patronizing edge. It would have been difficult to sustain without the omission of other passages in interviews which place the situation in Amsterdam in comparative perspective. For example, pressed to criticize his local public prosecutors for releasing drug dealers, Winkel also makes it clear that the solutions are not so easy, either here or abroad, in an untransmitted section of the interview:

INTERVIEWER: To the foreign observer of your policing methods in this city, it might appear that you turn a deliberately blind eye to drug use on the streets.

COMM. WINKEL: We did, in a way, in the beginning. And the drug addicts were not seen as criminals. They were, because according to our law they are criminals, only by possession of drugs and using drugs, but the prosecution and the political view on it, they were more victims than criminals. And we had to deal with this, that if we arrest someone with small amount for their own use of hard drugs, they didn't prosecute them. Some stopped it in arrangement with the local prosecutors, arresting those people for the possession of drugs.

INTERVIEWER: Did that upset you as a policeman?

COMM. WINKEL: No it doesn't upset me . . .

INTERVIEWER: Have you been given the power and resources to deal with the dealers enough?

COMM. WINKEL: We have got the normal Dutch power and the normal Dutch law and we are trying, within this law, to deal with it, and one of the things I always see if I speak or see other colleagues from other countries, they are always asking for more power and so do we, but I think, as a civilian, you have to be very careful with more power with the police, because you start to give the police more power for handling the drugs problem, but it soon arises that you use this power for other cases too and that's I think you have to be careful . . . In my opinion, I think also the opinion of our local government, is that we have to find other ways to deal with the problem, than only with the police force, the strong arm to find the solution to the problem. Which are, they are doing everywhere in the world. Everywhere in the world they put in more men, more power for the police, and they never succeeded in stopping the problem. America does already for 40 years, they have that problem already for forty years and all I hear is given the police more power, give the police more men and try to stop it by police, and I think you can't stop it by police. You just can try to control it in a way. (pp. 8–10, sound roll 1)

The clear acknowledgement in this part of the interview that prohibitionist and tough measures do not work, not only in The Netherlands, but everywhere, including in the United States where they have been tried for 40 (in fact 60) years, is inconsistent with the partial picture that emerged in the actual programme of a police force let down by the authorities. Only at the very end of the film was a part of the interview used that introduced complexity along these lines:

INTERVIEWER: Are they repressive methods?

COMM. WINKEL: They are repressive, yes.

INTERVIEWER: But you're not repressing the problem?

COMM. WINKEL: We are not repressing the problem we are doing just
the same as they do everywhere in Europe and everywhere in the
western world, we are repressing and in that way we try to see, make
the problem less feasible [i.e. visible]—what you do in England and
what they do in Germany, and what they do in America, they try to
make the problem less feasible [visible]—but you don't do anything at
the problem yourself. (Transcript, p. 24)

However, by this stage in the programme, the comparative
complexity of the problem world-wide comes too late to offset the
damning picture that has been given of the Dutch control system.
Moving straight into the discussion, David Mellor is prompted to
say: 'Well, I think it is an object lesson of how not to do it. I think
that they've made a lot of mistakes in Amsterdam, they had a
problem before we did (*sic*), so one perhaps shouldn't be too
critical, but we certainly want to learn from their grave mistakes
. . . They have had laws on the statute book which for many years
were not enforced, and that is not the position in England, we
enforce our laws with proper rigour . . .' (pp. 24–5). Ironically,
barely a year after that interview, the following case was reported
in an article in the *Observer* (Davies 1986a):

George is in heroin, moving about three kilos a week—buying at
£16,000 a kilo from a Turkish contact, selling at £23,000, earning about
£20,000 a week. The police know all about George. Eighteen months
ago, they infiltrated an undercover officer into his operation. But they
have not yet got around to arresting him. 'He's not a big target right
now. There are people like him queuing up to be arrested. There's so
much intelligence coming through that the operational side just can't
keep up.' George is one of hundreds . . .'

So much for 'proper rigour'.

Turning to the treatment side of the Dutch control strategy, the
programme unfortunately conveyed little of the scope and
character of the Amsterdam policy. Only towards the end of the
programme was this theme directly addressed, following a
sequence in which an addict was interviewed who admitted to an
everyday routine of petty criminality to finance his habit, for
which he had been arrested but never imprisoned:

COMMENTATOR: So the unpunished drug criminal goes back on the streets to do it again, unless the tolerant society can wean him off heroin and on to the bus. [*Music: theme of the Beatles' 'Musical Mystery Tour'*]

COMMENTATOR: This bizarre Amsterdam bus service picks up a thousand heroin addicts a day. Volunteers to try something a little less addictive, a substitute drug called Methadone. [*Music; Woman speaking in Dutch*]

COMMENTATOR: Nobody forces Jort to come here—nobody in Amsterdam's drug support operations forces anyone to do anything. Better they say to offer free Methadone and no questions asked, than coerce the addicts to give up. The success rate of this scheme—3%—but at least it keeps tabs on the users, persuades them into the clinics and allows them to be monitored. (Transcript, pp. 17–18)

This passage alludes, in the final sentence, to a major purpose of the 'methadone bus' while ignoring its primary function as a 'safety net': but the point is lost in the subsequent shift to an interview with Jort, solely to establish his continuing resort to cocaine despite the methadone; and overlaid by the initial assocation of the bus with the surrealism of the 1960s via the striking use of the *Magical Mystery Tour* music. Terming the experiment 'bizarre' and stating the success rate as 3 per cent (it is not the agency's policy to cite precise rates, but 5–10 per cent is thought more realistic) combined with the 'no questions asked' point, appear to justify David Mellor's assertion, in the discussion at the end of the programme, that 'what's missing in the Amsterdam dimension is treatment, they dish out drugs, not on a therapeutic basis, with doctors trying to wean people off drugs, but just as er, you know, here's your drugs for the day, and of course those drugs are dished around to other addicts and other people are brought into the game . . .' (transcript, p. 31). It was this statement, from a junior minister who had actually 'made a special study of Amsterdam in planning Britain's response to the heroin problem' (transcript p. 4) that particularly offended those who had been involved in the programme from the Dutch side.

Only one drugs specialist in Amsterdam was interviewed, and only one brief extract from that interview was shown on the programme:

COMMENTATOR 2   Cocaine, heroin, methadone, catch the dealers and solve the problem. Or do you?

DR ERNST BUNING: If there is still a demand for something, there will always be a way that people would get it. Um, I think that in Amsterdam the problem is on top of the table, and that means that people go to doctors if they have problems they come to us. Um, they don't have to do it in secrecy. I think that's important to help them not to damage themselves. On the moment the police comes down very hard on the addicts themselves, the addicts disappear. (Transcript p. 19)

No further attempt was made in the programme to expand on the principles underlying the treatment strategy, the main thrust of which was not only to avoid driving the addicts underground and even further into the arms of the black market in hard drugs, but also to stabilize their addiction, encourage them to 'come off' via less addictive life-styles and drugs theoretically less addictive (for the efficacy of methadone is highly problematic), and to do so via a variety of therapeutic strategies, not least that of doctor referral. Moreover, in the lengthy interview from which the extract was transmitted, Buning made the point that the signs were encouraging:

BUNING: Well, you know, we give them, by giving them methadone, by giving them basic care we hope they can stay alive and they can stay rather healthy persons in this particular phase.

INTERVIEWER: Is that a vain hope?

BUNING: No it's not. We have indications that this is working. We get less young addicts at the moment. The average age is increasing. So we think people finally, sooner or later, they decide to kick the habit, not so much due to what we are doing, I mean, not by pushing them so much.

· · · · · · · · · · · ·

INTERVIEWER: But there are 8 to 10,000 addicts.

BUNING: Yes, but they are not youngsters. You see, you have a group of people who became addicts in the '70s and they are still addicts today, or a lot of them are still addicts today, and if you are talking about attraction, I mean, young kids, teenagers who are attracted to heroin, that's not happening in Holland at the moment. (sound roll 7, pp. 1, 3)

These critical points were nowhere made or conveyed in the programme, thus leaving the viewer with the inescapable impression that little of any consequence was being said or practiced by way of treatment.

In a subsequent interview about the narcotic control system in

The Netherlands, Buning expressed disappointment in the way the programme had handled these and other issues. In his view, it failed to show how seriously the system was working. Indeed, 'it showed it to be somewhat stupid. Mellor implied there was no real treatment in Holland, but *half* of our money is spent on trying to get people off . . . The whole programme turned out to be an attack on the Dutch system of treating drug addicts and in favour of a hard Thatcher line. Of course, it is very difficult taking part in a programme for another country' (interview, 9 June 1985). A host of other points were contested: what was said by Mellor is 'a violation of the truth. First, we don't just dish out drugs. We try to stabilize them. And they have to drink the methadone there and then, so they can't re-sell it. Also, we have a *very* extensive treatment programme: 6 or 7 million guilders a year (about £3 million) on drug-free treatment programmes at the Jellinek Clinic. They keep a low profile. The trouble with the ''methadone bus'' is that everyone wants to see it, there is nothing else like it in the world. The Jellinek Clinic has 60 people at least working there, and it is like drug-free treatment across the world.' On the issue of drug-related crime, 'hard core heroin and cocaine users are quite criminal, but they will not do *anything*, as Winkel says. It is petty crime, car radio theft, pickpocketing, and shoplifting (but they are easily picked out) and prostitution (we have heroin prostitutes). The percentage of violent crime among addicts is no more than among other groups. Heroin makes people *less* aggressive. We have had contact with 10,000 addicts over the years and only very rare violence [has occurred] against our personnel' (interview, 9 June 1985).

That these kinds of points were either absent from or barely alluded to in the programme is not to say that it was entirely one-sided or lacking in any foundation for its many potent images of a city whose hard drugs problem is formidable, and whose policies for coping with it are in some disarray. But the reproofs offered by those who found it wanting in its coverage and commentary have real substance. Not least among the grounds for dismay was the contrast between the bravura professionalism with which the programme was filmed and edited, and what was felt to be an unwarrantedly distorted picture of a hard drugs problem completely out of control and a policy utterly unable to cope. Understandably, but in their own turn rather unfairly, this led the Dutch agencies concerned to see the programme as politically inspired: 'something of a propaganda film for [your] Government policies, which we don't like . . . It looked like a film for the Government to show how badly we do things, and how well the Government is going about things in England . . . We are very open, we have nothing to be ashamed about, we showed them both the good and the bad' (interview, Information Office, Amsterdam Town Hall, 13 June 1985). But only the bad was allowed to emerge, and another footnote was added to the history of the shift in the politics of drugs from '60s optimism to '70s disenchantment to the punitive policies of the '80s.

Drug dependence and its control in Amsterdam

Several phases can be discerned in the evolution of a relatively integrated narcotics control policy in Amsterdam. The first phase was simply ignoring the use of opium by the small and highly localized Chinese community in the traditional red-light district. The main drugs problem in the 1960s was the rise of experimentation with soft and hallucinogenic drugs, and on that front the city authorities adopted a policy of accommodation, with certain premises, notably the 'El Paradiso' youth centre, being virtually licensed for the sale and consumption of cannabis, a practice now selectively institutionalized throughout Amsterdam and even elsewhere in The Netherlands. This policy is viewed as—on balance—a success by the authorities both locally and nationally, though West Germany in particular has objected strongly to its operation in the border town of Enschede (Kaplan 1984). The second phase began in 1968, when heroin, unknown until then in Amsterdam, made its appearance, possibly brought in by addicted GIs from West Germany. 'It had to come from somewhere, and this was the scenario in youth circles' (Ed Leuw, interview, 12 June 1985). A sharp increase in its use occurred in 1972, and another much more dramatic increase in 1974, when 'heroin users rose in number from about a thousand to four to five thousand in Amsterdam' (Leuw). The figures are guesstimates from police and welfare sources, but the trend was downhill from that point on. The early shifts are conveyed in Table 5.1. Control at this phase seems to have been coloured both by an aversion to the two distinctive models on offer, the US prohibitionist and the UK clinic-based heroin maintenance, and by the earlier experience of accommodating soft drug use. The equation had been made between soft drug use and political and social non-conformity, to which the distinctive Dutch response of a politics of accommodation had been singularly appropriate. To adopt the same response to hard drug use was for a time seemingly justified on the grounds that a hard line would prove counter-productive, since it would serve to reinforce youthful non-conformity. In Leuw's view, the authorities were 'culturally deceived' by the young drugtakers, for the drugtaking of the 1970s was increasingly an index of despair, decreasingly of non-conformity (Leuw 1984).

TABLE 5.1   *Drugs used by drugtakers known to the Mental Health Department of the Amsterdam Municipal Health Authority, 1970–1980 (%)*

	1970	1971	1972	1973	1979/80
Opium	34	46	39	32	—
Heroin	7	4	21	30	93
Cocaine	28	32	29	24	35
Hashish	29	26	18	20	48
LSD	41	28	24	17	1
Speed	4	7	7	10	2
TOTAL no. drugtakers	220	271	335	377	632

Source: de Roij-Motshagen (1985: 8).

Note: Multiple drug use means that the sum of percentages exceeds 100.

Phase three began in the mid-1970s, and ended around 1980. Something of the nature of the escalation in the hard drug problem is captured by the figures from Amsterdam, which share the limitations inherent in those of officially registered addicts in other countries due to the ratio of several regular users to every officially registered user. The 600 or so heroin takers listed for 1979/80 would represent in reality a number of several thousand. The assumption of constancy between officially registered and actual numbers cannot be made, however, because over time the ratio may change for a variety of reasons. In London, the switch to methadone may have increased the disparity between 'hidden' and registered taking, and continuous monitoring is needed to ascertain the prevalence rate (Hartnoll *et al.* 1986) As the 'snowballing' methods used to estimate prevalence rates for the UK apart from London showed a rough ratio of 10 : 1, between actual and officially registered heroin use, we might assume the same for Amsterdam at this period. On that assumption, the number of persons dependent on heroin rose from roughly 200 in 1970 to 6,000 in 1979/80, a rate of increase far exceeding that of London, where the problem arose to a greater extent in the 1960s, and worsened more gradually in the 1970s. (Stimson and Oppenheimer 1982). Cocaine use rose threefold in the decade, without much change in its prevalence within the drugtaking population. The use of LSD and speed (amphetamines) fell quite remarkably, both in the UK and The Netherlands. The near-elimination of the use of LSD should not be taken literally, for it may reflect a change in the composition of the officially designated addict population: however, it is LSD, and not heroin, which is the obvious next step, both chemically and symbolically, for cannabis users. If its use really has declined as dramatically as the data suggest, that removes a powerful argument against the decriminalization of cannabis along Dutch lines.

Yet the most ambitious hope for the toleration of soft drug use—that it would block the rise of heroin addiction—failed to be realized. It may have kept the younger generation away from alcohol and solvent abuse relative to the experience of other countries, but such considerations were overridden by the steep and highly visible rise in heroin addiction in Amsterdam, a rise to which the civic authorities clearly had to be seen to be making some constructive response. Leuw sees the late 1970s as an era of 'limitless tolerance' in which 'the generation of ''flower power'' took a very liberal, subsidizing policy approach to problematic drug-users. Subsidies fed into the culture of de-professionalisation, critical of welfare and medical workers for their social distance from addicts.' The result was a somewhat chaotic era, with the main priority that of subsidizing addict and consumer-led community groups, and the legal and policing implications of such a policy left to sort themselves out. By about 1980, mounting financial scandals associated with the 'self-help' schemes, burgeoning evidence of police corruption and conspiracies of silence about the ineffectiveness of existing policies combined to bring this era to an end (Leuw 1984; Punch 1985). Noteworthy were the high-risk elements in the strategy which, in at least one case, allowed underworld agencies to run an open day centre for black drug users, in the hope that giving them greater autonomy would keep them off the streets. The promise was not kept: this and several other centres became venues for dealing and breeding grounds for drug use rather than contexts for its control. The temptation to fund groups and then 'turn their backs and claim the problem was solved' was, for a time, irresistible for the city authorities, particularly as the black drug-using groups resisted any involvement by white authorities. The tensions were to unfold in a series of running scandals, in particular that of Srefidensie, a black institution for black drug-users, which received a substantial annual grant. The group chose their own supervisory board, and selected as financial adviser the director's fiancée. When a deficit running into millions of guilders resulted, and links with the drug-dealing underworld were exposed, the agency collapsed in a welter of adverse publicity. In a climate of 'fantastic cynicism', as Leuw put it, most of the existing institutions based on this model, not all of them by any means so problematic, were wound up by 1980. The experience of Amsterdam is, of course, by no means unique. In his reportage of the strategy of eliciting welfare subsidies by symbolic threat, Tom Wolfe (1970) described much the same sort of situation in the inner urban areas of metropolitan America. By 1980, however, the limits of tolerance had clearly been reached, and 'limitless tolerance' as Leuw put it, was at an end; 'The official view was "never again" '.

The new era that was ushered in around 1980 was not, however, intolerant or repressive, as the *Out of Court* programme tended to assert. It was, rather, a question of 'limitless tolerance out, more controlled tolerance in. The priority became the reduction of social problems associated with drugtaking, rather than unlimited assistance for addicts. Now we're in a more pragmatic era, coinciding with cost-cutting' (Leuw interview). But policy still favours considerable subsidization of both addict and community groups: the change is that the city authorities, who resented being shut out of decision-making, now insist on having representatives on the boards.

At the same time, the amount of controlled experimentation with new ways of reaching addicts, and seeking to first stabilize and then reduce their degree of dependence on heroin, have been stepped up. The fourth phase in control strategies culminated in the announcement of an integrated drugs control policy in 1984. The high hopes invested in this policy are embodied in the personal influence of Mayor van Thijn, who pressed unsuccessfully for one element in the policy to be the introduction of a limited degree of heroin maintenance programme for addicts (City of Amsterdam 1985). Although ruled out by government opposition and opposed by many of the specialist drug agencies themselves, his defeat on that score should not obscure his ambitious attempt to co-ordinate the social, welfare, treatment, and preventive strategies with the legal and policing objectives of cracking down on the traffickers and heavy dealers, especially those operating with high visibility in and around the Zeedijk. It was the questioning of the success of this latter aspect of the policy by the BBC interviewers that led him to walk out of the interview, a factor which helped to shape the critical view taken in the programme of the policy. Neither the undue optimism of Van Thijn nor the undue scepticism of the progress made by the TV team should be allowed too much weight, though they testify eloquently to the intensity of emotion aroused by the issues at stake.

Narcotic control policies in Amsterdam in the 1980s

The integrated policy of 1984 sought to co-ordinate a variety of agencies and groups that had hitherto worked in relative isolation from each other. Institutional treatment is of both in-patient and out-patient forms, the second line of provision after the first line of 'safety-net' and crisis-reception work. General practitioners are viewed as the hub around which the system revolves, though the extent to which this is so remains highly variable. (See Roij-Motshagen 1985: 12 for an organizational sketch of the available assistance in Amsterdam.) Two elements in the policy will be discussed in greater detail below: the methadone programme and the experiment in long-term morphine maintenance treatment. The most important aspect of the policy is, however, the choice of methadone as the major element in treatment.

It is difficult to ascertain why heroin maintenance programmes were rejected from the outset in The Netherlands, but is is clear that there was very little support for them in the early 1970s, even though 'politically it was more feasible than now' (Jack Derks, interview, 10 June 1985). By contrast with England until 1968, general practitioners could not prescribe it, so the medical profession had no stake in such a system. Fears of becoming swamped by foreign addicts were both then and now to the fore in political circles. And the relatively sudden emergence of the problem in The Netherlands coincided with the early optimism about methadone based on US research that was later found to have been somewhat oversold. Also, 'the fact that the English were moving away from it did not help' (Derks). The reasons for rejecting heroin maintenance have remained much the same, despite the active championship of Peter Cohen, a sociologist specializing in drugs research, which won over the City Council but was vetoed by the government. Other specialists in the field were either sceptical or actively opposed to it. The fear of the 'Mecca effect' is very real in a country with such a flow of migrant workers and foreign tourists as The Netherlands, and with such open frontiers to the rest of the EEC. Amsterdam, where a 1960s ethos live on, is generally attractive to bohemian European youth, for cultural reasons not reducible to drug supply alone. However, as one specialist said: 'The problem with heroin is that it attracts in too many foreign addicts. And there is no possibility of checks on the border with other Common Market countries, since cars and trains are subject to only the most cursory checks.' Heroin maintenance for all comers is therefore ruled out, as it is for foreign addicts only. But why not for Dutch addicts only? On this score, the arguments falter a little. Firstly, there is the problem of differentiating between Dutch and foreign addicts. But that applies also to methadone:

That is why we don't treat foreign addicts except temporarily on production of a return ticket. They are mostly from Germany and Italy. We can't really supply methadone more to them because of the Mecca effect. We have parents on the phone from Germany asking if their addict kids can come here. There's the problem of 'outcast addicts' being dropped off at the border, good-looking girls hitch back and get here before the police do. We can handle the Dutch addicts [roughly 40 per cent of the addict population]. Surinamese addicts [roughly 30 per cent] are more difficult, not so integrated yet in Dutch society, they're a more serious challenge. But the big problem is young foreign addicts, especially girl prostitutes—they are a very big health risk from VD, a very high risk. The police need to have a much better way of sending them back, repeatedly, and by plane. At the same time, as a psychologist, I would want to help the individual foreign addict—but *en masse* they are our biggest problem [roughly 30 per cent of the addict population] (Ernst Buning, interview, 9 June 1985)

So the provision of heroin maintenance treatment, even if it was limited to Dutch addicts only, would heighten the Mecca effect and multiply the problems of exclusion and return. On the other hand, the foreign addicts who come for the methadone now can find heroin easily on the black-market. One outstanding feature of the heroin maintenance strategy is to undercut that market, a factor that would in part offset the heightened Mecca effect it would otherwise promote.

Secondly, and pragmatically, the police, the public, the politicians, and the world at large do not wish The Netherlands to dispense free heroin to addicts, even if the drug agencies and the Amsterdam authorities are prepared to contemplate it. The political argument is, however, about the politics of drug control, rather than the likely efficacy of such a policy. International pressure on the Dutch to resist heroin maintenance policies was in general seen as marginal by comparison with domestic opposition to it. Nevertheless, if Germany could object so strongly against the limited sale of cannabis in one youth centre in Enschede, one can logically surmise that any move towards a policy of heroin maintenance would provoke a major diplomatic outcry. Pressure against such developments has already been exerted by the United States and Sweden. At this level, the prohibitionist climate of fear concerning such controlled experimentation severely hampers both debate and policy options (Kaplan 1984).

Thirdly, it was argued that heroin maintenance would not do much to reduce the incidence of drug-related crime, since research has shown that 50 per cent of heroin addicts progressed to heroin from criminality rather than turning to crime to finance their habit in the first place (interview with A. J. de Roij-Motshagen, citing the work of Janssen *et al.*) Such findings set the argument in perspective rather than negate it, however. Two counter-arguments are that 50 per cent of addicts who are involved in crime *have* turned to it to feed their habit; and, for both groups, heroin may prolong what would otherwise have been a more short-lived or non-existent criminal career.

Hence the rejection of heroin and the active backing for methadone as the appropriate drug around which Amsterdam came to organize its narcotic control strategy. Within that constraint, the programmes are impressively resourced and funded. The aims are properly modest: containment, monitoring, and the provision of a safety net should be considered the main and perhaps the most important aspect of the methadone provision system (de Roij-Motshagen). The central methadone registration system was set up by the municipal health authority in Amsterdam in 1981 in an attempt to obtain as comprehensive a coverage of the scale and character of the addict population as possible. It is agency-based, and has no direct contact with addicts. By acting as a central registration point for agencies, and by holding data on each addict on a computer to which the police have no access, the aim is to provide as accurate a count as possible of trends in drug use, avoiding double-counting and too high a 'dark' figure of hidden addicts. With a lot of movement in and out of the system, it is vital to have as low a threshold for access into it as possible, and the methadone bus is seen as providing such a threshold. Other countries are seen as operating registration systems which suffer from much higher thresholds. 'The methadone bus goes like a hoover through the drug scene' (Ernst Buning), with a very high rate of contact (some 1,000 addicts per day). The use of such treatment appears irregular, offering a residual source when the street supply runs too low or becomes too costly. Though the aim is to get addicts off heroin and onto methadone as the first step in coming off drugs altogether, the programme functions mainly to keep tabs on what is happening. About 12,000 users are registered in Amsterdam, 70 per cent of whom are in some treatment programme or other, a far higher contact rate than exists in London. (They are not all necessarily resident in Amsterdam, even though they claim to be.) It is acknowledged that such counts may be an underestimate, since liaison with the police is complicated by fears of the invasion of privacy on the part of the drug assistance agencies. An elaborate protocol has therefore been devised to govern the disclosure of personal data from one agency to another, which may exacerbate problems of undercounting. Double-counting is avoided as far as possible by computerized screening of names, birthdays, identity documents, and aliases.

The main point of the methadone programme is viewed as the provision of a safety-net for addicts on a purely voluntary basis. This 'addict-led' strategy allows them to 'keep their life-style', unlike programmes in other countries which press addicts to give up their life-style as a pre-condition for treatment. Such strategies are seen as counter-productive, deterring addicts from contacting the agencies in the first place. The breadth of the threshold is as important as its height:

The whole point of methadone is to stave off any desperation for drugs. It is available seven days a week, on the bus and at four Community Centres. We try to motivate them to kick the habit. At the Community Centres, we have more control, urine tests, social workers, a programme to get them stablized, then we try to get the GPs to take over the methadone prescription. This would be the best system, to get them to mix with ordinary patients, and away from other junkies on the bus. Then we can tackle psychiatric problems (Ernst Buning).

Since it is very difficult to be an addict and keep out of contact with *all* agencies, the feeling is that they have a good idea of the size of the problem: 20,000 addicts in the country as a whole, give or take a few thousand, with half the population of Dutch addicts, plus the great bulk of the tourist addicts, concentrated in Amsterdam.

Success rates vary according to the time-span and criteria adopted, but were reckoned to be between 5 and 10 per cent. The principal route to kicking heroin and other hard drugs was seen as natural recovery, 'people just giving up', getting tired of the habit for a variety of reasons. Some faith was pinned on US research which suggested that 'getting clean' is linked with certain changes in life situations. Two examples given for The Netherlands were a woman who came into the agency and kicked the habit very quickly, despite a very high level of heroin addiction, once the man with whom she was living, a Turkish dealer in heroin, was deported; and a man who was rebuked by his son for missing the latter's winning of the national table tennis championship due to his drug habit. In both cases, the key variables seemed to be the nature of the personal relationships involved. Natural remission, addiction retirement (growing out of the habit), and addiction displacement (coming off heroin for methadone or another less addictive drug) were the three major processes for recovery: each stresses the need for stabilizing the habit as early in the user's career as possible, bolstering the more positive aspects of the life-situation as much as possible, keeping the addicts healthy to prevent physical deterioration, and keeping in contact by avoiding stigmatization. At the same time, the need to deter foreign addicts had led to the policy of the police dispersing the main drug-trafficking from the Zeedijk area only two minutes walk from the Central Station. 'The point of the Zeedijk policy is to clear the area near the Central Station where foreign addicts can within five minutes of their arrival buy heroin. Now they would have to go to Bijlmeer, where it is much more difficult for them to track it down' (Ernst Buning). At least some partial success is claimed for this policy.

Two facets of the drugs problem were seen as encouraging. Firstly, the average age of addicts is rising, having done so for the past five years at the rate of half a year per annum, from 26½ in 1980 to 29 in 1984. It is inferred from this trend that the flow of fresh recruits to heroin in adolescence has fallen sharply, and that the problem has therefore stabilized, consisting chiefly of an ageing generation of addicts who will gradually become attenuated by natural remission. The proportion of addicts under the age of 22 fell from 14.5 per cent in 1981 to 5.2 per cent in 1986. The main encouragement is drawn from the fact that very few under-19s are being recruited to heroin. Much the same trend is apparent in Germany, but the reverse is still occurring in Britain, outside London, where trends are complicated by the two-fold effect of an older and a rising addict generation: stabilization may now be inferred from trends in London, though not yet in the rest of the country. Secondly, the proportion of deaths from drug overdose among Dutch-born and Surinamese addicts fell in 1984 relative to those among foreign addicts, in particular those from Germany (see Table 5.2) although the absolute figures still rose. In 1984, 18 of those who died from drug overdose were Dutch-born, none were Surinamese, and 62 were foreign, half of whom were from Germany. This is taken to be an indication that Dutch policies are more effective than those, for example, in Denmark; in 1983, 145 deaths occurred in Copenhagen from drug overdose in a small addict population of 5,000 or so. It might be inferred from these comparative figures that the Dutch policy is more effective in keeping addicts alive by drawing them into a low-threshold therapeutic network and deglamourizing the drug subcultures from which they are being gradually detached. A parallel trend is seen as operating in connection with soft drug use, which is becoming less prevalent among children of school age—a product, it is argued, of destigmatization, the avoidance of panic among parents, and the provision of outlets which do not force users into hard drug dealing networks. Due to the opposition of the school authorities, however, inner Amsterdam was excluded from national coverage, which must raise doubts about the validity of the results of one of the surveys from which trends were inferred. Nevertheless, Utrecht, a city close to Amsterdam and with a reputedly growing drugs problem, was over-sampled for purposes of comparison with a 1976 survey there. In 1976, 3 per cent of the 15–16 year olds and 10 per cent of the 17–18 year olds had used cannabis at some time: the figures are now 2 per cent and 6 per cent respectively (Sylbing 1985: 18). On this basis the prevalence figures for The Netherlands compare favourably with those of countries pursuing relatively punitive policies towards cannabis.

TABLE 5.2 *Deaths of drugtakers in Amsterdam by country of origin, 1978–1985*

	1978	1979	1980	1981	1982	1983	1984	1985
Netherlands	9	12	14	15	12	20	35	26
Surinam	1	0	2	0	0	4	4	3
Germany	3	1	10	13	12	10	45	13
Britain	2	0	3	0	2	0	1	
Belgium	1	0	0	0	0	0	0	
Luxemburg	0	2	1	1	0	0	0	
France	0	0	1	1	0	1	5	13
Scandinavia	0	0	3	0	0	0	1	
USA	1	1	2	0	0	0	1	
Other	1	3	6	2	5	11	14	
Unknown	0	0	0	0	0	25	6	
TOTAL	18	19	44	34	33	71	114	55

Source: de Roij-Motshagen (1985 : 35). Data for 1978–82 are published police data; data for 1983–5 are from the CMR monitoring system.

Note: Figures are for all deaths, not only deaths due to drug overdose.

Figures for 1985 have been distinctly encouraging. Deaths went down sharply, though they remain higher than elsewhere except Copenhagen. The aim of discouraging drug tourists by cutting them off from methadone supplies, by strict registration of users and quantities, putting the dealers under more pressure and dispersing them from the centre of the city, was seen by the authorities as the turn of the tide (Van Stijgeren, interview, 13 May 1985).

One survival of the otherwise abandoned policy of heroin maintenance was the morphine-dispensing experiment carried out by the Amsterdam Municipal Health Organization (GG & GD) dispensing unit and the Stichting Drugshulp verlening Amsterdam (S.D.A.), an Amsterdam out-patient rehabilitation unit for long-term cases. The experiment was conducted by a psychologist, Jack Derks and evaluated by the independent Netherlands Institute of Mental Health. It was set up to assess how far the provision of injectable morphine to a small (n = *c* 40) number of 'extremely problematic drug users' (Derks 1983), under carefully regulated procedures, might assist in the management of drug problems. The provision for the user to inject the drug himself, with ampoules and syringes for a 24-hour supply, is monitored by urine tests (a non-damaging substance is added to the morphine to check that it has been used and not sold). Criteria for entry into the programme are stringent, and compounded by the relatively small number of addicts who *want* morphine: firstly, that users have been addicted to opiates for over five years; secondly, that they have tried other treatments; and thirdly, that they are medically or psychiatrically ill as well as addicted. So restrictive are these criteria that it has taken the project 18 months to contact 40 suitable cases, allowing for a drop-out rate of some 30 per cent, and the group concerned are mostly men, mostly in their mid-thirties. Set up in October 1983, the objectives are to enable the addicts to stabilize their habit and thus, progressively, the rest of their lives. At the end of 1987, a preliminary report remarked that the experiment could be counted a 'partial success' and could be finished, in terms of these objectives, 'without major difficulties', (Derks, personal communication 5 Jan 1988; see also Derks 1987). Considerable support is offered to the users, medically and psychiatrically, but the emphasis is on 'keeping them going till they get inclined to change their lives anyway.' The judicious hope is that the inclination will stand more chance of being realized within the context of better management of drug problems, rather than faced by drastic therapeutic, institutional or penal measures.

In summary, it is evident that the integrated policy in Amsterdam has assembled a variety of strategies for the better management, if not control, of the hard drugs problem, which shows signs of stabilization, if not diminution. It is plausible, but incorrect, to see the relatively short history of hard drug control there as moving from permissiveness to repression. It is more germane to see it as a move from limitless to controlled tolerance, in the social policy sphere; and from haphazard accommodation to a more co-ordinated and purposive experimentation in the field of treatment and welfare.

Drug-related crime

The problem of drug-related crime is one on which public, police, and criminological thinking tends to converge. With a few exceptions, addiction to heroin, cocaine, and hard drugs in general is viewed as highly criminogenic. The major exception is the situation, which prevailed in Britain for almost two decades, where heroin addiction is low in prevalence and dealt with by heroin maintenance strategies. But no society now pursues that strategy, or faces so modest a rate of prevalence as that which obtained in Britain until the mid-1970s. The simple equation is therefore drawn between high and/or rising rates of prevalence, and the need for addicts to finance by crime a habit which costs, even when street prices are relatively low, far more than the most generous welfare services provide. Unless the addict is in relatively well paid employment, the economic difference is seen as inevitably met partly by crime, usually of the petty theft variety—shoplifting, pilfering, and theft from cars—but embracing burglary and 'mugging' at the more serious extreme. Hard drug addiction is seen, therefore, as an exponential factor in crime: the basic processes of drug production, distribution, and exchange are in themselves illegal; their high costs are met by high rates of street crime; their high profits facilitate police, and even political, corruption; and the entire politcal economy of crime is transformed by the elaboration of sophisticated criminal organizations vying for a share of so immensely lucrative a market, and drawing prostitution, protection, and legitimate business into their control. Nor do the knock-on effects stop there. Governments and judiciaries, even if disinclined to jump on the law and order bandwagon, are prompted by the pressure of public opinion to resort to increasingly authoritarian measures to combat both the addiction and the climbing rates of crime. More and longer custodial sentences, high risk forms of policing, and high risk incursions into civil liberties become commonplace. Drug-related crime becomes an exponential factor in punishment (Ruter 1986).

Given that so momentous a set of consequences flows from a rising or high rate of illicit narcotic addiction, it is surprisingly difficult to find or establish any stringent attempt to measure its criminogenic potential. There is a great deal of rhetoric—for example, Nelson Rockefeller's notorious claim that 'about 135,000 addicts are robbing, mugging, murdering, day in and day out, for their money to fix their habit . . .' (Epstein, 1977: 44). As Epstein somewhat scathingly pointed out, such sensationalistic claims hardly fitted the police statistics, for if addicts had literally behaved that way, some 50 million serious crimes a year would have been committed—a bit on the high side even for New York City. In fact, only 110,000 such crimes were recorded in total, or less than one-four hundredth of the number Rockefeller claimed were being committed by addicts *alone*. A Hudson Institute study showed that less than 2 per cent of addicts financed their habit by robberies—and that there were far fewer addicts than Rockefeller stated. Moreover, only 4.4 per cent of those arrested for such felonies were even confirmed users, let alone addicts, who were far more likely to be involved in petty offences against property. On the other hand, it is easy to debunk such grotesque over simplifications as those uttered by Rockefeller (and later Nixon). Trebach is critical of Epstein for overdoing the criticism of these two arch-politicos alone: every other US president or presidential candidate from 1960 onwards mouthed much the same exaggerated fears. In the absence of more rigorous evidence, they are all too easily conjured up.

The difficulties of putting a figure on the extent of drug-related crime are compounded by the overlap between that and crime-related drug use. A study conducted in Utrecht that co-ordinated information on crime from police and other social agencies showed that about half of all burglaries were by drug addicts or users. No automatic causal assumption could be made about the links between burglary and drug use, since they both could be elements in a common subculture: burglars can turn to drugtaking as well as drugtakers to burglary—though the authorities see the need to 'score' every day as a rising factor in crime. The problems of disentangling drug-related crime from crime-related drug use are illustrated by a study of drugtakers in custody, which showed that some 50 per cent began their criminal careers before taking hard drugs, at least in the sense that they already had one or more convictions before the onset of drugtaking. (Erkelens and Janssen 1979) Over time, however, the trend for the drugtaking group was towards a higher proportion for whom criminality preceded drugtaking (see Table 5.3).

The authors' own inference is that, in The Netherlands at least, drug use is increasingly preceded by recorded criminality, though that interrelation may be affected by police and judicial action, i.e. in a prison sample, the population may well increasingly be composed of those whom the police arrest and who become prosecuted and imprisoned in the light of increasing concern about drugtaking.

One interesting aspect of these figures is that they show the

TABLE 5.3   *Recorded criminality prior to start of hard drug use*

Period of first use	Sample size	Criminal record (No.)	(%)	No record (No.)	(%)
Pre-1972	35	14	40.0	21	60.0
1972–4	39	21	53.8	18	46.2
1974–7	17	13	76.5	4	23.5
Total	91	48	52.7	43	47.3

Source: Erkelens and Janssen (1979), 4.

Note: $\chi^2 = 6.18$, df $= 2$, $0.01 < p < 0.05$.

reverse trend to that which one would anticipate from drugtaking becoming an increasingly important *source* of crime. However, it is possible to sustain the view that drugtaking is indeed an increasingly important source of crime if (*a*) it can be shown that—even for those who would become involved in crime anyway—criminal careers were prolonged by drug use, and (*b*) that the figures for prison populations only were unrepresentative of drugtakers who are involved in crime as a whole. On (*a*), Erkelens and Janssen (1979: 10) present data to show that the criminality level of users is both higher and more prolonged than that of non-users. On (*b*), there is observational evidence that police increasingly ignore petty offenders who are defined as drugtakers first and offenders second:

We have to select and catch the more serious type of criminal. In this city [Amsterdam] if a policeman is smelling hashish, he passes it by. In Utrecht, for example, the policeman does not smell hashish every day, and he catches that man. Here the decision is whether you have the time or not. Is the violation important enough? There are many other things going on. (Quoted in H. Johnson, 'Night Patrol in Amsterdam's Warmmoesstraat District', unpublished 1984)

Though the example may be a little overrestrained, encoded is a clear prescription for leaving the amateurs alone.

On this rather slender basis, it is possible to attempt a working idea of the contribution of hard drugtaking to crime. An upper limit may be set by taking the figure of about 50 per cent from the Utrecht study as that proportion of offences committed by people involved in some degree in hard drug use, and halving it in line with the figure given by Erkelens and Janssen for those whose criminality preceded drugtaking. The resulting figure of 25 per cent gains support from another source. It has been estimated that 20,000 addicts consume 50,000 guilders worth of heroin each per year, i.e. one billion guilders' worth. Assuming that crime pays for half this amount (the rest being paid for by prostitution, welfare payments, dealing, and labour), the addicts would still need to commit roughly 1 billion guilders' worth of property crimes to meet the bill, since fencing stolen goods would take at least half of their real value (Hoekstra 1983). The costs of property crime in general (excluding robbery, tax, and welfare fraud) have been calculated as amounting to 3.5 billion guilders (van Dijk 1984) in terms of the value of the goods stolen. If 1 billion of the 3.5–4 billion or so is attributable to drug-related crime, then again roughly 25 per cent can be derived as the contribution of the latter to the overall crime rate. If offences directly relating to trafficking and dealing were included, the contribution of drugtaking to the crime rate would be even higher.

It should be stressed that such estimates are problematic in the extreme. We know next to nothing either about sources of income and expenditure patterns among addicts and users of various degrees or about types of commitment to hard drug use. It may be that for many drugtakers, drug use is a substitute for crime rather than a stimulus to it. And some drugtakers steer well clear of even petty crime because they know they are more readily targeted than other deviants. Nevertheless, two other trends suggest the figure of 25 per cent may well be not too wide of the mark. Firstly, the real spurt in the Dutch crime rate occurred in the period from 1979 or so, when the addict population began to approach the rate of increase which would lift it from the 10,000 mark in the late 1970s to double that figure by the mid-1980s. Extrapolating the crime rate of the 1970s to the mid-1980s produces a figure some 25 per cent below what actually occurred. Secondly, the rise in crimes has been largely accounted for by petty offences against property, and burglary—offences associated with the kind of high turnover and low profitability of drug-related crime: crimes against the person have shown a less marked rise, and this accords with the view that addicts do not generate a higher rate of such offences than non-drugtakers.

The danger of such an exercise as trying to put a figure on the proportion of crime which is 'drug-related' is that it implies a neat demarcation exists between that and non-drug-related crime. Janssen and Swierstra (1983), in the most detailed documentation of the life-styles of 'hard core addicts', stress the reality of that concept, in terms of drugs driving many otherwise non-delinquent youths into crime, and prolonging into the 40s the age of desistance for those who might have been expected to drop out of crime somewhat younger. But drugs have also changed the whole pattern of criminality in other respects. 'Holland previously lacked large-scale criminality and organized crime, but now that has changed. Prostitution is now colonized by the heroin world. Pimps are often high-level dealers', (Swierstra, interview, 14 June 1985). Over the past decade, variegated worlds of drug use have been elaborated. The problem may be stabilizing, but it is doing so at a formidable level. The 'cultural rebels', former hippies with a long history of non-criminal drug use, have largely disappeared. The dominant worlds of drug use are now those of the 'ex-weekend adventurers', mainly white Dutch working-class males, who 'are shattered to find there is no easy cure' for what they thought was a recreational, leisure-time high. This group have found many recruits among the unemployed. Other white Dutch groups are the 'societal marginals' of both sexes who were heavily involved in delinquency before getting into drugs, but who have grafted hard drug use onto traditional patterns of delinquency. They are often involved also in small-time dealing, fencing, and links with older, larger dealers. By contrast, the 'down-and-outs', the long-termers of the drugs world, 'have no subcultural supports to speak of'. Another group, usually prone to very rapid addiction, are Dutch women termed by Janssen and Swierstra as 'home-leavers': runaways rebelling against family by embracing the drug-scene.

The social worlds of the Surinamers is viewed as a separate story, though Sansone sees the 'new fluidity of social organisation and structure' as increasingly salient. 'Youth crime (which is overwhelmingly petty crime) has lost, little by little, its centrality throughout the three social forms—the youth gang, the street corner and the youth style' (Sansone 1984: 33, 34). These are seen, however, as recent developments, signs that the young Surinamers have begun to overcome the culture shock they experienced on arrival in 1975. Their rapid swelling of the ranks of users and small dealers 'perhaps played a key role in disseminating drug use in Holland' (interview, Janssen and Swierstra) 'Hangers-on' are more victims than victimizers, though very small dealing may accompany their use of hard drugs. This group are most highly visible in Amsterdam, Rotterdam, and the big urban centres since they imported their own street-corner culture from Surinam and incorporated heroin into it. But by comparison with the Dutch addicts, they tended to have no prior criminal career in Surinam. Next up the ladder are the 'quarter-ounce dealers', who despite their addiction may achieve some prosperity by slightly larger dealing. A third group of earlier arrivals, the 'home-returners' have embraced heroin as a way of re-entering Surinamese society after experiencing prejudice and discrimination in The Netherlands. The big traffickers, however, are not from Surinam, but more likely from South-east, and, since 1979, South-west Asia, from Turkey for heroin, or from Latin America for cocaine. A distinction should be drawn, however, between traffickers who are integrated into organized crime, and those who try it as a 'one-off, get-rich-quick' scheme—migrant workers, for example, who may be recruited by the traffickers as couriers or act independently.

Such estimates, however, appear inflated when compared with available British work on the subject. Taking a different method of arriving at a figure for drug-related crime, Taylor carried out a study of the convictions of some 5,000 persons 'notified to the Home Office as narcotic drug addicts for the first time in England and Wales in the years 1979, 1980 and 1981' (Taylor 1986: 27–9). The persons in the study were on average convicted of about one offence every two years which, after adjustment to allow for offences 'taken into consideration' and 'not cleared up', mounts up to three offences annually. If there are 50,000 'regular opioid users' at any one time in the United Kingdom (Hartnoll *et al.* 1986), the group as a whole could be responsible for some 150,000 offences. This, however, is likely to be a maximum figure, since it includes 'drug' as well as 'non-drug' offences. 'In some areas, with large numbers of regular drug users, the proportion of offences they commit may be higher than 4%' (Taylor 1986: 28; see also Mott 1980, 1981).

One such area is the Wirral on Merseyside. In a rigorous and ingenious study of this problem (Parker *et al.* 1986), it was found that in the 1981–5 period, in this area, the rate of acquisitive crime by registered opioid users was double that by non-users, and about one-third of the users had reached this high rate of crime commission despite an almost unblemished official record pre-1981 (see Table 5.4).

TABLE 5.4   Convictions for acquisitive and non-acquisitive crimes: opioid users and non-users 1971–1985

	Sample size	Acquisitive crimes			Non-acquisitive crimes		
		'71–'75	'76–'80	'81–'85	'71–'75	'76–'80	'81–'85
Non-users	188	0.6	1.0	3.4	0.4	1.0	3.1
Users	91	0.6	1.3	6.0	0.2	1.1	2.1
Criminal record at age 16	59	0.9	2.0	6.1	0.3	1.7	2.6
No criminal record at age 16	32	0	0.1	5.8	0	0.2	1.2

Source: Parker *et al.* (1986: 17).

Note: 'Users' refers to people registered as opiod users, June 1984 to October 1985. The mean age for all groups was 21.

These findings enable one to distil to a degree the possible causal relation between drug use and crime. Though the authors are careful to avoid too pronounced a connection, they establish the reality of a drug-using 'new to offending' group that accounts in the 1981–5 period for roughly one-tenth of acquisitive crime in the Wirral. Moreover, the drug-using 'offending' group 'have broken loose of the already highly criminalized non user-offender 'control' group in that their rate of acquisitive crime convictions have rocketed over the past four years. This would appear to be due to the heroin factor, for whilst this group clearly were offenders before heroin arrived, their rate of conviction indicates the level of criminal activity has been accelerated, presumably by the need to purchase heroin' (Parker *et al.*: 18–19). Adding the putative heroin-related crime of this group to that of the 'new to crime' group raises the proportion of acquisitive crime attributable to heroin to something of the order of 20 per cent. For this area at least, the heady anomic brew long predicted as likely to be borne of high rates of youth unemployment interacting with the availability of hard drugs and triggering something of a crime explosion seems to have real substance (see also Farrington *et al.* 1986).

How can these results be squared with those of the Home Office study? Both used official data for indicators of crime and drug use, but the Wirral study, being later, took account of a more recent phenomenon. And the Home Office data were based on a national 'average', in terms of which the Wirral study was an extreme manifestation of skewed deviance. However, the Wirral study also revealed a particularly strong association between late adolescence, unemployment, drug use, and crime. If that effect was more general across the country, for that age group and period, then the effect on crime attributable to opioid use would be somewhat higher than that found in the Home Office study. A figure double that of the Home Office 4 per cent might logically flow from the Wirral finding that users offend at almost twice the rate as non-users for the forms of crime that dominate official crime statistics, i.e. 7–8 per cent seems not unreasonable, though still perhaps on the high side.

In relation to The Netherlands, the major disparity in estimates for drug-related crime derives from the methods employed to construct them: the tendency has been to work backwards from the rough correlation between the proportion of offenders with some declared involvement in drugs to the putative contribution that drug-use makes to crime, utilizing multipliers based on the street price of heroin to calculate the overall levels of consumption, licit compared with illicit sources of income, and so on. Such guesstimates are only too likely to overshoot the mark. What we lack are detailed ethnographies of the life-styles of different kinds of users, though in The Netherlands Janssen and Swierstra have made a notable beginning. The kinds of problems involved can be illustrated by taking, for example, the number of burglaries committed in The Netherlands in 1982. Of the official total, half—125,000—might notionally be attributable to drug users, and on average a loss to the victim of perhaps £100's worth of goods (the rough median for official figures on burglary in England). The total value of such burglaries of 50 million guilders (assuming a generous exchange rate of 4 guilders to the pound) would pay only 5 per cent of the notional one billion guilders' worth of opiates consumed in The Netherlands annually. Assuming (again) a generous fencing rate of 50 per cent of the value of the goods stolen (fences appear in such calculations to be far more benign than any other second-hand dealer) reduces the figure to 2.5 per cent of the drugs bill. In short, even in The Netherlands, if a sceptical view is taken of the valuation process, there is not enough crime to pay the drugs bill. What seems more likely is that the drugs bill is not so high. Most users are not one-gram-a-day addicts. And even addicts may stagger on from day to day by using other drugs, by milking their families or friends more heavily than is allowed for, by spells of near-abstinence before another source of supply materializes (Pearson *et al.* 1986). The other side of the coin is that victims, especially institutional victims, and particularly large stores, have a built-in incentive to over value 'shrinkage' due to theft for tax and insurance purposes. However, even if the amount of crime attributable to drug use in The Netherlands is scaled down to something nearer the notional figure for England above, that is still a not inconsiderable boost to the crime rate. And the effects of the drugs market for the political economy of crime and its control are clearly evident from the mid-1970s, whereas in Britain it became pressing only in the 1980s.

Policing has also been influenced by the drugs trade, though it has not undergone any marked transformation despite major changes in the political economy of crime (Punch 1985). The established patterns of accommodation and collusion with the older Chinese drug dealers became, as the stakes rose with the scale of the drugs trade, a ready soil for more ambitious forms of police 'protection'. Allegations of corruption became commonplace, but their investigation in the 1976–80 period 'unleashed four years of turmoil, bitterness, intrigue, and misery, and the result, in terms of combatting deviance and altering the organisation, was minimal' (Punch 1985: 200). On the other hand, by comparison with London, New York, and Hong Kong, 'fully fledged predatory "strategic" corruption did not exist in Amsterdam' (Punch 1985: 105), though some evidence suggests it may be on the way (p. 117). The bottom line, so to speak, in all these metropolitan centres, as well as increasingly in their provinces, is that drugs contaminate policing: by intensifying internal police conflicts, e.g. between specialized squads and beat police with local knowledge; by financing corrupter–corruptee relationships, which surface on occasion as scandals that damage the police more generally; by seeming to legitimize questionable police tactics and strategies in the face of an elusive 'victimless' crime, and so on. Most damaging of all, perhaps, is the lack of success in the 'war against drugs' despite the huge investment of time, energy, and resources. In England, one informed estimate was that the police, despite the expenditure of 'hundreds of millions' in resources, managed to seize perhaps 1 per cent of the annual amount of heroin imports (Stimson 1985). A Dutch police officer confided his thoughts in terms redolent of demoralization, cynicism, and role distance: 'What does it all mean? The clear-up rate for crimes in my district is 4 per cent. Who cares? I don't care any more. No one believes that a better performance leads to anything. What's there to motivate us? Nothing's done about the underlying problems' (Punch 1985: 191) This sort of generalized sense of anomie, embracing every form of deviance from violence to parking infractions, may represent the nadir of police morale in the inner cities, from which the attempt to co-ordinate police work with a policy for social and welfare initiatives may represent an advance.

Sentencing and penal policy have been influenced, and even—in some respects—distorted by the upsurge of drug-related crime, but seem to have withstood the kind of transformation that many anticipated from the adoption of sterner measures towards drug traffickers and dealers in particular. On the surface, it does appear that tougher sentences have blown a hole in Dutch penal policy. The proportion of sentences over a year in length has more than doubled since 1975, and a doubling of penal capacity over the decade 1980–90 is planned and partly fulfilled. But the fears that tougher measures towards drug traffickers and dealers would be automatically extended to the sentencing of other offenders have not yet been borne out (see Ch. 2); and even within the drug offence categories, what is happening is more in line with bifurcation concepts (Bottoms 1977) than with across-the-board increases in the severity of sentences.

Table 5.5 shows that the major change is the number of hard-drug offenders being brought before the courts by the police. The proportions waived and sentenced to the various forms of custody remain remarkably stable, as does mean sentence length. In the context of the Dutch prison system, however, the addition of such relatively large numbers annually, with such relatively long sentences, spells a considerable problem for penal capacity.

Within the prisons, the management of drug-control problems has become a major priority.

The proportion of hard drug addicts can be estimated at 20–30 per cent of the total prison population, that's about 4,000 prisoners [admissions] each year. The number of sentenced drug-traffickers rose also sharply to almost 1300 in 1982. This is 9% of the total number of inflicted prison sentences in that year, but as a consequence of the long duration of their sentences, they accounted for 21% of the total amount of imprisonment which had to be executed in 1982 . . . Results of scientific research, done in closed prisons for long-term offenders, made clear that drug dealers were to a large extent responsible for hard-drug traffic in these prisons. (Erkelens 1984)

A Netherlands Ministry of Justice (1983) Working Party Report recommended several measures to cope with the situation: (*a*) a registration system of imprisoned drug addicts; (*b*) development of such control measures as urine tests; (*c*) imprisonment of drug-dealers in a separate institution; and (*d*) creation of drug-free wings within prisons. It is recognized that 'a complete prevention of drugs can only be attained by very repressive measures. Doing so would affect negatively the relationships between prison officers and inmates and the treatment climate would undoubtedly deteriorate' (Erkelens 1984: 7). The resulting policy attempts to minimize coercion while encouraging admissions to drug-free wings. The former entails the confinement of the big dealers in

TABLE 5.5 *Sentencing of hard drug offenders in The Netherlands, 1978–1983*

	No. offenders		Sentencing (%)				Mean sentence (months)
	Charged	prosecuted	Waiver	Unconditional prison sentence	Partly suspended sentence	Otherwise dealt with	
1978	2,906	2,183	49.1	17.3	12.1	21.5	10.6
1980	3,554	2,902	65.6	16.5	8.1	9.8	13.6
1982	6,077	4,883	61.2	16.1	11.1	11.6	10.1
1983	5,672	4,662	60.5	18.2	9.6	11.7	13.0

Note: Percentages relate to offenders prosecuted, i.e. the total charged less cases dropped from the Public Prosecutors' statistics, e.g. 'not guilty' cases, as judged by the court; persons not available for trial; cases under appeal, etc.; 'mean length' is that for both unconditional and the prison part of partly suspended sentences of imprisonment.

one wing of the closed prison in The Hague. The latter has led to the development of drug-free wings at Rotterdam and Veenhuizen; admission is voluntary, but periodic urine tests are compulsory. The authorities have two working assumptions about motivation for prisoners who are already addicted or who are former addicts at risk of relapse: firstly, the more benign regimes of the open prisons can be offered as a reward for coming off hard-drugs; and secondly, drawing on Janssen and Swierstra's work, it seems that some addicts see imprisonment as a 'break: a way of getting rest, proper food and regaining a lower tolerance level' (Erkelens 1984: 3). Another set of choices can be made to divert drug-using offenders to an institute or clinic during remand in custody; or to allow transfer to a therapeutic community or suitable alternative during the second half of their sentence—both on a voluntary basis. These options so far affect only a small number of prisoners 120 and 43 respectively, in 1983 (Erkelens 1984: 9), but their numbers are likely to grow, and increasing liaison is planned for the role of the Centre for Alcohol and Drugs, probation officers, and both internal and external programmes for imprisoned addicts. The extent to which these measures can limit the diffusion of drugtaking cultures to specific wings within particular prisons, on the one hand, and can do so without damage to their generally humane character on the other, remains to be seen.

Conclusions

The rapid growth of hard-drug use and addiction since the mid-1970s had, by the end of that decade, convinced the authorities that the limits of tolerance had been reached for pragmatic, demand-led welfare policies. This trend was matched by a time-lagged steepening of the crime rate which, from 1979–81 onwards, came to be seen as predominantly a problem of drug-related crime. These parallel trends spelt the end of reductionism in penal policy, in the absolute sense that the attempt to reduce the prison population yet further was abandoned. In the relative sense, however, reductionism continued to prevail in the declining proportion of convicted offenders actually sentenced to custody, and in the maintenance of comparatively short sentences for all but a selected number of drug-related crimes. By the early 1980s, the ground was being prepared for more integrated social welfare and policing measures, and limited forms of penal expansion. Ironically, the one respect in which The Netherlands was less 'permissive' than Britain—in its refusal to countenance heroin maintenance policy as *one* element in drug control—may have left it less well defended against the upsurge of hard drug use than would otherwise have been the case. To see The Netherlands as moving from a soft to a hard line on drugs is to oversimplify greatly a move from relatively limitless tolerance, shorn of those elements which render a 'soft' policy coherent, to a mixture of hard and soft elements which aims at an integrated approach. The damage has so far been contained, as far as the basis of Dutch penal policy—a sparing use of imprisonment—is concerned, largely by trading off an increase in penal capacity for the continuation of the principle of one prisoner to a cell, consistently high rates of waiving prosecution, and—except for large-scale drug traffickers—short lengths of sentence by comparative standards. If, as some indicators suggest, hard drug use is stabilizing despite the threats of an epidemic in cocaine, the international community may be persuaded that Hobbes is no surer a guide than Rousseau to the control of deviance.

6 The Depth of Imprisonment: An Exploratory Study of The Netherlands and England

They treat you like a human being. They say, 'Enjoy your meal', 'Good morning'. They treat you like a man, they let you do things the way you like, they're not always looking up your arse for drugs, they don't guard you when you see the governor, with two warders either side. Even when you go to solitary, you take yourself there. You think, 'It can't be true, there must be a catch.' But there isn't. I just can't believe they don't despise you because you're a criminal. In England, they punish you for being a criminal. Then they punish you while they're punishing you. Then you're punished for the rest of your life. (English prisoner in a Dutch closed prison)

Dutch prisons are much better, especially at thinking how to bring prisoners back to the normal life. There is home leave every weekend or so—here there is no way you can get that experience. If they realize that you are not a thoroughgoing criminal, they will do their best to re-establish you in society. Here there is no real attempt to do that, and for the English prisoners that is very bad. He goes out to nothing, so he goes back to crime . . . (Dutch prisoner in English training prison)

Penal reformers, from John Howard onwards, have long preferred the Dutch penal system to that of England. Prisons in The Netherlands have traditionally been smaller, cleaner, and run in a more humane fashion than in England. That, at least, is how it appears from the vantage point of concerned middle-class inquiry. What remains an open question, however, is how far that view is shared by the prisoners themselves. Is the actual experience of imprisonment in the two systems as distinctively different as penal theory implies?

To go some way towards answering that question, and as part of the broader enquiry into post-war Dutch penal policy, I interviewed a small number of prisoners in each system, some of whom had experience of *both*. Interviews were carried out in June and July of 1985 with 12 British (and one Irish) prisoners in 5 Dutch jails, and 14 Dutch prisoners in 4 English jails. This was about a third of the number available in each system coming from their respective countries. Seven of the British and six of the Dutch prisoners interviewed had also been imprisoned in their own countries. Their experience is not necessarily representative, but it would be surprising if those not interviewed felt significantly at odds with the views expressed, for on certain issues there was near unanimity—above all, on the strong preference expressed by both British and Dutch prisoners for the Dutch penal system. This was despite the fact that none of the four prisons selected by the Prison Department for interviews with Dutch prisoners in England was a local prison, where problems of under-staffing and over-crowding are at their most unrelieved.

It is probable that the Dutch prisons chosen for interview were more representative of the system than those selected for me in England. Permission to conduct the interviews was granted initially from the Prison Department of the Home Office in England, and the Prison Department of the Ministry of Justice in The Netherlands. It was then sought and granted by the governors of the prisons concerned. In England, the Prison Department assembled the list of four prisons where Dutch prisoners were held in custody, and it was left to me to contact the appropriate member of staff to arrange the most appropriate time. Prisoners were asked, in advance of my arrival, if they wished to take part in the interviews and none refused. In The Netherlands I was allowed to contact *any* prison at which British prisoners were held, and asked to write a letter to the prisoners outlining the purpose of the interviews, though in practice only a few of the prisoners actually received the letter. None refused an interview when permission was sought at the outset, however. The number of interviews in other prisons could have been extended in The Netherlands once official permission had been granted. Only constraints of time precluded interviewing more than 13. There was only one prisoner whom I was refused permission to interview. In England, if more interviews had been possible, I would have had to re-apply for official permission afresh. Another difference in the interviewing lay in the constraints which governed the time they could take. In the Dutch prisons, once entry had been gained, there was no particular time limit set to the interview beyond the interviewee's own wishes. In English prisons, strict time limits—usually those of the hours of visiting—were adhered to in all but one case. All interviews in The Netherlands were in private, and in all but one prison in England this was also the case. Interviews were tape-recorded with the prisoners' permission, except for three refusals in The Netherlands and two interviews in England which could not be taped because they took place in general visiting conditions.

In The Netherlands permisssion to inspect prisoners' files would have been needed from the prisoners themselves, but no such constraint applied in England. Cross-checking details of offence and sentence were carried out in three cases of Dutch prisoners in England, and prisoners' and file accounts tallied in all main respects. Convergence was also the case on occasions that prisoners had been convicted jointly. Otherwise, I had no marked inclination to cross-check that which had already been conveyed in confidence. The interviews were of a frankly exploratory nature. The main focus was explicitly on the prisoners' experience of the criminal justice system in general and of imprisonment in particular, and it was thought useful to ask for such perceptions even where they had no experience of their own system. Where they had such experience, they were asked about the similarities and differences between the two systems, again in terms of their own experience.

The contrast between the British and Dutch penal systems is usually drawn in terms of the *length* of sentences of imprisonment. The average Dutch sentence—three months or so—is far shorter than the average British sentence of roughly ten months, a difference which principally accounts for the much smaller proportionate size of the Dutch prison population relative to that of Britain. The two sets of prisoners interviewed were, however, closer to each other in terms of sentence length than the average. The British prisoners in Dutch jails were typically in prison for hard drug offences, mainly dealing and trafficking in cocaine, and in three cases for heavy crimes of violence: armed robbery, attempted murder, and murder. Their average length of sentence of 25 months was several times the Dutch average, compared with an average sentence of 39 months for the Dutch prisoners in English jails, which is still four times the average for this country. The principal offence committed by the Dutch prisoners was 'soft' drug smuggling, typically large consignments of cannabis, though in five cases cocaine or heroin was involved. In practice, parole etc. would reduce each average term by one-third, to 16 months for British prisoners in The Netherlands and 26 months for Dutch prisoners in England.

Important as this magnitude of difference is for the individuals concerned, and for the operation of the system as a whole, the main contrast in the interviews between the two systems was couched in terms of the *depth* rather than the length of imprisonment.[1] In a variety of ways, some gross, some nuanced, prison in The Netherlands is experienced as a far less damaging and repressive phenomenon than in Britain. Another way of putting it is to say that even the less unpleasant end of the prison system in Britain holds few positive features for the prisoners. The main impact of the system here, even the training prisons, is to blunt sensibilities rather than—as in the Dutch system in general—making some attempt to preserve or even sharpen them. This sense of a contrast in terms of psychological invasion by the prison was expressed on a variety of levels: relations with staff; relations with other prisoners; rights and privileges; material standards and conditions; and a sense of the overall quality of life which the prison regime made possible or witheld.

Relations with staff

As the first of the accounts implied (p. 163) relations with staff were among the more unexpected as well as welcome features of prison life in The Netherlands, particularly for prisoners who had experience of the British system. With the exception of open prisons in Britain, whose atmosphere corresponds most closely to that in the majority of Dutch prisons, British jails were regarded as unnecessarily oppressive. Some saw this difference as lodged in system and broader societal terms:

The main difference is the attitude of your fellow prisoners and staff . . . In Wormwood Scrubs, . . . the staff are not particularly friendly—that's a polite way of putting it—and the system is unnecessarily degrading. Whereas in Zutphen [a Dutch remand prison] you didn't have to do anything that wasn't common sense; there was nothing that was done completely pointlessly, just to punish you . . . The whole atmosphere was different. The staff seemed to treat you as a human being, whereas

---

[1] The 'depth of imprisonment' is one of those familiar sounding phrases which strike one as obvious but which have not been coined before. It was first used, to my knowledge, by Mr T. Robinson, an adult educationist with long experience of the Dutch penal system, at the 1985 Abolitionist Congress in Amsterdam. It is not to be confused with the 'depths of imprisonment', a more literary phrase connoting the hidden miseries and squalor to be found in the recesses of Victorian prisons—but not, for that reason, unknown today.

the staff in Britain would treat you as, well 'animal' is too strong a word, basically with a lack of any humanity. The way that going to the toilet is arranged, the lack of showers, the way staff would shout at people continually, that wouldn't work in Holland, they'd go on strike or something. It's basically alien to the Dutch character to have that sort of divide between people.

Others prisoners were less constrained in describing their experience of the British local prisons in particular: 'barbaric', 'inhuman', 'degrading', and 'makes you an animal because it treats you like one' were commonly employed. Even the least critical made such points as 'guards here are more human, you can joke with them; in England, guards are much more strict'. The Dutch attitude was summed up by one English prisoner: 'They've got your liberty and that's enough. They don't have to make your life complete hell.'

Three points emerged, or were made, that undercut some of the more common objections to staff–prisoner relations assuming too 'normal' or sociable a form. Firstly, the lessening of what one prisoner called 'physical and mental control' did *not* entail more indiscipline and risk to staff safety. It was asserted that staff were trained to spot trouble coming, and to deal with it quickly and without animosity, using verbal rather than physical means to defuse potentially violent situations. Secondly, what King and Morgan have termed the 'normalization' of the prison is much enhanced by the presence of women staff. Women do not serve as guards in men's prisons in The Netherlands but as governors, social workers, and secretaries, as well as psychologists and teachers; their presence is now taken for granted. They are abused neither physically nor verbally: 'nobody has ever tried anything on'. Indeed, their presence is said to lower the aggressive atmosphere that builds up in all-male environments: 'If there are men and women in prison, you relate to them as human beings. If there are only men, you relate to them only as men', as one prisoner put it. A women deputy director stated that until a few years ago, the Ministry of Justice's fear that sexual attacks would occur inhibited such appointments as her own; but there have been no 'incidents' of any kind over the two-year period of her employment. Not least, 'they can speak about emotional problems as they can't with a man.' Under the impact of equal opportunities legislation, similar developments have occurred in England, so that by 1988 there is no type of male penal establishment in which women are not represented at governor grades. Though few have as yet been recruited as prison officers in male prisons, this is an encouraging trend. Thirdly, the view is often expressed, both by and on behalf of prison officers in Britain, that the presence of social workers and other 'caring' staff in jails strips the prison officers of their welfare roles, and reduces them to mere turnkeys (J. E. Thomas 1972). The Dutch experience shows that this need not be so.

The experience of Dutch prisoners in English training prisons was not a symmetrical mirror-image of their counterparts in Dutch prisons. There were no accounts of physical brutality or sadistic mind control. But, despite several accounts of acts of individual kindness by particular officers, the picture that emerged was of an absence of humanity or normal human relations. Both staff and prisoners were said to be caught up in a deadening routine imposition of 'niggling' and 'silly' rules. Three of the 14 Dutch prisoners had landed favourable jobs within the system, such as probation orderly and library work. These jobs meant friendlier staff relations, and some small freedoms which made doing time without extra problems more feasible. But the theme which recurred most frequently was the all-pervasive character of being pinned down within walls by what Cohen and Taylor (1978) have called 'rules-within-rules-within-rules'. These could be both opaque and varied from prison to prison. 'It is very hard and impersonal here. Rules here are very complicated, even the guards don't know them.' Even in the prison that was least 'closed' in character, examples were given of 'silly rules' entailing such penalties as loss of seven days' remission for going to the dining room at the wrong time; certain common toiletries were not allowed to be purchased; lying outside on the grass instead of going to gym was sometimes okay, and sometimes not. 'A cup of tea under a tree—not even that is allowed on a summer's day—just silly walking round in circles.' When asked about the chief difference between prisons in England and The Netherlands, one prisoner summed them up in terms reminiscent of Alexander Paterson's remark that 'prisons should be *as,* not *for,* punishment':

The most important comparison is that you are in prison to be taught how to behave in society. So, in The Netherlands, they take your freedom, but that's it. You work, to teach you how to be in society as a normal working man. People who work in prisons there treat you as a human being, not as a child or as a mental patient. Here, it's so different . . . It's so difficult for us, they expect you to behave yourself. Okay—so then they should treat you as a grown man, not as a child, coming at you with children's rules. For example, you're supposed to wear slippers on the Wing, and a shirt. A week ago, there is a library visit once a week, some still had shoes on from work. They had to wait for an officer to go for a shirt, since they only had a T-shirt on. Little things. To write a letter, you have to ask for a letter. In Holland, you buy 15 envelopes and stamps from the shop and write as many letters you like. Here two letters are impossible. Buying two letters and stamps leaves no money for tobacco.

In such examples, staff–prisoner relations are clearly determined by the fine mesh of institutional rules. It is by such minute particulars that the depth of imprisonment is partly to be plumbed. Censoriousness, in terms of an appeal to the yardstick of the rules of equity in society at large, was seen by Mathiesen (1965) as one of the principal 'defences of the weak'. It was notably absent, however, from British prisoners' accounts of their experience in Dutch jails.

Relations with other prisoners

Relations with other prisoners were not, in general, experienced as a problem by British prisoners in Dutch jails. The one-to-a-cell system made for privacy when it was wanted, and the relatively generous amount of time allowed for association and recreation did not make isolation the other side of the coin. Dutch prisoners in English jails tended to feel under constant pressure from the conflicts arising in part from the deprivations of prison life, in part from over-crowding even in the less congested end of the penal system. Only one British prisoner in The Netherlands, in a remand prison, felt cell-sharing was less onerous than enforced privacy, for the company it provided. The rest, who often called their cell their 'room', valued the one-to-a-cell arrangement. British prisoners in British jails were seen as 'tougher, more out to prove themselves . . . Discipline is more severe in England. They don't like violence at all here, it leads to quick transfers, which are not so much in England unless it's real bad.' Another British prisoner in a Dutch jail recalled that one of Scotland's more notorious jails was very strong in the ' "hard man" gang thing'. Dutch jails are hardly trouble-free, but the prisoners there felt that trouble could be avoided relatively easily. By contrast, the Dutch prisoners in British jails felt the restrictive discipline was counter-productive, generating tensions and making it more difficult for

them to mix with prisoners they liked and to avoid those they did
not. 'Here, not a minute, not a second, privacy—never.'
Relations with other prisoners could hardly be easy and relaxed
where substandard rights and conditions made for 'nervousness'
all round. For one prisoner at least, the combination of restrictive
discipline and a turbulent inmate culture that was as inescapable
as the prison itself proved almost unbearable: 'Here, it is a
nightmare when you wake. Only when you go to sleep you live
again.'

Rights, privileges, and conditions

Rights, privileges, and conditions were almost overwhelmingly
regarded as far superior in Dutch prisons by comparison with
those in England by both sets of prisoners. The major exception to
this picture concerned remand prisoners at the pre-trial, or at least
the investigative, stage of their confinement in police and prison
cells. 'What was not so good was that after arrest I was kept
incommunicado in Zutphen for three months, and for a few weeks
my wife and family didn't know where I was.' Another prisoner
saw the pre-trial remand system in Britain as '10 times better'
than that in The Netherlands: 'Here they do things in reverse: you
get real privileges in England on remand until proven guilty, your
own clothes, food, visits every day, lager, cigs. and so on . . . here
they deny you all privileges, no visits and for two months no letters
were either sent or received. My brother actually came over from
England but was denied a visit.' This young prisoner said he had
attempted suicide, 'but that didn't change things.' Things only
changed when his plea changed, otherwise he could have been
kept in isolation for up to 106 days. The Dutch authorities were
seen as using isolation as a weapon in the investigative process.
'You're treated like an animal before conviction, even if you're
innocent, then you get all the privileges afterwards. Seems the
wrong way round to me.' Another prisoner commented: 'If you're
remanded in custody in England, you can see your family every
day, they can bring you food and so on[2], but here you can be held
in isolation. They start the punishment straight away . . .
Underneath the nice, liberal facade in Holland, I think suspects
are dealt with far more severely, initially.'

---

[2]   The right of remand prisoners to have their own food and drink sent in was
ended on March 1, 1988.

In this one major respect, however, it is doubtful if the differences between the two systems are as pronounced as the prisoners maintained. In their study of remand prisoners in Winchester local prison, King and Morgan (1976) concluded that 'the special provisions for the protection of unconvicted persons in custody, which are valuable but slender enough in theory, mean very little in practice' (p. 39). 'In our wider comparative study of prison regimes there was a good deal of evidence to suggest that unconvicted prisoners experienced more constraining regimes than convicted prisoners . . .' (p. 40). Nor is solitary confinement, for periods far longer than those reported by the prisoners in Dutch jails, unknown in comparable cases in England. 'Arrested some nine months ago, my client is still in custody awaiting trial . . . Since his arrest—except for periods totalling 10 days—he has been held in solitary confinement as a Category A prisoner. The regime in which he has been held consists of 23 hours a day cellular solitary confinement, no association with other prisoners and exercise for the remaining hour each day' (Letter to the editor, *Guardian*, 12 Sept. 1987, from James Butler, Offenbach & Co.). The provisions protecting the rights of unconvicted prisoners are grounded in the presumption of innocence, but that is 'tempered by a second principle, namely, that the course of justice must proceed unhindered by the activities of those who would seek to subvert it' (King and Morgan 1976: 32). In practice, therefore, the English presumption of innocence affords little more protection than the European convention that any case not proven falls. At the investigative stage, therefore, there is less to choose between the two systems than the above accounts asserted. Nevertheless, the right to visits, under however inhibiting a set of conditions, and letters, does remain inviolate in the English system at this stage, and in that signal respect it is superior to the Dutch.

There are, however, worrying instances of that right being curtailed in practice by sudden transfers for security reasons (as in the case of McAvoy, 1984, on which see Richardson 1985: 57) or for reasons arising from conflicts over staffing levels (Ballantyne 1988).

What all prisoners agree upon is that, once the investigative stage is over in The Netherlands, things dramatically improve for the prisoners; and once conviction is secured in Britain, things rapidly change for the worse.

Accommodation

Accommodation provides the basis for much that differentiates the two systems' standards. With one exception, all the British prisoners preferred the one-to-a-cell system which the Dutch have placed a high premium on retaining. (It is made possible by the system of prisoners 'waiting' for a prison place and will be further facilitated by a planned expansion of penal capacity that, if implemented, will double the number of places from 3,683 in 1980 to 7,070 by 1990.) The commitment to the one-to-a-cell rule was sharply expressed by a senior member of staff in an Amsterdam prison who was willing to resign if it was abandoned: 'If two to a cell, I go.' The closed prisons allow for more individualization of cell furnishing and decoration than is the case in the remand prisons, where even convicted prisoners may have to wait several months for a place in the closed prisons to become available. But even there cells are usually open from 7.00 in the morning until 9.30 at night, with prisoners not otherwise on work duties or under discipline being allowed to leave their cells or not as they wished. TV can be rented at a cost well within the weekly pay budget, floors can be carpeted, 'one man even has an aquarium in his cell'. 'Here you can control the lighting system in your room, so you can read [at night] if you want to—that's not so in England—very small things make a big difference.' By contrast, even in the less-congested 'C' category training prisons in England, accommodation is often shared, in dormitories with three, four, or five prisoners in one space. Far more time is spent in the cells, and less scope exists for private effects to be there. In only one of the Dutch remand prisons did conditions verge on the British, with confinement to cells being the norm except for work and an hour's recreation a day, with two hours additional recreation every other evening. Staff shortages at night also involved slopping-out, as in England. In no Dutch prison, however, were the prisoners 'locked down' for 23 hours a day, or anything like it.

Food and clothing

Clothing was left to the prisoners' choice in The Netherlands, not so in England: few chose to comment on this, but those that did preferred choice, and it is clearly the most visible signifier of prisoner status. Food elicited varied responses, which differed more by prison than by country. The greater preference shown by some British prisoners for the fresh milk, fruit, and yoghurt that was more frequently available in Dutch prisons was offset by that of others for the cooked (rather than cold, buffet-style food) which was the norm in British prisons. The food in Dutch jails seemed more varied. In one, a barbecue for all the prisoners was being prepared with three different kinds of meat for different religious groupings. The festival of Ramadan was the occasion for Turkish prisoners being allowed to prepare their own food in the kitchens. In England, food was 'dumped on disgusting plastic plates'; real plates were used in The Netherlands. Washing and toilet facilities were clearly superior in the Dutch prisons. Prisoners could have four showers a week, and could in general leave their cells to use the toilet where cells had no integral flushing toilets. One Dutch prisoner who had been in Wandsworth called it a 'real hell. Eighty persons for four toilets, one shower a week, mice, cockroaches, you had to sleep fully clothed, you were 23 hours in a cell.' (On the continued postponement of integral sanitation in Wandsworth Prison, see Stern 1987: 182:) Training prisons in England were not so bad, but some still had no access to toilets during the night in shared cells.

Work and pay

Work and pay are basic determinants of the experience of prison. Work offers a break from the cell, a chance to socialize, and at best some form of training that offers a marketable skill on release. The two systems were not so very different as far as foreign prisoners were concerned, though Dutch prisoners in Dutch jails were said to have better training opportunities than British prisoners in British jails. Pay, however, differed greatly between the two systems, with the prisoners in The Netherlands earning roughly £12 a week, compared to a *maximum* £2.98 a week in England. The effect of this extremely low rate of pay was seen by Dutch prisoners in English jails as much needless friction and pointless deprivation. 'You get at most three packets of cigarettes. So if they buy [extra] letters, something happens in the family, then they can't buy the tobacco. So they feel bad, they get things out of proportion, then trouble breaks out without reasons.' Tobacco is the mainstay of prison life, but prison pay does not stretch to more than three packets a week—a source of constant haggling when soap, toiletries, extra letters, confectionery and so on have to come out of wages. 'Two stabbings over a quarter-ounce of tobacco—I can't believe it.' Dutch prisoners were also keenly aware that tobacco for roll-ups was four times as expensive in England as in The Netherlands—in effect a tobacco allowance ratio of 1 : 16, since wages there are four times as high. A further irritation was that even if one had the money, the discretion allowed to prison governors meant that, for example, the sale of toiletries could be severely restricted—in one jail to powdered toothpaste. 'They take everything here. They take your freedom but they also take your smokes.' 'At the end of the week, people come to you for dog-ends. At first, I thought it was to do with a dog!' 'A lot go down over Rule 43 due to debt over dope and tobacco.' By contrast, in The Netherlands the wages enable prisoners to buy extra food: 'In the canteen here you can get everything you can in a supermarket outside—muesli, yoghourt, cans of fruit. You can live decently.' The low rates of pay were seen by Dutch prisoners in England as derisory for work that was often both long and demanding. 'One girl did 35 metres of tasselling a week and she got £2.67. Kitchen work is very demanding, no time off, a 7-day week from 6.00 in the morning until the evening.' 'The wages are really stupid. My family can't believe it.' Ironically, the less the prisoners earned, the higher the premium attached to wages. 'There is education here . . . but few go. It takes time off work, so you lose money from earnings.' Yet educational provision was one of the few features of the English system praised by the Dutch prisoners.

Communication with the outside world

The depth of imprisonment is most graphically conveyed by the rules governing letters, phoning, and visits. It is here, for foreign prisoners ineligible for home leave, that the differences between the two systems were most starkly inscribed. 'Prisons are certainly more comfortable here [in The Netherlands] than in Britain. But comfort is beside the point—the main thing is more letters, visits, and so on. There is no reason to deny any number of letters. But in England I had to ask my girl-friend to write fewer letters.' In Dutch prisons, there is no limit to the number of letters prisoners can write or receive. There is random censorship, but it is not a pretext for limiting correspondence. Postage has to be paid for, but the more generous wages mean this is no problem. In English prisons, there is one free letter a week; the number of additional letters that prisoners can buy varies between prisons. Some are limited to one, others more—but affording envelopes and stamps out of prison wages becomes a major obstacle. The Dutch prisoners complained in one or two cases about unexplained delays in receiving mail, and censorship was cited as more prevalent than in The Netherlands. At the remand stage in Britain, however, prisoners can write as many letters as they like, at their own expense.

Use of the phone could vary even more between the two systems. In The Netherlands it was taken for granted that prisoners have the right to make at least one free foreign call a week, two or possibly more by permission of the governor on welfare or other grounds. One prisoner stated calls within The Netherlands could be made daily 'to encourage personal contact'. In England, phoning was unusual, either abroad or domestically. It is very much a privilege, to be granted only on application to the governor. It varied from prison to prison on a discretionary basis: 'one call every six to seven weeks', 'one after application to the governor', 'one call a month but had to wait three months for her first call', 'no phoning was allowed at all in Holloway', 'possible with governor's permission, but costs too much, so I have only made one', 'no phoning at all here' and so on. The picture was of a sparely given privilege for which the prisoner had to mobilize considerable welfare support.

Visits are the most fundamental of prisoners' rights, the main way in which the prison's hold over the prisoner is temporarily reduced by the presence of family, friends, or other contacts from the outside world. But even here the prison can and does intrude via the host of variables that make up the context in which visits take place, the degree of monitoring that pervades them, the length of time they are allowed to last, and so on. The character of visits is therefore a prime determinant of the depth of imprisonment. At its most developed, in the long-term closed prisons, the Dutch system allows three visits of up to three hours weekly, plus one 'private visit' a month, with extra visits if the case can be made. In remand prisons, convicted prisoners could receive visitors twice a week for up to two hours each, but facilities did not exist for private visits. The frequency of visits in English training prisons was markedly less, one visit of up to two hours being allowed only once fortnightly. Some prisons are more flexible than others, and where families found difficulty in visiting from abroad, daily visits were in one case arranged for three days running. However, for prisoners remanded in custody, visiting arrangements are more generous in English than in Dutch prisons. (They may, however, be of very short duration; daily visits for prisoners remanded in custody in Holloway last only quarter of an hour.)

Both British and Dutch prisoners argued that private visits should be introduced into British prisons, though the likelihood in the foreseeable future is, to put it mildly, remote. Their arguments go to the heart of the debate about whether imprisonment should be as, not for, punishment. The main argument was ' . . . that relationships are kept alive. You have sexual contacts and they keep you alive.' The result was seen as less dependence on drugs, less homosexuality, and less violence—in prisons and after release. It was argued that in British prisons, as in British society, 'people are too controlled, so they go mad when they get out'. Another prisoner made the point that private visits were not only or mainly for sex, but allowed an intimacy and self-expression not possible on a routine visit: 'Sometimes we just cuddle each other and weep.' Another prisoner linked the significance of the length and depth of imprisonment: 'They don't put people away here for 12, 15, 18 years, when your marriage breaks down, you come out, you've got nothing. Here, you can have private visits, you can have sex, you can plan a family, you've got something to come out to.' Others affirmed that family relations had been kept together by the visits. Such visits are not possible in British prisons, and their introduction is opposed by the Prison Officers' Association, partly because they may be subject to abuse. One reply to this criticism by a Dutch prison deputy director was that such abuses as, for example, drugs being brought into the prison, exist as a possibility with *any* visiting. In both systems, body searches can take place after visits as a check against illicit substances or weapons being brought in from the outside. And the British prisoners were emphatic that both soft and hard drugs were as prevalent in the British as in Dutch jails. What *is* apparent is that the Dutch authorities regard the benefits of such visits as outweighing the costs.

While visiting arrangements have improved in English jails over the past few decades, the Dutch prisoners in English jails seemed to have had fewer visitors than their counterparts in The Netherlands. The difference may in part be due to the British prisoners having more settled relationships in The Netherlands, in part because the size of the country means it is possible for visitors from abroad to reach even the more remote prisons without the extensive travel needed to reach British prisons outside the East Coast and the Home Counties from The Netherlands.But the main conclusion must be that the incentive to undertake such long and costly journeys is seriously diminished when the visiting arrangements are too restrictive. Even when family visit periods had accumulated over three to four months, for example, one Dutch prisoner stated that the visit could still last only one and half to two hours. Rules vary, and elsewhere allowance had been made to extend the number of visits to allow to some extent for previous non-take-up. The arrangements another prisoner had made with his girl-friend had to be cancelled due to a missing Visiting Order slip. The picture is of sparse and relatively inflexible visiting arrangements, occasionally modified on welfare grounds but generally not. The setting in which the standard visits take place is not so very different between Dutch and English training prisons—in both, several visits take place simultaneously in rooms where guards are in general out of earshot. Refreshments may be available, and the atmosphere can be relaxed. The glass screens that one Scottish prisoner remembered between prisoners and visitors in Barlinnie in 1983 seem exceptional even for Britain. But the relative infrequency and lack of privacy in visiting arrangements in British prisons combined with the much more restrictive rules governing letters and telephoning markedly diminish the prisoners' social bonds with the outside world, and correspondingly deepen those within the world of the prison.

Welfare

Welfare considerations loom larger in the Dutch than in the British system. When asked about the chief differences between the two, one English prisoner in The Netherlands replied that it lay in a 'lot of emphasis on rehabilitation', though (as discussed below) this was regarded as applying mainly to Dutch rather than to foreign prisoners. 'If you want rehabilitation, they will do anything for you.' By 'rehabilitation' or 'resocialization' was implied a set of helping strategies akin to Bottoms and

McWilliams's (1979) 'non-treatment paradigm': work training facilities that can be tailored for the individual, generous educational provision, ample time and facilities for sport and recreation, minimal discipline consonant with security, and ease of access to social work and specialist assistance. 'The main asset here is the resocialization. Children aren't ashamed to come here. Welfare payments are kept up . . . whereas stigma in England is very powerful. I had friends who refused me permission to see their children after I'd been in prison for cannabis . . . In England, the attitude is "once a criminal, always a criminal". Here, they think maybe next time you'll be different.'

The situation in English training prisons is not simply the obverse of that which exists in The Netherlands. Educational provision in two of the prisons was singled out for praise by Dutch prisoners, and library facilities were seen as adequate. One prisoner stated: 'What is very good here is education, better than Holland. You can even transfer between prisons here for educational reasons. Here they have a school—I do English, typing, and mathematics. Nothing else is better here than in Holland.' These best practices were not referred to in the two other prisons where interviews took place, though in one the scope for hobbies such as photography and computing were seen as very good; sport and keeping fit in the gym were also stressed as important outlets. If only for reasons of the time allotted to these activities, however, they came across as more marginal to prisons in England than in The Netherlands, despite the fact that they were cited as the best features of the prison life here.

Discipline

Discipline was clearly more severe in English than in Dutch prisons, and less subject to rights of appeal. 'There is no democracy inside the prison [in England]. Every prison officer is like God. No complaints are possible. In The Netherlands, if the governor says no, and you think you have a right, you can appeal to a Commission one of whom has to be a jurist, and you might get your right.' Punishments were seen (sometimes exaggeratedly) as heavier in England than in The Netherlands. 'I'm on three days' punishment [solitary] for having a bit of hash . . . In England, you'd get three more months on your sentence for that.' A parallel case cited by a Dutch prisoner in England had actually cost him 14 days' remission—not three months—but the disparity in punishment was still marked, in part perhaps a reflection of the greater tolerance towards 'soft' drug use in The Netherlands in general. But even legal drug use is penalized in England more than in The Netherlands: 'Going on report here can be just for giving another prisoner tobacco . . . You can get on report so easily here.' 'A £6 fine could do for you if you are a smoker.' Nor can money and tobacco be sent in from the outside quite legally, as it can in The Netherlands. Tobacco baroning is relatively unknown there: the depth of imprisonment and the strength of inmate hierarchy built on scarce resources and their illicit distribution are no doubt correlated to some degree. The contrast in disciplinary terms is that of constraints within constraints as the pattern of prison life in England, many of which are seen as both unnecessary and arbitrarily imposed, 'just to remind you you are a convict, not a human being' (Dutch prisoner in English jail). In The Netherlands, the constraints are more acceptable not simply because they are less severe, but because they are recognized as kept to a minimum consonant with security and good order.

Quality of life

The quality of life was not explicitly addressed as a theme in the interviews, but implicitly linked the otherwise uneven perceptions of the prisoners that a marked difference obtained between the two systems. It was evidently just possible, given a level of self-control none too common in the world at large and not noted for its presence among those officially cast as deviant, to do time quietly in English training prisons. Keeping one's nose clean—avoiding illicit drugs, spinning out the tobacco, making the most of the few hours a day allotted to education, work, and leisure, and keeping on the right side of the staff—would with luck see one through without extra penalties. But it remained an ordeal, an assault on the self to be survived, time out of life. In Dutch prisons, the rupture is not so marked, the passage of time less prolonged, the sense of social distance from society less acute, and the problems of psychological survival less chronic. Allusions to such differences occurred repeatedly in such statements from both sets of prisoners as: 'In Britain, you *always* know you're in prison. Here, you can for a time forget about it . . . Here, you are a person, not just a number in the system.' 'Here there is much more to do, time goes much quicker here. You are only locked in your rooms at night.' 'Here they *want* you to take advantage of what's offered. You have more chance afterwards.' 'There's a chance to keep a bit of your own life going.' 'You are still a member of society.' When asked what features of the Dutch prison system should be introduced into England, British and Dutch alike responded both in holistic terms—'the whole attitude', and so on—and in terms of specific points, ranging from fresh fruit and milk to friendlier and better trained officers, to home leave and more frequent visits. By contrast, the reverse question, on which features of the English penal system should be introduced in The Netherlands, almost invariably produced a strong negative: 'Not a thing from here should be introduced in Holland.' 'England has nothing to offer the Dutch, just to mind their own fucking business.' 'It's not just bull shitting for Holland. The prisons there really are better—stay in there for two days or so and you'll see.'

The near-unanimity among both sets of prisoners on the comparison between prisons favouring the Dutch was in sharp contrast to the much more disparate responses to questions about policing and the criminal justice sytem in general. There, answers were more in line with a belief in the superiority of one's own system, or on there being no substantial difference at all. It is especially disturbing that the comparison between the two prison systems would have been even more marked if interviews with Dutch prisoners had taken place in the more congested local prisons. The only exception was the greater stated preference for the English system in the early stages of remand in custody, though women prisoners who had been at Holloway did not share this preference.

Double punishment? Prisoners abroad

What makes the generally favourable response of British prisoners to Dutch prisons even more notable is that, as foreign prisoners, they felt relatively more discriminated against, by comparison with Dutch prisoners, than did Dutch prisoners in the English system with their English counterparts. Their perceived discrimination—along with other foreign prisoners—began with the sentences they received and extended to the withholding from them of such major rights as home leave and 'interruptions' to sentence. As these latter rights do not exist anyway in the English system, except in very limited respects in the small number of open prisons, the Dutch prisoners in our jails had fewer grounds on which perceptions of discrimination could arise in the first place. In their case, the sense of discrimination was largely limited to the operation of parole.

Though a research project conducted by Jongman, Bosma and Tildemans of the University of Groningen[3] did not in general support the view that foreign offenders were more severely sentenced than Dutch nationals, the usual assertion by British prisoners was that on average foreigners were subject to sentences of imprisonment roughly double the length of those passed on nationals. The great majority of the British prisoners interviewed were imprisoned for hard drug offences, mainly smuggling or dealing in cocaine. As the Dutch authorities have been under strong domestic and international pressure to toughen sanctions against hard drug offenders in particular, this claim is not altogether implausible, and Jongman's team did not include drug offences in their research coverage of the issue. Moreover, drug offenders in The Netherlands were liable to find themselves assessed for hefty tax bills and sequestration of assets. For example, one British prisoner sentenced to three and a half years' imprisonment for dealing in and possession of 215 grams of cocaine had a tax bill for 87,000 guilders (about £20,000), and possessions such as TV and video taken from his house in part payment. When the maximum sentence for an offence is greater than six years, such prisoners are liable to instant deportation on release. It is difficult to sustain the image of The Netherlands as soft on hard drugs in the light of this kind of penalty. If was felt that foreign drug offenders were particularly liable to such additional penalties, since welfare workers would have intervened on behalf of Dutch nationals to forestall such actions. Nevertheless, resentment at such perceived differences of sentence were largely offset by the conviction that comparable sentences in England would have been far stiffer. For example, a prisoner convicted of smuggling 200 grams of cocaine and sentenced to 18 months' imprisonment reckoned he would have received at least five years in England. Another prisoner

---

[3] Summarized in an interview by one of the participants, Mr Tildemans, as showing for male larceny cases a greater chance of custody for non-Dutch first offenders but the reverse for recidivists (interview, 14 Jan. 1985).

sentenced to four and a half years in prison for armed robbery thought he would have received a 15-year sentence in Britain. Estimates of the difference were roughly in the range of English prison sentences being three times as long.

By contrast, Dutch prisoners in England tended to feel a rough parity with English prisoners on sentence length, though they also felt that in The Netherlands their sentence would either have been non-custodial or for a far shorter term, especially for the cannabis-related offences. They did, however, feel discriminated against in terms of parole, an issue which did not arise for English prisoners in The Netherlands, where parole is more akin to remission, being both automatic (for all sentences of over nine months) and not subject to licence and recall in the same way. 'There is no way foreigners can get parole [in England]. Even for good behaviour, you can't get out earlier.' Another prisoner, jailed for two years for smuggling cannabis and a recent recipient of a parole 'nodback' (refusal), was told by his probation officer not to waste his time asking for a review as 'drugs offenders never get parole anyway'. This statement may reflect one consequence of the then home secretary Leon Brittan's withdrawal of parole rights for—in effect—all drug offenders imprisoned for over five years. This restriction may have become informally extended to all drug offenders regardless of the length of their sentence. Dutch prisoners were uncertain whether or not to attribute the cause of their 'nodbacks' to being foreign or being drug offenders or both. But whatever the reasons—and the prospects of supervizing foreigners so close to home as the Dutch may be among them—the withholding of parole was experienced as a major form of double punishment, particularly as in half the cases the type and length of sentence were felt to be far heavier than would have been incurred in The Netherlands.

Discrimination against foreign prisoners in The Netherlands by their denial of home leave and interruptions to sentence must be seen in the context of the far more extensively developed system of such forms of 'time out' by comparison with Britain. The system of home leave and allied forms of time out is largely confined to the long-term prison population, roughly half the overall prison population in that country, who are Dutch by birth or adoption, or who, as foreigners, have five-year residency permits. As roughly one-third of this sector have foreign nationality, of whom only a small number have the necessary residency, the exclusion of this group from home leave arrangements is clearly of quite major significance. At least one of the British prisoners intended to challenge the exclusionary workings of this rule. Nevertheless, the system was otherwise seen and praised by them as *the* cardinal feature of the greater commitment of the Dutch system to prisoners' welfare: 'There is a striking amount of home leave for the Dutch, and this is a good thing. I was never allowed out at Leyhill even when near the end of my sentence. Here, they let you go out for home leave so you have something to go out to. There, you are completely cut off [in England]. Here, you are still a member of society.' It is normal for 60 hours' home leave to be granted every eight weeks in the long-term institutions. In addition, 'interruptions' may be allowed, that is, breaks in the sentence for welfare reasons but which, unlike home leave, do not count as time served.

Another issue in terms of relative deprivation is the refusal of the relevant Dutch authorities to allow foreign prisoners the alternative sanction of TBR—indefinite stay in the closed mental hospitals for offenders which offer therapeutic regimes of varying sorts. Biennial reviews are mandatory for offenders kept in TBR institutions. The main reason given for the general exclusion of foreign offenders from TBR is that therapy would be unduly inhibited by lack of mastery of the Dutch language. None of those interviewed had sought TBR but the case of Alan Reeve (1983) was cited as an example of a prisoner who might more appropriately be placed in such an institution. (Reeve was the only British prisoner in The Netherlands whom I was informally refused permission to interview. The extent to which his then recent hunger strike was connected with that decision, and with the TBR issue, is unknown.)

The imprisonment of women could not be contrasted in the same way as that of the men. There were no British women prisoners in Dutch jails at the time of the interviews. One Irish woman prisoner, who had no prior experience of the criminal justice system in any country, stated that the situation for women differed for the worse from that for men since her entire sentence had to be served in the only closed prison for women in Amsterdam. Also, whereas key decisions about such issues as home leave were taken locally for men, and only exceptionally referred to the Ministry of Justice in The Hague, in the case of women the site of decision-making was much more likely to be The Hague. Four Dutch women prisoners were interviewed in an English training prison, and their views on the similarities and differences between the two systems corresponded broadly with those of the men.

Recidivism and deterrence

Considerations of recidivism and deterrence loom large in the minds of those concerned with criminal justice policy, in part because 'public opinion' and political representatives alike tend to make a commonsensical link betwen harsh penalties and effective deterrence. Such considerations tend to have been more prominent in Britain than in The Netherlands until the very recent past. As stated above (pp. 118–19), direct comparisons of recidivism rates are not possible, since such data are not routinely available in The Netherlands. (60 per cent is the rate given for the whole sample, 66 per cent for the sample excluding those convicted of serious traffic offences; see van der Werff 1978: 10, 28). This one comparison, however, suggests that Dutch reconviction rates are no higher, and may be lower, than those for England.

Crime rates offer a problem-strewn check on the effectiveness of penal policy for reasons which are by now amply documented (see, for example, Bottomley and Coleman 1981; Carr-Hill and Stern 1979). Victim surveys do confirm the official statistical view that crime has increased in the post-war period, though they provide a cross-check only for the past 12 years in The Netherlands and the past 3 years in Britain (van Dijk and Steinmetz 1980, Hough and Mayhew 1985). But they usually chart both a far greater incidence of crime than the official figures, along with a slower rate of increase, in part due to changes in public reporting and police recording practices. Raw crime rates show a broad parallelism in trends between the two countries over the past three decades, with that in Britain rising relatively faster in the first half of the period, that in The Netherlands 'catching up' in the second half. The great bulk of both rates remain petty property crime. It may be that drug and drug-related offences have contributed to the relatively greater increase in standard crime rates in The Netherlands than in England, though the situation in England may have changed significantly in that respect over the past four or five years; whereas serious offences against public order have been relatively more marked in the recent past in England by comparison with The Netherlands. Again, however, it would be rash to link the trends in crime to differences in sentencing severity and penal harshness.

The easy assumption that longer sentences necessarily spell more deterrence was challenged by one young British prisoner, who argued in effect for the view that long sentences entail 'prisonization' and subsequent recidivism, whereas shorter sentences do not automatically mean painless confinement:

Twenty-one months is enough for me. Just not having your freedom, just being away from your wife and kids, it's killing me. More than 5, 10 and so on, it's giving no-one a chance. So it's well and truly enough for me—I don't want to be locked away again. It's completely cured me, and it's humane here. In an English prison, I'd probably be full of hate and want to get back at the system. Here brings it home to you even more. Three in a cell in England, there's no way you can think, it's just down to survival. Here I've got a cell to myself, all the comforts of home *except* your family and freedom—that really brings it home to you. When I ring home, I just want to crawl down the phone. Dogs barking, kids shouting—it brings it all home to you.

Despite the elements of overstatement in that account, it manages to specify how tough measures can simply lead to desensitization, and so-called soft measures to a more acute sense of the fundamental reality of imprisonment, the loss of liberty and personal relationships. Nor are the measures that keep such relationships alive all that costly: the annual costs of the prison system per capita (of the population) are estimated to be 114 per cent higher in England than The Netherlands, and 144 per cent higher as a proportion of the GNP (Netherlands, Ministry of Justice 1984*b*: 77).

Finally, an attempt was made to tap reasons for British offenders in The Netherlands, and Dutch offenders in Britain, having come to commit their offences abroad. The Netherlands may have come to experience, in the criminal justice sphere, some of the problems associated with 'socialism in one country'.[4] How far does its relative leniency in punishment, especially in the drug

---

[4] The reference is to the debate associated with Stalin and Trotsky in the 1920s: Stalin argued that 'socialism in one country' was possible despite capitalist encirclement, Trotsky that the first priority was that revolutionary struggle in other countries should be actively promoted, or the gains of the Revolution would be undermined by such encirclement. Needless to say, Stalin won.

field, attract career criminals from other countries? When asked why they had come to The Netherlands in the first place, not one prisoner replied in terms of instrumental planning for lighter sentences. They had come looking for work, had stayed on, and had subsequently become involved in the drug scene; or they had come to The Netherlands to buy drugs for use and/or sale in England, but without knowing that sentences may be lighter; in one case, fear of reconviction for cannabis use in England led to the move; in another case, the prisoner had left Britain having skipped bail and needed to stay abroad. In some cases, an initial attraction to the general ambience and drug scene in Amsterdam played a role; but in no case did penal policy as such figure explicitly in the process.

The Dutch offenders, who were all in prison for smuggling drugs into Britain, had not been deterred by the tougher sentencing. In some cases, they had not realized sentences *were* tougher; the rest thought the risk had been worth it. Two women had been arrested at Heathrow Airport where they had simply been in transit to Schiphol with a large consignment of cannabis intended for The Netherlands. Quite what we are doing hauling Dutch nationals off Schiphol-bound planes instead of wiring suspicions to the Dutch Customs at their destination is an open question. But as one was a single parent with two children under 18 (one only 10), for whom imprisonment outside The Netherlands was singularly cruel, it seems an aspect of policy long overdue for change. It is also clear that drug traffickers target novices to do their dirty work for them, people without a record whom they hope will be waved through at Customs. The pool of such novices is vast, and it would need truly draconian sentences to filter through to that level abroad with any deterrent effect.

Discussion

The experience of imprisonment varies in terms of depth as well as length. Comparative work on the subject has tended to concentrate on length, in part because it lends itself to quantitative analysis. Recent work on social control trends has focused on its *breadth*, ways in which the 'carceral society' is generated by the permeation of disciplinary modes of supervision by 'penal agents' throughout non-custodial community-based forms of correction (Foucault 1979; Garland and Young 1983; Cohen 1985). The bleakest view of the future of social control is offered by Cohen's depiction of a remorseless increase in the extent of and correlation between the length, depth, and breadth of imprisonment.

The difficulties of comparing whole societies in terms of their 'carcerality' has been discussed above (Ch. 3). However, the extent of the penetration of penal control into civil society may be more concisely addressed in terms of such indicators as the numbers and percentages of ex-prisoners recalled to custody for breach of parole; the volume and character of conditions attached to parole; the scale of imprisonment for breach of non-custodial penalties, such as the fine or probation; and the extent to which penal agents continue to exercise supervision over the lives of those released from custody above and beyond normal limits, e.g. over 'lifers' released on licence in England. Though no attempt has been made here to contrast the two systems in terms of such indicators of the 'breadth' of imprisonment, and even allowing for the extension of control implicit in the 'call-up' system of awaiting a prison place, it is most probable that penal control in The Netherlands is less constraining in these respects than is the case in Britain in general, or England in particular.

The Netherlands has traditionally offered an alternative way forward, one which embraced a 'reductionist' approach to all forms of penality (Rutherford 1984). Recent developments in The Netherlands, however, suggest that even there the early 1980s have been something of a watershed in penal policy. Sentence lengths are creeping up; the prison population is likely to double in the decade 1980–90, and prison capacity is being increased to accommodate it (though the latest official projections, as shown in Fig. 1.1, suggest a lower increase, to 5,900 rather than 7,000 by 1990); staffing ratios are being reduced, implicitly threatening the relatively humane character of the regimes; and Community Service Orders have been introduced to divert offenders from custody, a measure which in Britain has tended to supplement rather than displace imprisonment for a significantly large proportion of offenders. It remains the case, however, that on the three indicators of length, breadth, and depth, The Netherlands, even by 1990, on present trends, will remain substantially less carceral a society than Britain and the great majority of other industrial societies.

In conclusion, all prisoners interviewed expressed a clear and strong preference for the Dutch system over that of England and (where it had been experienced) Scotland. The only exception to that opinion concerned a reversal of preferences at the pre-charge stage of remand in custody. The depth of imprisonment in The Netherlands is markedly shallower than that in Britain; the length of prison sentences is substantially shorter (Tulkens 1979, Hulsman, *et al.* 1978, Downes 1982) and the breadth of imprisonment remains prima facie less developed than that in Britain. If the prisoners' voice counts for anything in the debate on crime and punishment, it is at one with those who argue that the benefits of reductionist policies tangibly outweigh the as yet undemonstrated costs.

7 Contrasts in Tolerance: Criminal Justice Policies in The Netherlands and England

In September 1986, in his opening address to the Penal Congress convened to celebrate the centenary of the Dutch Penal Code, Jan van Dijk, head of the Research and Documentation Centre of the Ministry of Justice, spoke of the criminal justice system in The Netherlands as being 'in serious trouble'. Though no equivalent congress was held, or is readily imaginable, in England, the phrase could equally well, in a year which saw serious rioting in several prisons—one of which was so badly damaged that it has been closed—have been employed to describe the situation there. Although linked by the fact that in both societies rising crime has produced a crisis in penal capacity, the two sorts of 'serious trouble' have otherwise profoundly different characters. In England, the obligation of the prison service to accept all persons custodially sentenced by the courts has led to its functioning as a depository for the failure of 'the system' to diminish the flow of inmates. The failures of the system are both those of the criminal justice process to use non-custodial measures, and of the larger society to check the rise in crime which feeds it. In The Netherlands, the commitment to keep the size of the prison population within the limit set by penal capacity, on a one-to-a-cell basis, has meant that the 'serious trouble' arises earlier in the criminal justice process: at the point where, for example, serious offenders have been released from remand in custody because of lack of cell space. The shape of the policies to address the problems also differ quite profoundly.

Rutherford (1984) has put forward the view that three main policy options are available in penal policy: expansionist, standstill, and reductionist. The first is linked strongly with what he terms, in Dickensian metaphor, 'Great Expectations', the belief that the criminal justice and penal systems have a significant impact on the levels and character of crime and allied social problems. The third is associated with a more sceptical 'Bleak House' view of the likely marginality of control processes to the nature of the crime problem. The second is the likely outcome of a series of alternations or postponement of choice between the two. The Netherlands is seen as taking the reductionist course, England a combination of standstill and expansionist courses at different times. To complicate matters further, 'policy' is only one variable among others in governing what actually happens. Policy may be influential only to a degree or not at all. It may be clear or fudged. It may work successfully at some stages of the criminal justice process, and misfire badly at others. Most of all, policy may mean one thing in Whitehall or The Hague, quite another in Swindon or Zutphen. Policy may misfire not only because it is inefficiently or half-heartedly implemented. It may be implemented perfectly but generate unanticipated side-effects. For example, schemes to divert people from the criminal justice process may draw in more people at an earlier stage of offending than before (Cohen 1985, Pratt 1986).

Moreover, the knowledge base on which the policy options might be evaluated remains not only slender but also subject to a variety of interpretations. For example, in 1975, by virtue of his *Thinking About Crime*, James Q. Wilson became perhaps the world's most influential criminologist when his arguments for incapacitation ushered in 10 years in which the custodial population of the United States virtually doubled. From 1980, the crime rate in the States has fallen, apparently a vindication of the view that, however immense the costs of rapid expansionism, it pays off in terms of less crime. Putting around 1 in every 300 of the 'at risk' population behind bars must have some effect—indeed, if the ratio of prisoners to sub groups of the population at risk (such as young black males) is taken, a quite grotesque proportion must be incarcerated at any one time? However, as Blumstein has argued:

Indeed, crime rates peaked in 1980 and have been going down steadily ever since. That turnaround, however, was influenced to a very large degree by the changing age composition of the US population: the post-war baby boom cohorts (beginning in 1947 and reaching a peak in 1961, with the decline continuing until 1976) were in the high-crime ages in the 1970s (the peak 1961 cohort was 16 in 1977) and receding from those high-crime late-teenage years in the 1980s' (Blumstein 1986: 253).

Demographic relief is not due to occur in Britain and The Netherlands until four to five years later than in the States, since the peak cohorts were born in the mid and not the early 1960s. 'Demographic change represents one of the few observable factors that affect the criminal justice system in reasonably known ways that can be anticipated well in advance' (ibid. p. 255). However, since demographic trends in The Netherlands and England are rather similar, we can hold this constant in comparing trends.

What inferences might be drawn from the Dutch experience? First, it has to be said that there are no easy reformist inferences to be drawn from the past 10 years' experience of crime and its control in The Netherlands. Secondly, the character of the policies pursued in The Netherlands continue to be, despite anomalies, markedly more reductionist than those in England. Thirdly, the co-ordination of policies seems more effectively accomplished than in England. Fourthly, the roots of reductionism seem to derive not so much from a free-floating tolerance on the part of people in general but from the convictions of the most influential élites that crime is to be best combatted by social and institutional, rather than specifically penal, means. Fifthly, if such objectives are to be followed, then an array of policies are needed, not simply one or two initiatives to influence sentencing process. It is worth looking at these points in turn.

The fact that there are no simple reformist conclusions to be drawn from the Dutch experience is due not so much to their record in the penal sphere—which remains by any standards outstandingly humane—but more to the last 10 years' experience of something resembling the proverbial crime 'explosion'. Although crime rates in The Netherlands have levelled off in the past two years while in England they have continued to climb, the steepness of the rise in the 1975–84 period brought an end to the traditional insulation of the Dutch judiciary from exposure to an increasingly restive sense of 'public opinion' as pressing hard for tougher measures. Especially worrying were the rises in the most serious crimes against the person. Although the Dutch murder rate remains much the same as that of England, it would appear to have risen more rapidly than in England, though official aggregation of the 'completed' and 'attempted' murders and manslaughters in the figures before 1983 confounds comparisons of a more precise nature. Trends in rape are similar: though the Dutch rate is higher than that in England, the rates for indecent assault are considerably lower, and some definitional artefacts may account for much of the gap. Pre-1978 figures for crimes known to the police for rape are unfortunately not available, nor are those for robbery, the rate of which is much the same in

England. But if convictions and waivers are used, the Dutch rates for rape and robbery rose at double the rate for England between 1960 and 1981. The continuation of these trends into the 1980s made some hardening of public response virtually inevitable.

Accounting for these trends has been attempted in Chapter 4. Though the interpretation of crime figures, especially on a comparative basis, is notoriously hazardous, what seems most plausibly to have happened is a process of The Netherlands catching up with trends already under way in England as well as other countries. For the Dutch, the most crucial development has been the 'depillarization' of society, the 'collapse of the columns' of denominationalism which guaranteed social order to a high degree on the basis of informal social controls (Lijphart 1975, Bryant 1981, van Dijk *et al.* 1986). The erosion of informal social controls both removes the major constraints against whatever pressures generate rising crime, and also generate demands for tougher formal controls. Though England never developed so dense a network of community controls as Dutch denominationalism, much the same process seemed to occur far earlier in the post-war period, the era of affluence and the beginnings of the breakdown of many working-class communities. As Pearson has noted (1983), people tend throughout history to hark back to an apparently mythical Golden Age of higher standards and lower levels of crime and disorder. But despite their vagaries, crime figures do tend to support such a view for the immediate post-war period. Unless we are to discount them altogether—and victim surveys suggest that would be unwise—the official trends, at least over this period, can be taken to reflect some measure of social reality. The changes in political economy that gradually destabilized the British social order came thicker and faster in The Netherlands (Ch. 3). Drug-related crime, which would make some impact on crimes against property, including robbery, seems to have become a variable of significance in The Netherlands sooner than in Britain. The possibility that leniency in sentencing played a role cannot be discounted. But the fact that crime rates in general have climbed to even higher levels in England than in The Netherlands, despite much more severe sentencing and penal policies, remains the most salient fact, leading one to conclude that the role of such policies has been negligible by comparison with the more profound structural changes at work in both societies.

The broad parallelism between the rising crime rates of the two societies over the past 40 years has been met, as we have seen, with very different responses. These might be characterized as corresponding to Durkheim's conception of *restitutive* and *repressive* models of social control (for a succinct summary of those models, see Lukes and Scull 1983). In the former case, justice is designed to minimize disruption and restore the *status quo ante* with the least possible sanctions to ensure future compliance. In the latter, the offence is defined as a threat to the social order which warrants the stigmatization and punishment of the offender, not only to ensure future compliance but also to reaffirm the inviolability of the rule transgressed. These are 'ideal types', most usefully employed in empirical fashion rather than in Durkheim's original and highly suspect evolutionary schema. All systems combine elements of the two, varying the weight assigned to each. In England restitutive justice is seen at work in the compliance strategies pursued in such fields as environmental and pollution control or revenue offences such as tax evasion (see, for example, Hawkins 1984 and Hutter 1988; and NACRO 1986 for a comparison of the regulation of tax and social security offences). In The Netherlands, resort to repressive modes of justice is maintained in connection with the most heinous offences. But The Netherlands has gone further than most societies in extending the restitutive mode seemingly as far as possible under existing social arrangements. In what amounted to a massive programme of pre-trial diversion, prosecution policy was modulated to take the strain of the rising crime rate away from the courts and the prisons. In effect, the absorptive capacities of the community were relied on to accommodate it. By contrast, the criminal justice system in England maintained a repressive policy (in Durkheim's sense) pretty well intact with regard to routine crimes, limiting restitutive measures to the younger end of the juvenile age-range, and to such fields as traffic and revenue offences, in which repressive law had never been dominant.

For the prisons, these strategies resulted in a contrast between shielding and dumping. In The Netherlands, the small prison system was shielded by not only the waiving policies of the public prosecutors but also by the co-operation of the courts in lenient sentencing and the falling clear-up rate. In England, the prison system became progressively more swollen as offenders passed through the criminal justice system to be dumped inside its walls. Rising crime in The Netherlands was handled by extending the shields in even more flexible ways. In England, attempts were made to manage the growing size of the dumps more effectively. The rise in crime rates into the 1980s brought crises at the pressure points of each system. In The Netherlands, defendants charged with crimes of an unacceptably heinous character were on occasion released due to lack of cell space. (It is facile to overdo this contrast, however. The case of Winston Silcott, who was convicted of the murder of PC Blakelock whilst on bail for a murder charge, in 1985, brought to public attention the small minority of those charged with murder or manslaughter who are released on bail.) In England, simmering conflict broke into outright riots in the wake of the prison officers' strike in certain prisons in 1986. Responses to the crises have also been characteristic. In The Netherlands, the latest policy plan emphasizes social rather than penal measures; in England, penal measures take priority over social initiatives.

The report entitled *Society and Crime* may turn out to be a watershed in Dutch criminal justice policy or a temporary if ingenious holding operation. The second and third phases discerned at the end of Chapter 4 are, from another point of view, one phase only—that of the implementation and development of a new paradigm in criminal justice (t'Hart 1986). The new paradigm solved the problem of increasing crime by reversing the principle of expediency, and by treating law as an instrument of welfare rather than as a substantive realm of justice. For two decades or so, the solution worked, though with increasing resort to *ad hoc* pragmatic remedies for increasing anomalies. At the 1986 Penal Congress in Amsterdam, three stances were discernible in relation to the paradigm. The first, represented most eloquently by van Dijk, a principal architect of *Society and Crime,* aims to keep the existing system intact as far as possible. Some extra penal capacity is needed to restore credibility to the system, but no extra judicial manpower is to be provided to reduce the overloading of capacity in the criminal justice process itself. The main emphasis, however, is on social measures as an antidote to rising crime, and rising fear of crime: in particular, more occupational forms of surveillance are to be developed, better modes of crime prevention are to be explored, and more help and advice for victims is to be provided. But the system will remain fundamentally that which has developed since the 1960s. The most salient forms of tightening-up would be the reduction of the number of waiting prisoners, and the halving of the number of unconditional waivers.

The second stance, represented most strongly by Steenhuis, was that the present system could not function without far more effective managerial strategies. The judiciary should be better integrated into the system, whose parts lack proper co-ordination. The system lacks a coherent philosophy 'on the basis of which the effectiveness (i.e. the outcome) can be determined and the production process adjusted where necessary' (Steenhuis 1986: 231).

The third stance, that of t'Hart and Peters, was far more critical. The paradigm now constituted a problem rather than a solution: 'not waiving but drowning'. The public prosecutorial 'executive' had re-organized and re-orientated the criminal justice process from a case to a policy basis. The executive has become the prime mover in the criminal justice sphere (t'Hart 1986: 87).

The contribution of t'Hart to the Penal Congress was of particular interest, as the first real stirrings of a principled opposition to the whole trend both of criminal justice and of welfare state policies in general. The 'hyper-active State' is viewed as over-involved in the dissemination of justice and altruism. The post-war growth of the 'welfare state' has itself undermined pillarization, since its stress on the individual as the unit of administration is inevitably at the expense of the 'midfield' (pp. 84–5). Not only that, but the 'welfare state is unable to satisfy the expectations which it itself has raised' (p. 89). Ironically, a new form of deprivation is created for those unable to find their way around the system. In sum, the welfare state has generated sectionalism and a standardised construct of the individual which is both fragmenting and alienating (p. 89). It is worth remembering that these criticisms, not entirely unfamiliar in the British context, concern a welfare system which is now more extensive and financed by a larger share of GNP than the British system is.

The crisis of the 'welfare state' is seen, therefore, as self-generating. It is only in that context that the crisis of the criminal justice system can be understood. For the welfare state has laid increasing claim to criminal justice as one aspect of its operations. The law is deployed as a means of instrumental and functional control at the expense of its intrinsic substantive rationality and capacity to act as a curb on discretionary power. 'Modification not codification' is the result (t'Hart 1986: 84–5). Statute thus becomes the minimal requirement rather than the real basis for law enforcement. As the system became progressively overloaded in the 1980s, 'priority' was added to legality and social expediency as an operative criterion. A flood of reports brought a host of changes for administrative convenience rather than the better dispensation of justice. 'Crime is approached . . . as a gigantic problem of organization', to be met by instrumental use of law and policy measures, which overlooks 'crime in terms of a response to behaviour and situations' (p. 69). Most trenchantly, t'Hart regards the powers of the executive as mediated through the public prosecutors as having gone too far.

As in the Dutch situation detection, reporting, prosecution and execution of sentences can already be controlled and co-ordinated [according to the official conception] by the Minister of Justice and the OM [Openbaar Ministerie—the Dutch Public Prosecutors' Office], the aim [of drawing the senior judiciary into guideline setting] is evidently to ensure that the sole remaining link in the entire criminal justice system, namely the independent judiciary, is forced into the straitjacket of a centrally directed criminal law machinery. (t'Hart 1986: 97)

Even so, room for manoeuvre has effectively run out, and with the rise of public concern about criminal victimization, and the fear of vigilantism on the part of the authorities, 'criminal law policy is becoming less offender-orientated. A certain toughening of attitudes would also appear to be on the cards' (pp. 98–9). Hence, *Society and Crime* can be a holding operation only, shoring up a paradigm whose time has gone.

There are naturally a number of points of omission and interpretation that might be made about t'Hart's critique. First, although he appears to want an alternative to the welfare state and present ways of running the criminal justice system in The Netherlands, he is extremely vague about what such alternatives might be. Secondly, he could be seen as misrecognizing the enemy: there are other candidates for the responsibility for undermining pillarization than the welfare state, notably the operations of post-war consumer capitalism (Bryant 1981). Thirdly, the 'new paradigm' may not be so different from earlier developments as he contends. The reversal of the principle of expediency was an acknowledgement of trends already well under way, rather than a fresh initiative. However, it is certainly the case that these tendencies were to become greatly elaborated and systematized in policy terms after 1970, so that in effect a new paradigm may be inferred. And fourthly, he is not overtly at odds with the direction of specifically penal policy, which is simply left out of the equation. Yet is is difficult to see how, if the criminal justice system were to proceed on some strict basis of adherence to cases, anything other than a greatly enlarged penal system would result. Not only routine crimes of victimization but also the entire range of economic offences, such as tax evasion, would be funnelled through the courts. A hyperactive criminal justice system would replace the filters and shields, and without necessarily making much impact on the overall weight of the hyperactive state.

Durkheim once remarked that 'a hypertrophied State, confronting a mass of disaggregated individuals, would be a veritable sociological monstrosity'. What is bound to result from present developments is, to t'Hart, Durkheim's nightmare, ironically brought about by the neo-Durkheimianism of the followers of Vrij who adapted the prosecutorial system to restitutive ends. To Steenhuis, however, the problem is not so much one of overintegration as of too little integration. 'The co-ordination between the different links in the criminal justice system was so deficient that the functioning of the system as a whole was seriously impaired and the credibility of the criminal justice system was being undermined' (Steenhuis 1986: 230). The system lacks a coherent philosophy 'on the basis of which the effectiveness (i.e. the outcome) can be determined and the production process adjusted where necessary'. He points to 'singular lack of agreement' and 'deep divisions of opinion' both within and between the parts of the system (p. 231). Because the system is not to be expanded as a whole, better use must be made of existing capacity at the pre-penal phases. Yet the system seems almost to have been designed 'to impede as far as possible a smooth throughput based on a coherent concept of the products to be manufactured' (pp. 238–9). The OM are not really able to integrate policy as well as the authors of *Society and Crime* envisage. All the main actors in the criminal justice system should therefore be subject to new forms of cultural training aimed at sensitizing them to 'teamwork' and greater coherence. 'What is important from the point of view of integration here is how the various parts of the criminal justice system can be induced to operate on the basis of such a philosophy or such premises. Minzberg speaks quite openly in this connection of "indoctrination" ' (p. 244; the reference is to Minzberg's *The Structuring of Organisations,* 1979). A new 'basic training course' should be devized, culled largely from business management teaching, as a two-year prelude to specialist training.

The main problem with Steenhuis's approach is that of Hamlet without the prince. Nowhere does he convey the nature of the underlying philosophy which he wishes to be more efficiently transmitted. Nor does he analyze the problems endemic in integrating parts of a system which indeed *has* been designed, at least in part, to 'impede as far as possible a smooth throughput based on a coherent concept of the products to be manufactured'. As Blumstein (1986) points out rather devastatingly, the separation of powers *requires* a degree of intentional incoherence in the criminal justice systems of democratic societies.

The business school imagery of inputs, outputs, throughputs, and production flows can become seriously misleading when transposed to the criminal justice sphere. Blumstein argues that intentional incoherence is justified at the micro level, where often necessarily conflicting objectives, rights, checks and balances, and due process, on the one hand, and speed, efficiency, and accountability on the other will necessarily make for inefficiencies that would plunge any business into bankruptcy. Such inherent 'inefficiencies' are to be distinguished from those which are just plain inefficient, however. At the macro level, by contrast, the incoherencies which are eminently justifiable at the micro level become impediments to co-ordination and integration where they *are* needed. Here Blumstein invokes naturalistic rather than business metaphors of 'upstream' and 'downstream' stages to make his point. For example, 'upstream changes' of a demographic sort can be planned into 'downstream' policies for more or less prison places. In criticism of Blumstein, it might be said that such macro-level planning does entail *some* micro-level integration. It is difficult to see how otherwise the policy plans at macro level can be translated into appropriate practices. Blumstein is a little disingenuous on this score. For example, Steenhuis's most powerful instance of incoherence in the Dutch criminal justice system was the degree of priority accorded one group of cases above virtually all others in the processing of cases: drunken drivers (see Table 7.1).

Part of the reason for the disproportionately high rate of

TABLE 7.1   *Composition of 'offence packages' of police, public prosecutors, and courts, 1985 (percentages)*

Law violated	Police	Prosecutors	Courts
Criminal Code	90	66	46
Road Traffic Act	8	25	42
Other Acts (firearms, narcotics)	2	9	12

Source: Steenhuis (1986: 234).

processing road traffic offences is that they are 'solved' at the point of becoming known to the police, unlike the bulk of Criminal Code offences. But that does not account for the extent to which they are brought to court so readily by contrast with Criminal Code offences. Differential definitions of seriousness are again partly responsible, no doubt, but it is odd for so overloaded a system to devote so high a level of resources to such offences. As Steenhuis points out, the data mean that 'of every 100 convictions by the courts, 42 are pronounced in respect of traffic offences . . . 1 in every 3 convictions for an indictable offence relates to driving under the influence' (Steenhuis 1986: 234). It is doubly odd, since one of the pieces of research most quoted in interviews by the judiciary was Steenhuis's own project on blood-alcohol levels and sentencing policies in contrasting areas of The Netherlands (1977). No difference was found in alcohol levels despite major sentencing variation. Six years later, such sentencing remains severe, a practice at odds both with research findings and some comparative data. In England, for example, where sentencing in such cases is actually milder than in The Netherlands, rates of death on the road are lower than in The Netherlands, though this difference may be accounted for in other terms (e.g. traffic densities). It is, however, a sign that sentencing in The Netherlands is less 'rational' than is often supposed, and less 'integrated' than may be feared. To an outsider it seems inappropriate for so many of such cases to be passed onto the court, when a range of conditional waivers are available at the prosecutorial stage, a policy which would free both criminal justice and penal capacity for more serious cases.

These polar views of trends in criminal justice policy in The Netherlands find some partial resolution in *Society and Crime*. Its central themes of differentiation and consistency are in essence those of the Home Office in Britain. Petty crime is viewed as the numerical bulk of the crime problem, and is to be differentiated from serious crimes such as crimes against life and the person, drug-trafficking and robbery. Bottoms's (1977) notion of 'bifurcation' is clearly at work. Consistency is the attempt to ensure equity without too much local variation. The Dutch modified version of a 'back to justice' movement in the work of t'Hart and Peters is hardly in evidence, other than in the recommendation that the public prosecutors halve the number of unconditional waivers; and in the determination that extra capacity will be found for offenders remanded in custody, the latter being, in t'Hart's view, 'the most obvious example of deficient planning in the entire field of criminal law policy and a considerable threat to the credibility of the criminal justice system' (t'Hart 1986: 92). Whether or not the policy of unblocking the system and creating extra capacity at crucial points, notably the remand prisons, will meet the problem and restore credibility depends greatly on rises in crime staying within projected limits, and levels of sentencing remaining much the same as now.

Some criminologists in Britain (Blom-Cooper 1986, Bottomley 1986) have noted that in one key respect the main point of the recent debate in The Netherlands about criminal justice policy is that it takes a form very different from that in Britain. '. . . the Dutch policy plan is one of a carefully constructed strategy—whatever may be one's view of the inherent merits of its content. Beginning with an analysis of the perceived nature of the crime problem, it establishes a number of broadbased working principles, which are then systematically followed through in an examination of their practical and organisational consequences' (Bottomley 1986: 209). In contrast, the closest British equivalents, *A Review of Criminal Justice Policy* (Home Office 1976) and *Criminal Justice: Working Paper* (Home Office 1984) 'list objectives, underlying themes and preoccupations, in such a way that they fail to provide an integrated sense of direction for decision-makers, who are likely instead to concentrate on the practical directives for efficient management in their own particular sphere' (ibid. p. 213-4). 'Such initiatives as the proposals of the Control Review Committee (Home Office 1984*b*), and Fresh Start, are components towards a penal policy, rather than a policy in their own right.' Bottomley (1986: 214) calls for 'an authoritative "supra-agency" statement of objectives and principles, applicable in practice, so that the experience of law enforcement and the administration of justice is as coherent and consistent as it can be throughout the many jurisdictions in different parts of the country'. Overall co-ordination is seen as the prime need, though it was barely mentioned in the Home Office working paper—'perhaps because of an acute awareness of the lack of any overall organising principles or policy to follow?' (ibid). By contrast, Hudson (1987: 82 ff.) discerns the growing influence of 'justice model thinking' in Home Office commendations of Court of Appeal guidelines to sentencers, in the extending scope of the guidelines, and in their active dissemination by the Judicial Studies Board set up in 1983. Steady penal expansion is bound to result from such measures, since their objective of reducing disparities in sentencing is to be achieved by evening out variations around an average 'tariff' which is already severe by comparative standards.

The problem in England, however, is even more intractable than the absence of a clear set of policy directives and a strategy for their overall co-ordination. It is not so much a lack of means for the construction of such a policy. That could be the task of the Home Office acting as prime mover in setting up an inter-departmental and joint body with the senior judiciary to tackle the job. A National Criminal Policy Committee such as was suggested by the Home Affairs Committee in 1981, but rejected by the government, could also be established. The first main problem is that significant resistance to any such move is embodied in the judiciary, at least at senior levels. Criminal justice policy is seen almost as a contradiction in terms by the judiciary, since it is defined as encroaching on their own preserve. The second main problem is that, even if we had such a policy, we lack the framework for its implementation. We have no constitutional equivalent to the Openbaar Ministerie, with its multi-agency role enabling prosecutors to mediate policy from the minister accountable to Parliament through to the police, the local authorities, and the courts. Given the resistance of the judiciary on the one hand, and the policy framework vacuum on the other, it is hardly surprising that no very substantial attempt has been made to enunciate an overall criminal justice policy.

A subsidiary reason for the lack of attention to this policy vacuum is that the prisons in England take almost the entire strain of the system's problems. In The Netherlands the problems spill out into the community at earlier stages; this is perhaps why the Dutch have come to respond to them, after a series of pragmatic attempts at their resolution, with so forthright and open a policy document as *Society and Crime*. In England, the inadequacies of the system are unceremoniously dumped in the lap of the prisons, which are left to cope with the consequences as best they can. The consequent crises of prison administration and conditions are, however, less visible and accorded far lower priority than those in the community, so that less urgency is felt about the need to address them in a properly co-ordinated way. In so far as they *are* addressed, however, they are usually defined as problems specific to the penal sphere. Attention is therefore paid to exclusively prison matters, such as over-crowding and industrial relations. Almost all the policy initiatives of the past 20 years have been devoted to reducing the pressure on the penal system, by earlier release, by the creation of non-custodial alternatives, by occasional exhortations to the courts to trim the length of sentences, and—finally—by acceding to the narrow logic employed and financing the building of 26 new prisons. Over the past five years, the search for means of reducing pressure on the prison system has shifted somewhat from *external* 'input' and release measures to *internal* modes of relieving the pressure in more effective ways. For example, welcome as many of the proposals of the Control Review Committee may be, (Home Office 1984*b*), such as the aim to move towards a much greater variety of work programmes for prisoners, they coincided with the decisive abandonment of the more fundamental aim of relieving pressure by reducing the size of the prison population. The problems endemic in the criminal justice system as a whole, and in the larger society, are thereby deflected, displaced, and defused by this linkage with the prison context.

An extensive and rigorous literature has grown up in the past decade on the generally adverse fate of successive attempts to deploy alternatives to custody as a means of reducing the pressure on the prison population (see especially Bottomley 1984; Bottoms 1977, 1983, 1986; King and Morgan 1979, 1980). A major problem inheres in the tendency for such alternatives to be used interchangeably rather than as substitutes for custody. Moreover, they promote secondary and unanticipated conflicts over their role in the tariff, the notional hierarchy of sentence severity, which may lead to 'net-widening' (Cohen 1985, Pratt 1986). Perceived as experimental and even soft in relation to custody, they prompt politicians to balance their introduction with some compensatory tough measure for the more serious offenders, the classic example being Leon Brittan's virtual withdrawal of parole for all offenders sentenced to over five years' imprisonment for violence and drug-trafficking. Piecemeal and pragmatic innovations, defended less in their own terms than as designed to reduce prison overcrowding, or save money, they tend to arouse hostility among those who see sentencing as a process of a strictly judicial character, which should not be contaminated by the availability of prison places. For these and other reasons, the limited success they may have cumulatively wrought in moderating custodial sentencing now seems to have evaporated. In 1984, a larger proportion of indictable offenders were jailed than in 1974, despite a decade of ministerial exhortation, intermittent judicial advice, and several new custodial alternatives aimed at tempering the use of imprisonment. In 1974, 11.8 per cent, and in 1984, 16.4 per cent of all indictable offenders were imprisoned, a rise approaching 50 per cent. By failing to maintain, let alone reduce, the level of resort to custody of 1974, we have ensured that the average daily prison population is swollen by at least several thousand more prisoners than would otherwise have been the case. And the crime rate has continued to rise despite such severity.

Yet the current obsession in ministerial and judicial circles seems to be with leniency rather than severity (see for example, 'Crackdown on Soft Judges', *Sunday Telegraph*, 26 Oct. 1986). Thinking is beginning to turn towards new ways of financing expansionism, rather than continuing to grapple with the problems of reducing the resort to custody ('MP's Say Private US Gaols Show Way for Britain', *Guardian*, 28 Oct. 1986). Unlike The Netherlands, where—*pace* Steenhuis—there is *some* philosophical coherence among the judiciary concerning the damage wrought by imprisonment (see Chs. 3 and 6 above), in England the judiciary continues, in the teeth of formidable evidence, to regard imprisonment as at best an effective antidote to crime, and at worst a justified form of incapacitation, even for petty, persistent offenders. At the same time, some concessions are made to the view that guidelines and directives may be needed to promote some degree of equity. The resulting ambivalence leaves the judiciary prey to every populist tremor, so that it sometimes seems as if a single banner headline in the *Sun* carries more weight

than the combined findings of the Home Office's own redoubtable
Research and Planning Unit. By contrast, the Research and
Documentation Centre of the Ministry of Justice in the Hague is
centrally involved in the consultation processes of policymaking,
and in the monitoring of the implementation of policy. Not only
that, but its members are free to speak out on such issues, in ways
that would be frowned on or forbidden in England.

It may well be contended that public opinion ultimately and
rightly constrains policymaking, in the criminal justice field, and
that too great a deviation from that opinion will undermine the
credibility of the system, as the Dutch have now discovered.
Leaving aside the problematic ways in which such opinion is
defined, it may well be that perhaps the ultimate contrast between
the two systems lies in the greater reliance on community
tolerance in The Netherlands than in Britain. It may well be the
case that the limits of that tolerance were reached in the early
1980s, largely as a result of the highly visible and concentrated
nature of drug abuse and drug-related crime in the major cities.
However, the key indicators of unease hardly show greater
credibility in Britain than in The Netherlands. Vigilantism is no
more apparent in The Netherlands than in Britain; indeed, the
prevalence of racially motivated attacks, and corresponding rises
in self-defence groupings, may be higher in Britain. Most
vigilantism in The Netherlands related to narcotic abuse and
trafficking and is now on the decline. Rioting is markedly more
prevalent in Britain, despite the fact that unemployment has been
as high, and problems of ethnic minority group assimilation more
substantial. A higher degree of laxity had developed in The
Netherlands in such matters as the payment of public transport
fares and fine repayments—matters specifically addressed by the
Roethof Committee, and already ameliorated due to tighter
inspections of enforcement practices. In short, there are no grounds
for asserting that, taken as a whole, the Dutch criminal justice
system lacks credibility any more than the British.

We have scant knowledge of community tolerance, though it
occupies a central place in theories of deviance and control. Its
variability across groups and communities is little understood.
Some societies display surprising flexibility and elasticity in
accommodating deviance and dissent, others barely countenance
mild infractions. Both Britain and The Netherlands lay claim to a
culture of tolerance, notably in the expression of opinions and

ideology. In relation to deviant behaviour, however, the Dutch have fashioned a culture of tolerance that seeks to accommodate it, wherever possible, to a greater extent than in Britain. They do not seem to have suffered unduly as a result. Indeed, in certain respects, we are beginning to learn, slowly and painfully, lessons they could have taught us. Such experiments as the Priority Estates Projects embody forms of community work foreshadowed in much of the community relations work on large housing estates in The Netherlands.[1] There élites have a distinct appreciation of the extent to which community tolerance cannot be taken for granted, but needs active elicitation and encouragement. British élites tend to assume its absence or even malign character. Hence, it is to be pre empted by tough policies or at best left to its own devices.

It does not do to overdraw the comparison between Britain and The Netherlands. The two countries have more in common than divides them. There is much justice of a restitutive kind in Britain, notably in the fields of economic offences, such as tax evasion, pollution control, and industrial safety. The Dutch can act more repressively than the British: their police are armed and employ tear gas and water cannon to disperse 'riotous assemblies'; perimeter guards of their top security prisons are armed. But in almost every other respect, their prisons demonstrate that genuinely humane containment is possible, and that is an important lesson. The means to that end seem to be several rather than one. The drastic shortening of sentences to custody is the major route, but other measures are needed for a properly co-ordinated response. These would include setting limits to the size of the penal estate; introducing minimum and legally enforceable standards for prison conditions; conditionally diverting petty offenders, with their consent, from prosecution; experimenting with victim restitution in suitable cases; co-ordinating crime prevention, occupational surveillance, and youth employment measures; and resisting the use of imprisonment for petty offenders when persistence rather than the gravity of offences constitutes a problem (see also Rutherford 1984, final chapter). As

---

[1] Priority Estates Projects are a linked set of initiatives sponsored by the Department of the Environment to improve the quality of life on public housing estates by *inter alia*, decentralized management, more rapid response to tenants' complaint, and better inter-agency co-ordination (see Power 1987).

many commentators have suggested, a suitably authoritative body should be created to review the most appropriate strategy for the components of such a policy to be evaluated.

It would be a mistake for the British judiciary to infer from the current debate in The Netherlands that their criminal justice system is in such disarray, and so dominated by the executive, that nothing is to be learnt from it except what to avoid. For the simmering but largely hidden crisis in the British criminal justice system needs to be addressed in the same open fashion adopted by the Dutch in relation to theirs. Nor need the judiciary fear that some subversive constitutional movement is going on whenever anyone suggests the need for sentencing policy to be subject to analysis and discussion outside their ranks. As Ashworth has tirelessly pointed out, sentencing policy is not the preserve of the judiciary.[2] Its discussion by other bodies is not some act of *lèse-majesté* but an essential part of the democratic process. The judiciary in Britain holds such undisputed sway over sentencing that it can afford to be receptive. No-one is about to suggest its takeover by a British version of the Openbaar Ministerie. There is, however, a clear need for a policy framework capable of formulating and guiding the implementation of criminal justice priorities. The new Crown Prosecution Service should be allowed to envisage a more robust role than that which it is currently allotted. At present, it is little more than a renamed police prosecution department. Some means has to be found for situating a much more sparing use of imprisonment within a reformed criminal justice system. We in England can edge a great deal closer to the Dutch example without running comparable risks, for we would do so from a position of such grossly inflated use of custody that much can be cut without serious backlash. The Dutch judiciary have shown great courage in insisting on humane standards and the minimum use of pain in the dispensation of criminal justice. It is to be hoped they can keep their nerve in the face of adverse criticism. It is also to be hoped that we find sufficient nerve to follow their example.

---

[2]   But cf. Lord McCluskey's Reith Lecture, *Listener*, 6 Nov. 1986.

References

ACPS (Advisory Council on the Penal System) (1978). *Sentences of Imprisonment: A Review of Maximum Penalties.* London: HMSO.

AMSTERDAM. CITY OF (1985). *The Amsterdam Policy on Drugs.* City Information Office

ASHWORTH, A. (1983). *Sentencing and Penal Policy.* London: Weidenfeld and Nicholson.

BAGLEY, C. (1973). *The Dutch Plural Society.* Oxford: University Press.

BAGLEY, C. (1983). 'Dutch Social Structure and the Alienation of Black Youth' in Bagley, C., and Verma, G. (eds.), *Multicultural Childhood.* Farnborough: Gower.

BALDOCK, J. C. (1980). 'Why the Prison Population has Grown Larger and Younger' *Howard Journal* 19: 142–55

BALLANTYNE, A. (1988). 'Warning of Violence at Remand Centre', *Guardian,* 9 Jan.

BANTING , K. (1979). *Poverty, Politics and Policy.* London: Macmillan.

BBC-2 (1985). *Out of Court,* transcript of programme 15, 28 Feb. 1985.

BERGHUIS, A. C., and ESSERS, J. J. A. (1985). *Het toekennen van prioriteiten bij de tenvitvoertegging van voorlopige hechtenis* (The scaling of priorities in the actual implementation of remands in custody). The Hague: WODC.

BIANCHI, H. (1975). 'Social Control and Deviance in The Netherlands', in his (co-ed) *Deviance and Control in Europe.* London: Wiley.

BIANCHI, H., and SWAANINGEN, R. van (eds.), (1986). *Abolitionism: Towards a Non-Repressive Approach to Crime.* Amsterdam: Free University Press.

BLOCK, R. (1986). 'Crime in Your Neighbourhood: A Comparison of England/Wales and The Netherlands'. Paper delivered at Home Office Research and Planning Unit Seminar, 11 June 1986.

BLOM-COOPER, L. (1986). 'A Freedom-loving Nation Is Forced To Think Again', *Guardian* 12 Sept. 1986.

BLUMSTEIN, A. (1986). 'Coherence, Co-ordination and Integration in the Administration of Criminal Justice', in Dijk, J. J. M. van *et al.* (eds.), 1986.

BLUMSTEIN, A., and COHEN, J. (1973). 'A Theory of the Stability of Punishment', *Journal of Criminal Law and Criminology* 64: 198–207.

BOTTOMLEY, A. K.(1984). 'Dilemmas of Parole in a Penal Crisis', *Howard Journal* 23: 24–40.

BOTTOMLEY, A. K. (1986). 'Blue-prints for Criminal Justice: Reflections on a Policy Plan for the Netherlands', *Howard Journal* 25:199–251.

BOTTOMLEY, A. K., and COLEMAN, C. (1981). *Understanding Crime Rates.* Farnborough: Gower.

BOTTOMS, A. E. (1977). 'Reflections on the Renaissance of Dangerousness', *Howard Journal* 16: 70–96.

BOTTOMS, A. E., (1983). 'Neglected Features of Contemporary Penal Systems'. in Garland, D., and Young, P. (eds.) 1983.

BOTTOMS, A. E., (1986). 'Limiting Prison Use: Experience in England and Wales', in Dijk, J. J. M. van *et al* (eds.) 1986.

BOTTOMS, A. E., and MCWILLIAMS, W. (1979). 'A Non-treatment Paradigm for Probation Practice', *British Journal of Social Work* 9: 159–202.

BOTTOMS, A.E., MAWBY, R. I. and WALKER, M. (1987). 'Localised Crime Rates', *British Journal of Criminology* 27: 125–54.

BOX, S. (1983). *Power, Crime and Mystification.* London: Tavistock.

BOYLE, J. (1977). *A Sense of Freedom.* London: Pan.

BOYLE, J. (1984). *The Pain of Confinement: Prison Diaries.* Edinburgh: Canongate.

BRAND-KOOLEN, M. (forthcoming). 'The Dutch Penal System and its Prisons', in her (ed.), *Studies in the Dutch Prison System.* The Hague: WODC.

BRYANT, C. G. A. (1981). 'Depillarisation in The Netherlands', *British Journal of Sociology* 22:56–74.

BUIKHUISEN, W. and DIJK, J. J. M. van (1975). *Official Police Reporting of Criminal Offences.* The Hague: Research and Documentation Centre, Ministry of Justice.

BULMER, M. (1985). *The Chicago School.* Chicago University Press.

CARR-HILL, R. A., and STERN, N. H. (1979). *Crime, the Police, and Criminal Statistics.* London: Academic Press.

CHAN, J. B. L., and ERICSON, R. V. (1981). *Decarceration and the Economy of Penal Reform,* Toronto: University of Toronto, Centre of Criminology Research Report 14.

CHATTERTON, M. R. (1983). 'Police Work and Assault Charges', in Punch, M. (ed.), *Control in the Police Organisation.* Cambridge, Mass.: MIT Press.

CITY OF AMSTERDAM (1985). 'The Amsterdam Policy on Drugs'. Amsterdam: City Information Office.

COHEN, S. (1979). 'The Punitive City', *Contemporary Crises* 3: 339–63

COHEN, S. (1982). 'Western Crime Control Models in the Third World: Benign or Malignant?', in Simon, R. and Spitzer S. (eds.), *Research in Law, Deviance and Social Control,* vol. 4. Greenwich: JAI Press.

COHEN, S. (1985). *Visions of Social Control.* Cambridge: Polity Press.

COHEN, S., and TAYLOR, L. (1972). *Psychological Survival.* Harmondsworth: Penguin.

COHEN, S., and TAYLOR, L. (1978). *Prison Secrets.* London: Radical Alternatives to Prison/National Council for Civil Liberties.

CROSS, R. (1975). *The English Sentencing System.* 2nd rev. edn. London: Butterworths.

DAHRENDORF, R. (1985). *Law and Order.* (The Hamlyn Lectures.) London: Stevens.

DANIELS, A. (1981). 'Future of Alternatives', *Correctional Options* 1.

DAVIES, N. (1986a). 'Heroin: Have We Got It Right?', *Observer* 16 Mar. 1986.

DAVIES, N. (1986b). 'More Policemen Confirm Crime Figures Scandal', *Observer* 20 July 1986.

DERKS, J. (1983). 'The Amsterdam Morphine-dispensing Experiment', Paper delivered at Utrecht, Netherlands Institute of Mental Health (unpublished).

DERKS, J. (1987). 'The Amsterdam Morphine-dispensing Experiment', 160–3 in Kaplan, C. D., and Kooyman, M., *Responding to a World of Drugs: Intentional and Unintentional Effects of Control, Treatment and Prevention.* Proceedings of the 15th International Conference on the Prevention and Treatment of Drug Dependence, April 1986. Rotterdam: Erasmus University.

DHSS (Department of Health and Social Security) 1987. *Mental Illness and Mental Handicap Hospitals and Units in England: Legal Status Statistics, 1982–1985.* DHSS Statistical Bulletin: London: HMSO.

DIEDERIKS, H. (1980). 'Patterns of Criminality and Law-enforcement During the Ancien Regime: The Dutch Case', in *Criminal Justice History: An International Annual,* Vol. 1. New York.

DIEDERICKS, H. (1981).'Punishment During the Ancien Regime: The Case of the Eighteenth-century Dutch Republic', in Knafla, L. A. (ed.), *Crime and Criminal Justice in Europe and Canada.* Waterloo, Ontario.

DIJK, J. J. M. van (1980). *Some Characteristics of the Sentencing Process.* The Hague: Research and Documentation Centre, Ministry of Justice.

DIJK, J. J. M. van (1983) *The Use of Guidelines by Prosecutors in The Netherlands.* The Hague: WODC.

DIJK, J. J. M. van (1984). 'Financiele-economische aspecten van misdaad en misdaadbestrigding' (Financial and economic aspects of crime and its control), *Economisch statistische berichten* 19: 1248–52 (26 Dec. 1984).

DIJK, J. J. M. van, and STEINMETZ, C. D. (1980). *The Burden of Crime on Dutch Society.* The Hague: Research and Documentation Centre, Ministry of Justice.

DIJK, J. J. M. van, HAFFMANS, C., RUTER, F., SCHUTTE J., and STOLWIJK, S. EDS., (1986). *Criminal Law in Action: An Overview of Current Issues in Western Societies.* Arnhem: Gouda Quint.

DITTON, J. (1977). *Part-time Crime.* London: Macmillan.

DOLE, V. P., and NYSWANDER, M. E., (1968). 'Successful Treatment of 750 Criminal Addicts', *Journal of the American Medical Association,* 206: 2708–11.

DONZELOT, J. (1979). *The Policing of Families.* London: Hutchinson.

Downes, D. M. (1982). 'The Origins and Consequences of Dutch Penal Policy since 1945: A Preliminary Analysis', *British Journal of Criminology* 22: 325-62.

Durkheim, E. ([1895],trans. 1952). *The Rules of Sociological Method*. London: Routledge and Kegan Paul.

Edwards, G (1979). 'British Policies on Opiate Addition: Ten Years' Working of the Revised Response, and Options for the Future', *British Journal Of Psychiatry* 134: 1-13.

Edwards G. and Busch C. (eds.) (1981). *Drug Problems in Britain: A Review of Ten Years*. London: Academic Press.

Emmerick, J. L. van (1982). *Detained at the Government's Pleasure*. The Hague: WODC.

Epstein, E. J. (1977). *Agency of Fear: Opiates and Political Power in America*. New York: Putnam.

Erikson, K. (1966). *Wayward Puritans*. New York: Wiley.

Erkelens, L. H. (1984). 'Main Characteristics of and Some Special Topics in the Drug Policy of the Dutch Prison Administration'. Internal paper, Prison Dept. of The Netherlands Ministry of Justice.

Erkelens, L. H. and Janssen, O. J. A. (1979). 'Hard-drug Use and Crime'. Paper presented at the International Sociological Association: The Hague, unpublished.

Farrington, D. P., Gallagher, G., Morley, L., St. Ledger, R. J., and West, D. J. (1986). 'Unemployment, School Leaving and Crime', *British Journal of Criminology* 26: 335-56.

Feldbrugge, J. T. T. M. and Werdmuller von Elgg Y. A., eds., (1981). *Involuntary Institutionalisation: Changing Concepts in the Treatment of Delinquency*. Amsterdam: Excerpta Medica.

Fiselier, J. P. S. (1978). *Slachtoffers van delicten*. (Victims of Crime). Utrecht: Ars Aequi Libri.

Fitzgerald, M., and Sim, J. (1982). *British Prisons*. 2nd. edn. Oxford: Blackwell.

Foucault, M. (1977). *Discipline and Punish*. Harmondsworth: Penguin.

Garland, D. (1981). 'The Birth of the Welfare Sanction', *British Journal of Law and Society,* 8: 29-45.

Garland, D. (1985). *Punishment and Welfare: A History of Penal Strategies*. Aldershot: Gower.

Garland, D. (1986a). 'Foucault's *Discipline and Punish:* An Exposition and Critique', *American Bar Foundation Research Journal* 847-80

Garland, D. (1986b). 'The Punitive Mentality: Its Socio-historic Development and Decline' (review essay on P. Spierenburg's *The Spectacle of Suffering,* 1984), *Contemporary Crises* 10: 305-20

Garland, D. and Young, P., eds., (1983) *The Power to Punish*. London: Heinemann.

Haan, W. De. (1986). 'Abolitionism and the Politics of Bad Conscience', 157-77 in Bianchi, H., and van Swaaningen, R. (eds.)

Abolitionism: Towards a Non-repressive Approach to Crime. Proceedings of the Second International Conference on Prison Abolition. Amsterdam: Free University Press.

HALL, S., CRICHTER, C., JEFFERSON, T., CLARKE, J., and ROBERTS, B. (1978). *Policing the Crisis*. London: Macmillan.

HALL WILLIAMS, J. E., and LEIGH, L. H. (1981). *The Management of the Prosecution Process in Denmark, Sweden and The Netherlands*. Leamington Spa: James Hall.

HART, A. C. 't (1986). 'Criminal Law Policy in The Netherlands', in Dijk, J. J. M. van *et al*. (eds.), 1986.

HARTNOLL, R., LEWIS R., and MITCHESON M. (1986). 'Estimating the Prevalence of Opioid Dependence', *Lancet* 26 Jan. 1986.

HAWKINS, K. (1984). *Environment and Enforcement: Regulation and the Social Definition of Pollution*. Oxford: Clarendon Press

HOEKSTRA, J. (1983). 'Financiele consequenties van een gereguleerde heroineverstrekking' (The costs of controlling heroin trafficking), in *Discussienota over heroineverstrekking'*, Uitgave Stichting Ultgeverij De Oude Stadt, (March).

HOFER, H. von (1975). *Dutch Prison Population*. Nordic Research Council for Criminology.

HOME OFFICE. (1976). *A Review of Criminal Justice Policy*. London: HMSO.

HOME OFFICE. CRIMINAL STATISTICS (1979). *Criminal Statistics, England and Wales*. London: HMSO.

HOME OFFICE. (1981) *Report of HM Chief Inspector of Prisons for England and Wales*. London: HMSO.

HOME OFFICE (1984a). *Criminal Justice: Working Paper*, London: HMSO.

HOME OFFICE. (1984b) *Managing the Long-term Prison System: Report of the Control Review Committee*. London: HMSO.

HOME OFFICE. (1985) *Report of the Committee on the Prison Disciplinary System*. London: HMSO.

HOME OFFICE. PRISON STATISTICS (1978). *Prison Statistics, England and Wales*, 1984 London: HMSO.

HOME OFFICE. (1986). *Criminal Justice: Working Paper*, London: HMSO. (rev. ed.).

HOME OFFICE. (1986a). *A Fresh Start*. London: HMSO.

HOUGH, M., and MAYHEW, P. (1983). *British Crime Survey*. London: HMSO.

HOUGH, M., and MAYHEW, P. (1985). *Taking Account of Crime*, London: HMSO.

HOWARD J. (1784). *The State of the Prisons in England and Wales: With Preliminary Observations and an Account of Some Foreign Prisons and Hospitals*. (3rd. rev. edn.) London.

HUDSON B. (1987). *Justice Through Punishment: A Critique of the 'Justice' Model of Corrections*. London: Macmillan.

HULSMAN, L. H. C., BEERLING, H. W. R., and DIJK, E. van (1978). 'The Dutch Criminal Justice System from a Comparative Legal Perspective', in Fokkema, D. C., *et al* (eds.) *Introduction to Dutch Law for Foreign Lawyers*, Netherlands: Kluwer.

HUTTER, B. M. (1988). *The Reasonable Arm of the Law? The Law Enforcement Procedures of Environmental Health Officers.* Oxford: University Press.

IGNATIEFF, M. (1978). *A Just Measure of Pain: The Penitentiary in the Industrial Revolution 1750–1850.* London: Macmillan.

JANSSEN, O. J. A. and SWIERSTRA, K. (1983). 'On Defining "Hard Core Addicts"'. Paper presented at Symposium on the Care of Hard Core Addicts, Strasburg, 14–16 March 1983 (unpublished).

JOHNSON, E. H. (1984). 'Night Patrol in Amsterdam's Warmoestraat District', University of Southern Illinois (unpublished).

JOHNSON, E. H. and HEIJDER, A. (1983). 'The Dutch Deemphasise Imprisonment: A Sociocultural and Structural Explanation'. *International Journal of Comparative and Applied Justice* 7: 3–19.

JONGMAN, R. W. (1981). *Klasse Elementen in de Rechtsgang.* (Class elements in sentencing). Groningen: Institute of Criminology.

JOWELL, R., WITHERSPOON S., and BROOK, L., eds. (1986). *British Social Attitudes: The 1986 Report.* Aldershot: Gower.

JUNGER-TAS, J. (1979). *Juvenile Court Structures: Problems and Dilemmas,* The Hague: Research and Documentation Centre, Ministry of Justice.

KAPLAN, C. D. (1984). 'The Uneasy Consensus: Prohibitionist and Experimentalist Expectancies Behind the International Narcotics Control System', *Tijdschrift Voor Criminologie* 26: 98–109.

KELK, C. (1983). 'The Humanity of the Dutch Prison System and the Prisoners' Consciousness of their Legal Rights', *Contemporary Crises* 7: 155–70.

KING, R., and MORGAN, R. (1976). *'A Taste of Prison: Custodial Conditions for Trial and Remand Prisoners.* London: Routledge and Kegan Paul.

KING, R., and MORGAN, R. (1979). 'Crisis in the Prisons: The Way Out'. Paper based on evidence to the Inquiry into the UK Prison Service. (Universities on Bath and Southampton).

KING, R., and MORGAN, R. (1980). *The Future of the Prison System.* Farnborough: Gower.

KOENRADT, F. (1983). 'Forensic Psychiatric Expertise and Enforced Treatment in The Netherlands', *Contemporary Crises 7: 171–82.*

LEUW, E. (1984). 'Door schade en schande: de geschiedenis van drug hulpverlening als sociaal belied in Amsterdam' (Through shame and scandal: The history of drug assistance as social policy in Amsterdam), *Tijdschrift Voor Criminologie,* 26.

LIJPHART, A. (1975). *The Politics of Accommodation* (2nd. rev. edn.) Berkeley and Los Angeles: University of California Press.

LUKES, S., and SCULL, A., eds. (1983). *Durkheim and the Law.* Oxford: Martin Robertson.

MCCLUSKEY, J. (1986). 'Law, Justice and Democracy'. Reith Lecture 1, *Listener* 6 Nov.

MANGEN, S. (1985). 'Psychiatric Policies: Developments and Constraints', in his (ed.) *Mental Health Care in the European Community.* London: Croom Helm.

MANNHEIM, H. (1939). *The Dilemma of Penal Reform,* London: Allen and Unwin.

MANNHEIM, H. (1965), *Comparative Criminology.* London: Routledge and Kegan Paul.

MANNING, P. K. (1977). *Police Work,* Cambridge, Mass.: MIT. Press.

MASON, H. L. (1952). *The Purge of Dutch Quislings.* The Hague: Nijhoff.

MATHIESEN, T. (1965). *The Defences of the Weak.* London: Tavistock.

MATHIESEN, T. (1983). 'The Future of Control Systems: The Case of Norway', in Garland, D., and Young, (eds.) 1983.

MAWBY, R. (1979). *Policing the City.* Farnborough: Gower.

MAY, MR JUSTICE (1979). *Report of the Committee of Inquiry into the United Kingdom Prison Services.* London: HMSO (Cmnd. 7673).

MOEDIKDO, P. (1976). 'De Utrechtse school van Pompe, Baan en Kempe', in Kelk, C. *et al.* (eds.), *Recht, Macht en Manipulatie.* Utrecht and Antwerp: Uitgeverig het Spectrum.

MORRIS, P. (1969). *Put Away.* London: Routledge and Kegan Paul.

MOTT, J. (1980). 'Opiate Use and Crime in the United Kingdom', *Contemporary Drug Problems* 437-51.

MOTT, J. (1981). 'Criminal Involvement and Penal Response', in EDWARDS, G., and BUSCH, C. (eds.). London: Academic Press.

MOTT, J. (1986). 'Estimating the Prevalence of Drugs Misuse'. *Home Office Research Bulletin* 21: 57-60.

NACRO (1986). *Enforcement of the Law relating to Social Security* NACRO: London.

NETHERLANDS, CENTRAL BUREAU OF STATISTICS (1986). *One Hundred Years of Penal Code in The Netherlands: A Statistical View of 1886-1986.* The Hague.

NETHERLANDS, MINISTRY OF JUSTICE (1947). *Rapport van de Commissie voor de Verdere Uitbouw het Gevangeniswezen* (Report of the Committee for the Further Development of the Prison System). [The Fick Committee Report.] The Hague: State Publications.

NETHERLANDS, MINISTRY OF JUSTICE (1977). *Detention at the Government's Pleasure: Treatment of Criminal Psychopaths in The Netherlands.* The Hague: State Publications.

NETHERLANDS, MINISTRY OF JUSTICE (1981). *De capaciteitsproblemen bij het gevangeniswezen* (The problems of capacity in the prison system). The Hague: Report of the Working Group.

NETHERLANDS, MINISTRY OF JUSTICE (1983a). *Rapport van de Commissie*

Psychiatrische/Therapeutische Voorzieningen Gevangeniswezen. [The Mulder Committee Report.] The Hague: State Publications.

NETHERLANDS, MINISTRY OF JUSTICE (1983b). *Rapport ven der werkgroep druggerbruik en handel in de inrichtingen van het gevangeniswezen.* (Report of the Working Committee on Drug use and the Drug-trade in the Dutch Penal System). The Hague: State Publications.

NETHERLANDS, MINISTRY OF JUSTICE (1984). *Interimrapport van de Commissie Kleine Criminaliteit* (Interim report of the Committee on Petty Crime). [The Roethof Committee Report.]. The Hague: State Publications.

NETHERLANDS, MINISTRY OF JUSTICE (1985a). *Samenleving en Criminaliteit: Een beleidsplan voor de komende jaren.* (Society and Crime: A policy plan for the future). The Hague: State Publications.

NETHERLANDS, MINISTRY OF JUSTICE (1985b). *Society and Crime: A policy Plan for The Netherlands.* (Eng. trans. of the summary and two chs. of 1985a.) Schiedam: Van Rossum.

NETHERLANDS, MINISTRY OF JUSTICE (1985c). Structuurplan Penitentiaire Capaciteit: Rapport van de projectgroep ingesteld bij beschikking DD. 8. Nov. 1984 van der Staatssecretaris van Justitie (Plan for the Construction of Penal Capacity: Report of the project group established on 8 Nov. 1984 on behalf of the Secretary of State for Justice). The Hague: State publications.

NETHERLANDS, MINISTRY OF JUSTICE (1985d). *6e Follow-up van het onderzoek van de werkgroep capaciteit TBR-inrichtingen* (Sixth follow-up report of the inquiry of the working party on the capacity of the TBR institution). Directie TBR en Reclassering (Department of Mental Institutions and Probation).

NETHERLANDS, MINISTRY OF JUSTICE (1985e). Table A: Onvoorwarrdelijk ter beschikking van de Regering gestelden per 1 Januari 1985. (Unconditional TBR inmates on 1 January 1985.) Directie TBR en Reclassering (Department of Mental Institutions and Probation).

NETHERLANDS, MINISTRY OF JUSTICE (1986). Namlist leiden rechtereijke macht (Directory of principal members of the judiciary). The Hague: State Publications.

NIJBOER, J. A., and PLOEG, G. J. (1985). 'Grievance procedures in The Netherlands', in Maguire, M., Vagg, J., and Morgan, R. (eds.), *Accountability and Prisons: Opening up a Closed World.* London: Tavistock.

O'CONNOR; J. (1973). *The Fiscal Crisis of the State.* New York: St Martin's Press.

PARKER, H., NEWCOMBE, R., and BAKX, K. (1986). 'Heroin and Crime: the Impact of Heroin Use on the Rate of Acquisitive Crime and the Offending Behaviour of Young Drug Users'. Liverpool: Misuse of Drugs Research Project, University of Liverpool.

PEARSON, G. (1983). *Hooligan: A History of Respectable Fears.* London: Macmillan.

PEARSON, G., GILMAND, M., and MILNER, S. (1986). *Young People and Heroin: An Examination of Heroin Use in The North of England.* Aldershot: Gower.

PEASE, K. (1980). *Prison Population: Using Statistics to Estimate the Effects of Policy Changes.* Milton Keynes: Open University Press.

PETERS, A. A. G. (1986). 'Main Currents in Criminal Law Theory', in Dijk, J. J. M. van *et al* (eds.), 1986.

POMPE, W. P. J. (1959). *Handboek van het Nederlandse Strafrecht* (Guide to Dutch Criminal Law). 5th edn. Haarlem.

POWER, A. (1987). *PEP Guide to Local Housing Management,* 3 vols. London: Department of the Environment.

PRATT, J. (1985). 'Delinquency as a Scarce Resource', *Howard Journal* 24: 108–17.

PRATT, J. (1986). 'Diversion from the Juvenile Court', *British Journal of Criminology* 26: 212–33.

PUNCH, M. (1979a). *Policing the Inner City: A Study of Amsterdam's Warmoestraat.* London: Macmillan.

PUNCH, M. (1979b). 'A Mild Case of Corruption', *British Journal of Law and Society* 6: 243–53.

PUNCH, M. (1985). *Conduct Unbecoming: The Social Construction of Police Deviance and Control,* London: Tavistock.

RADZINOWICZ, L. (1966). *Ideology and Crime: A Study of Crime in its Social and Historical Context.* London: Heinemann.

RADZINOWICZ, L., and HOOD, R. (1980). 'Incapacitating the Habitual Criminal: The English Experience', *Michigan Law Review* 78: 1305–89.

RADZINOWICZ, L., and HOOD, R. (1986). *History of the English Criminal Law,* vol. 5. London: Stevens.

REEVE, A. (1983). *Notes From a Waiting Room.* London: Heretic Books.

REISS, A. J., Jr. (1971). *The Police and the Public.* New Haven: Yale University Press.

REMMELINK, J. (1980). 'Actuele Stromingen in het Nederlands Strafrecht'. (Actual Tendencies in Dutch Penal Law), in *Strafrecht in Perspectief,* Arnhem: Gouda Quint.

RICHARDSON, G. (1985). 'Judicial Intervention in Prison Life', in Maguire, M., Vagg, J., and Morgan, R. (eds.), *Accountability and Prisons.* London: Tavistock.

RIJKSEN, R. (1958). *Meningen van Gedetineerden over de Strafrechts-pleging* (Prisoners Speak Out). Assen: van Gorcum.

ROBERTSON, R. and TAYLOR, L. (1973). *Deviance, Crime and Socio-legal Control.* Oxford: Martin Robertson.

ROCK, P. E. (1979). *The Making of Symbolic Interactionism.* London: Macmillan.

ROCK, P. E. (1980). *Public Opinion and Criminal Legislation,* Strasburg: Council of Europe.

ROIJ-MOTSHAGEN, A. J. de (1985). 'Multicity-study: Drug Abuse in Amsterdam'. Amsterdam: GG and GD (unpublished).

ROLLESTON COMMITTEE, (1926). *Report of the Departmental Committee on Drug Dependence.* London: HMSO.

ROSETT, A. (1972). 'Trial and discretion in Dutch Criminal Justice'. *University of California at Los Angeles Law Review,* vol. 19.

ROTHMAN, D. J. (1971). *The Discovery of the Asylum,* Boston, Mass.: Little, Brown.

RULLER, S. van (1981). 'Het aantal gevangenen in Nederland sinds 1837: Een analyse van 140 jaar gevangenisstatistieken' (The number of prisoners in The Netherlands since 1837: An analysis of 140 years' imprisonment statistics), *Tijdschrift voor criminologie* 23: 209–23.

RULLER, S. van (1985). 'The End of Decarceration', in *International Conference on Prison Abolition,* Amsterdam: Free University.

RUSCHE, G. and KIRCHHEIMER, O. (1939). *Punishment and Social Structure.* New York: Columbia University Press.

RUTER, F. (1986). 'Drugs and the Criminal Law in The Netherlands', in Dijk, J. J. M. van *et al* (eds.), (1986).

RUTHERFORD, A. ([1984] [1986a]) *Prisons and the Process of Justice.* London: Heinemann and Oxford: Oxford University Press.

RUTHERFORD, A. (1986b). *Growing out of Crime.* Harmondsworth: Penguin.

SANSONE, L. (1984). *!...And Leisure Time Is Mine! The Creole Youth of Amsterdam in Social Welfare, Vocational Education and Leisure Time.* Amsterdam: Gemeente Amsterdam Afdeling Bestuursinformatie (August).

SCHUTZ, A. (1967). 'The Stranger': Collected Papers II. Hague: Nijdhof.

SCPB [SOCIAL and CULTURAL PLANNING BUREAU] (1979–). *Social and Cultural Report* (published biennially). Rijswijk.

SCULL, A. (1977). *Decarceration: Community Treatment and The Deviant.* Englewood Cliffs, N. J.: Prentice-Hall.

SHAPLAND, J. M. (1981). *Between Conviction and Sentence.* London: Routledge and Kegan Paul.

SHARPLES, K. S. (1972). *The Legal Framework of Judicial Sentencing Policy.* Amsterdam: University Press.

SHAW, S. (1980). *Paying the Penalty: An Analysis of the Cost of Penal Sanctions.* London: National Association for the Care and Resettlement of Offenders. (NACRO)

SIMPKIN, M. (1979). *Trapped Within Welfare: Surviving Social Work.* London: Macmillan.

SMIT, N. W. de (1976). 'On the Babylonic Confusion Between Psychiatry and Criminal Law: Moving Forensic Psychiatry Beyond

Its Expert Function', *Psychiatrische Praxis*. May (in Dutch).

SMITH, R. (1984a). 'Deaths in Prison', *British Medical Journal* 288 (21 Jan.): 208-12.

SMITH, R. (1984b). 'Medical Care in the Dutch Penal System', *British Medical Journal* 288 (24 Mar.):925-7.

SOETENHORST -De SAVORNIN LOHMAN, J. (1981). 'Kritische kanttekeningen bij het rapport *De capaciteitsproblemen big het gevangeniswezen* (Critical annotations on *Capacity Problems of the Penal System*), *Delikt en Delinkwent*, 11: 721-32.

SPARKS, R. F., GENN, H. G., and DODD, D. J. (1977). *Surveying Victims*. London: Wiley.

SPIERENBURG, P. (1986). 'Deviance and Repression in The Netherlands: Historical Evidence and Contemporary Problems', *Historische socialforschung* 37: 4-16.

STEENHUIS, D. W. (1977). *General Deterrence and Drunken Driving*. The Hague: Research and Documentation Centre, Ministry of Justice.

STEENHUIS, D. W. (1986). 'Coherence and Co-ordination in the Administration of Criminal Justice', in Dijk, J. J. M. van *et al* (eds.), 1986.

STEENHUIS, D. W., TIGGES, A. C. M. and ESSERS, J. J. H. (1981). 'The Penal Climate in The Netherlands: Sunny or Cloudy?,' *British Journal of Criminology* 23: 1-16.

STERN, V. (1987). *Bricks of Shame: Britain's Prisons*. Harmondsworth: Penguin.

STIMSON, G. V. (1985). 'Can a War on Drugs Succeed?' *New Society* 15 Nov.

STIMSON, G. V., and OPPENHEIMER, E. (1982). *Heroin Addiction: Treatment and Control in Britain*. London: Tavistock.

STOLWIJK, S. A. M. (1986). 'Alternatives to Custodial Sentences', in Dijk, J. J. M. van *et al* (eds.), 1986.

SYLBING, G. (1985). *The Use of Drugs, Alcohol and Tobacco: Results of a Survey among Young People in The Netherlands Aged 15-24 years*. Amsterdam: Foundation for the Scientific Study of Alcohol and Drug Use. (SWOAD).

TAYLOR, R. (1986). 'Criminal Convictions of Persons First Notified as Narcotic Drug Addicts in 1979-81', *Home Office Research Bulletin* 20: 27-29.

THOMAS D. A. ([1970], 1979). *Principles of Sentencing*. London: Heinemann. 2nd ed., rev.

THOMAS D. A. (1982). 'The Partly Suspended Sentence' *Criminal Law Review* vol. 288.

THOMAS D. A. (1986). 'Out of Court', *Guardian* 16 May.

THOMAS, J. E. (1972). *The English Prison Officer Since 1850*. London: Routledge and Kegan Paul.

TITMUSS, R. (1970). *The Gift Relationship: From Human Blood to Social*

Policy. London: Allen and Unwin.

TOWNSEND, P. (1963). *The Last Refuge*. London: Routledge and Kegan Paul.

TREBACH, A. (1982). *The Heroin Solution*. New Haven: Yale University Press.

TREBACH, A. (1986). 'The Loyal Opposition to the War on Drugs: Drugs and the Criminal Law in Western Societies', 215–28 in Dijk, J. J. M. van *et al* (eds.), 1986.

TULKENS, H. (1979). *Some Developments in Penal Policy and Practice in Holland*. Chichester: Barry Rose (for London: National Association for the Care and Resettlement of Offenders).

VINSON, T. (1985). *Impressions of the Dutch Prison System*. The Hague: WODC.

VRIJ, M. P. (1956). *Verzameling uit zijn Geschriften op het Gebied van Strafrecht en Criminologie* (Collected Works in Criminal Law and Criminology) Zwolle.

WALKER, N. D. (1985). *Sentencing: Theory, Law and Practice*, London: Butterworths.

WALLER, I. (1982). *Canadian Crime and Justice in Comparative Perspective: Selected Indicators for Selected Countries, 1900–1980*, rev. edn. Ontario: University of Ottawa.

WERFF, C. van der (1978). *Recidivism and Special Deterrence*. The Hague: WODC.

WERFF, C. van der (1986). *Recidive 1977: Recidivecijfers van in 1977 wegens misdijf veroordeeldem en mit vervolgden*, (Recidivism 1977: Data on recidivism among convicted and non-prosecuted suspects for felony in 1977). The Hague: WODC:

WHEELER, S., BONIACH, E., CRAMER M. R., and ZOLA, I. K. (1968). 'Agents of Delinquency Control: A Comparative Analysis', in his (ed.) *Controlling Delinquents*. London: Wiley.

WILSON, J. Q. (1975). *Thinking About Crime*. New York: Basic Books.

WOLFE, T. (1970). 'Mau-mauing the Flak-Catchers' in his *Radical Chic and Mau-mauing the Flak Catchers*. New York: Farrar, Straus, and Giroux.

WOOTTON, B. (1978). *Crime and the Penal System*. London: Allen and Unwin.

YANAGIMOTO, M. (1970). 'Some Features of the Japanese Prison System', *British Journal of Criminology* 10: 209–24.

ZOOMER, O. (1979). *Sanctioning in Cases of Serious Offence*. The Hague: Research and Documentation Centre, Ministry of Justice.

Index